A guide to sports medicine

Frank Mullija.

A guide to sports medicine

Edited by Peter G. Stokes, MNZSP.

CHURCHILL LIVINGSTONE EDINBURGH LONDON AND NEW YORK 1979

Longman Paul Limited
182–190 Wairau Road, Auckland 10,
New Zealand

CHURCHILL LIVINGSTONE
Medical Division of Longman Group Limited
Robert Stevenson House,
1–3 Baxter's Place, Leith Walk, Edinburgh, EHI 3AF.

Distributed in the United States of America by
Churchill Livingstone Inc., 19 West 44th Street, New York,
NY 10036 and in New Zealand
by N.M. Peryer Limited,
93–97 Cambridge Terrace,
Christchurch 1, New Zealand.

Associated companies, branches
and representatives throughout the world

ISBN 0-582-71768-X

Printed in Singapore by Multiprint Services Pte Ltd.
Illustrated by Mike Richardson

British Library Cataloguing in Publication Data

A guide to sports medicine.
  1. Sports medicine
  I. Title   II. Stokes, Peter G
  617^1.1027   RC1210   79-40208

The cover incorporates graphic symbols taken from
Handbook of Pictorial Symbols, Rudolf Modley with the
assistance of William R. Myers, Dover Publications,
Inc., 1976.

Contents

My sincere thanks to all contributors to
this book. At last a start has been made in
the study of sports medicine within New
Zealand which others, in future, will
continue.

Peter G. Stokes

Acknowledgements

The author and publishers wish to thank the following for permission to reproduce copyright material:

Federated Mountain Club of New Zealand, International Cycling Federation of Rome, National Mountain Safety Council, New Zealand Federation of Sports Medicine, *Australian Journal of Sports Medicine*, *Journal of the American Medical Association*, *Nebraska State Medical Association Journal*, *The French Olympic Review*, *The Lancet*, *The Travellers Health Guide* (Lascelles), *Science*, and *Swimming Technique*.

The author would like to take this opportunity of sincerely thanking all contributors, both those who allowed the reproduction of already published material, and, in particular, those who wrote articles especially for the book.

1 Diet and the athlete

Eating for superior athletic performance

Prof. R.H. Hall

Professor Ross Hume Hall, Professor of Biochemistry at McMaster University, Hamilton, Ontario, former Principle Cancer Research Scientist at the Roswell Park Memorial Institute in Buffalo, New York, was Assistant Professor of Medicinal Chemistry and Associate Professor of Biochemistry at the State University of New York before his present appointment. An associate editor of numerous journals, he has received over one million dollars in grants towards his research, and has written numerous books and articles.

Professor Hall is a member of the Medical Committee of the International Federation of Bodybuilders and wrote the following article for the I.F.B.B. in response to requests from many coaches for the latest information on the value of food in athletic performance.

Getting the most out of what you eat

Superior athletic endeavour, regardless of the sport, requires total concentration of mental and physical powers; it requires that the total body biochemistry function at its peak efficiency. To obtain that peak efficiency every cell in your body must be bathed in its optimum nutritional requirements. All nutrients must be present and in the correct balance. Most nutrients needed by the cells are made in the body starting from the basic foodstuffs you eat, but some of the nutrients required cannot be made by the human body, and therefore you must eat plant or animal food that when alive synthesised those obligatory nutrients for their own healthful purposes. The substances needed by your cells and manufactured by the body are provided to the cells in the correct proportions through automatic biochemical balancing mechanisms. You cannot consciously control these processes, but through your choice of food, you can control those obligatory requirements that you take in. There are essentially two aspects to nutrition for athletic endeavour, eating sufficient quantity and eating foods for their nutritional quality. Athletes seem to readily consume the correct quantity of food for their weight and type of sport, so this article will concentrate on how to get the most nutritional quality out of your food in order to get the most out of your body biochemistry.

Limits to nutrition knowledge

Athletes probably more than any other group have been conscious of the need to eat well for high performance, and in their search for information on how to eat well they have turned to the science of nutrition for guidance. But the advice that the science of nutrition can give, while helpful, is limited by the state of its art. The demands of athletes for specific information goes far beyond what nutrition science is capable of offering. However, the increasing knowledge of biological phenomena in general gives us certain principles we can use. Therefore to know how to get superior nutrition from the food available you need to understand how to use the information nutrition science provides, how to apply basic biological principles and finally how to synthesise creatively this information into your choice of food.

It is important to recognise the limits of nutritional knowledge in the context of the athletes' world. I emphasise the limitations of nutrition science because although this science gives us basic data and ideas, it has not developed to the point of being able to detail the specifics. It is like visualising a forest from a distance. You see the general outline and the mass of green but you cannot make out the individual trees, their shape, size, and species. We can discuss the nutrient needs of the body cells but only in a general way can we specify what the cells need and in what sort of balance. We are really very ignorant and it is not just a question of not having done the experiments. It is a question of not knowing how to do the experiments.

To illustrate, scientists can culture human cells in bottles using a complex nutrient broth containing known vitamins, minerals and amino acids. But because scientists do not know exactly what the cells require they must add as well a whole substance such as blood serum. There are unknown substances in correct balances in that serum which are essential to the survival of the cells.

When we examine the kinds of specific nutritional experiments conducted in athletics we find that they furnish only the most general information. Experiments, for example, show that a marathon athlete running at 16 k.p.h. will expend about 1200 kilocalories per hour.[2] These experiments can specify the amount of sugar and fat burned by the body to generate that energy, and illustrate the fact that the muscles are completely exhausted of glycogen (sugar storage form) at the end of the run. But science cannot determine precisely what other nutrients are being consumed in order to metabolise the fat and sugar for energy production. It has been shown that in an endurance sport an athlete can double the maximum amount of glycogen stored in the muscles by first depleting the muscles a few days in advance of the competition and then eating a high carbohydrate diet up to the day of the performance.[3,12] The experiments, however, do not specify what foods specifically to eat or what other nutrients are especially required by the body biochemistry to produce this phenomenon.

In top athletic competition the athlete does not compete against persons whose body biochemistry ticks over at an average level; the athlete competes with others as superbly trained as himself. Under these circumstances the nuances in nutrition which contribute to a small percentage improvement in body efficiency are what make the difference between non-champion and champion. This article will provide information on how to choose foods to gain those all important incremental advantages.

How nutrition science started and stopped

To be able to choose food wisely we need to know about the information basic nutrition science offers. Why do we try to describe human nourishment in terms of vitamins, fats and proteins and what are the limitations to expressing nourishment in this form? We can gain some insight by briefly looking at the history of nutrition science.

In the middle of the last century the scientific problem that attracted the greatest attention of biological scientists was the question: 'How is it possible to convert a chicken into a man?' Or, to put it more precisely: 'What happens to convert the dead flesh of the chicken into the living flesh of the man?' The best scientific brains of the day studied this problem and through the use of the tools of analytical chemistry they determined that the chicken's flesh consisted of three classes of substances: carbohydrates, fats and proteins. Moreover, so did the flesh of man. They decided, therefore, that what was happening was that the human digestive processes were converting the three nutritional classes of substances from one flesh to the other.

This concept of nutrition was embellished in the first half of this century when a series of accessory factors essential to human metabolism was discovered. Today we know of sixteen vitamins and at least seventeen minerals that are essential. All these discoveries were made using the techniques of analytical chemistry. This science calculates how much of a vitamin or a mineral is present in a food or in human tissue but it gives precious little insight into the actual biological involvement of these nutrients in the body biochemistry. Outside of knowing that the human body needs the accessory factors and some of the specific biochemical reactions in which they participate, science cannot offer much knowledge about the specifics of accessory factor usage. For example, we know that the vitamins and minerals function as a team but we don't know how. In other words, supplying the body amply with one or a few vitamins may be useless if their team-mates are lacking.

All the nutritional problems solved
Nutrition science arrived at the middle of the twentieth century thus, with a definite concept of human nourishment: nutrition could be defined in terms of carbohydrates, fat proteins and the accessory factors. There was a feeling that nutrition science had gone as far as it could go. Professor Hugh Sinclair of Oxford University, England, tells the story that in 1946 his university was offered a large sum of money to found an Institute of Human Nutrition but the university turned it down because the authorities believed that after ten years there would be no human nutritional problems to study![21] Scientists in general seemed to have agreed with that conclusion and although biological science has flowered magnificently in many directions it left nutrition science in a sort of a backwater. Some thirty years later, with the reawakening interest among biological scientists in nutritional problems, there is general realisation that instead of having a mature and complete science, scientific knowledge of the phenomenon of human nourishment remains in its infancy.

All the essential vitamins have not been discovered and nutrition science still speaks in terms of fats, carbohydrates and proteins when it should be defining more precisely the molecular architecture of these substances. Science has dissected the phenomenon of human nourishment giving us bare facts. Having outlined the skeleton of nourishment, science must now flesh out the skeleton into a dynamic and useful whole phenomenon.

Your nourishment is unique
No one doubts that every person has a unique appearance and unique personality but science does not allow you to have a unique body biochemistry. The study of sociology is the study of groups of people; the study of psychology is the study of the

individual. We can derive much useful knowledge from both types of study. Modern biochemistry, like sociology, studies man the species without any acknowledgement of the biochemistry of the individual. There is no science of biochemistry which is the equivalent of psychology. The lack of emphasis on personal biochemistry concerns the eminent nutritionist Roger J. Williams of the University of Texas, who has made a serious study to prove that biochemical individuality exists.[22] Dr William's studies have done much to show that because of a personal biochemistry everyone has unique nutritional requirements. You may have a need for a certain vitamin in your diet several times greater than that of your friend. Moreover, your requirement for dietary nutrients varies, depending on your activities and what you are eating. Nevertheless, pick up any book on nutrition and you will find tables of required nutrients couched in terms of the average man and woman. These tables lack two features important to athletes. First, the [given] values of required nutrients (in the United States termed the 'Recommended Daily Allowance', RDA) are the basic minimum necessary to avoid illness. For athletes a vitamin deficiency illness should not be a problem; the athlete is interested in nutrition for optimum performance and of that the tables say nothing. Second, these tables, set for the mythical standard man and woman, ignore the individuality of the individual eater. I could add a third feature: when you recognise a face, you do not consciously measure the length of the nose, the distance between the eyes, the circularity of the mouth, but unconsciously and simultaneously integrate all the features of the face into a unique whole. Similarly your personal nutrition cannot be easily synthesised from a quantitative list of the bare bones, vitamins, minerals, proteins, carbohydrates and fats. You need to approach your personal nutrition as a whole.

The fact that we require vitamins, minerals, fats, carbohydrates and proteins is useful information and I will refer to some quantitative data, but we must realise that nutrition science has not progressed to the point to be able to designate, except in a very general way, how much of each class of nutrients, or the quality, you require in your particular life style. The human body adapts readily to whatever quality of food is eaten and because of this adaptability quality usually receives less attention than quantity. I refer to nutritional quality here, not the cosmetic qualities of appearance or shelf life that envelopes much of modern food. The fact that the body appears to adapt to a wide range of nutritional qualities does not mean that the body achieves optimum biochemical performance on food of less than optimum nutritional quality. Adaptation of the body to poor diets is a survival mechanism designed to keep the body at least alive and mobile. Athletic performance lies at the other end of the activity scale and people desiring peak physical and mental performance must strive for peak quality in what they eat within the context of their own unique body biochemistry.

The effects of modern food processing

Chemical technology restructures the molecular architecture of food
A standard work on sport and nutrition suggests that athletes divide their daily calorie pie into a 15 per cent slice for protein, 30 per cent slice for fat and a 55 per cent slice for carbohydrates.[9] This type of advice is helpful to a certain point but it does not tell you what kinds of proteins, fat or carbohydrates to eat. This sort of

advice is based on the analytical approach of the nutritionists of the last century who might have wished to specify more precise information at the time but could not do so owing to the limitation of their scientific approaches. In the intervening years two things have happened that have consequences for modern nutrition.

First, a considerable body of knowledge about the precise biochemistry of the three classes of tissue substances has been acquired although very little of this information has been expressed in nutritional terms. We know in intimate detail the structure and biochemical function of hundreds of protein molecules but we know nothing about the differing nutritional importance of these different protein molecules. Science knows about the function of these proteins in their host tissues but nothing about what happens when the proteins are transferred into another being, which is what nutrition is all about. Second, the most drastic change that has occurred since the beginning of nutrition science a hundred years ago and probably the fact of most practical importance to our study is the change in form in which food is available. It really doesn't help to suggest that athletes should obtain 55 per cent of their daily calorie requirements from carbohydrates without providing advice on the form of carbohydrates actually sold in the store. The point of this comment is that while nutrition science tends to provide information in terms suited to the market conditions of the last century the real world of food supply has changed markedly.

The whole technology of food raising, processing and merchandising has changed and is changing rapidly. In order for you to choose wisely in today's food market it is necessary to understand the major technological trends. Food processing has been part of human culture for thousands of years. Home cooking is a form of food processing. Until the time of World War II, factory processing of food was similar to home cooking except that it was on a grander scale. This type of processing involves mostly mixing and heating. Starting about the time of World War II, factory processing embraced chemical technology and it is this infusion of chemical technology that has transformed the food industry. Chemical technology confers the power to modify and rearrange the very molecular architecture of food substances. With its new technology the food industry now takes the three original classifications of nutritional substances and within each class restructures the molecular architecture to suit the manufacturing goals of the industry, but not necessarily the nutritional goals of athletes.

Textured vegetable protein (TVP)

Athletes feel that protein, particularly animal protein, is their main source of strength, and their diets tend to include a lot of meat. To give you an example of how chemical technology is deployed in the food industry we might examine the response of the industry to the demand for meat. The response is to provide a product that looks like, feels like, and tastes like meat but is a product derived from less expensive soybeans. The transformation of soybeans into beef steak takes a great deal of chemical sophistication.

Soybeans consist of about 40 per cent protein, and of all the plant proteins, they come closest to human protein in terms of amino acid composition. To convert soy protein into beef steak the soybeans are first crushed and extracted with gasoline or similar petroleum solvent in order to remove the oil (20 per cent of the original weight). The defatted flour is treated with industrial alcohol or acid to remove part

6

of the carbohydrate, a process that increases the protein content of the flour to about 70 per cent. The protein is dissolved in lye and this alkaline solution is forced through tiny orifices into a bath of dilute acid. The protein solidifies in the form of fine threads which are spun and cemented into large bundles. The spun protein has an affinity for artificial flavour and synthetic dyes; it retains juices and has a meat-like texture. The bundles can be cut into desired shapes then cooked or artificially smoked to simulate chicken, turkey, beef, bacon.[14] These products are labelled textured vegetable protein (TVP) and are promoted as satisfying meat substitutes.

The whole soybean contains 1½ times as much protein as lean beef, 3½ times as much as eggs or cheese; it contains several vitamins, thirteen identified minerals and over 2 per cent by weight of lecithin. The protein of soybean retains its normal high quality only if soybeans are eaten as soybeans or a minimally processed soy flour which I will mention in the section on supplementation. The chemical processing necessary to make the textured protein product destroys most of two of the essential amino acids, lysine and methionine. Your body cannot synthesise either of these two components of protein so if they are lacking in the diet you will not survive. The manufacturers of TVP try to circumvent the loss of lysine by adding free lysine. They balk at adding free methionine because it imparts a characteristic rotten egg odour to the product.

The textured vegetable protein is a set of naked molecules devoid of the complementary components of the soybean essential for balanced nourishment. Meat at one time was living flesh, it retains the cellular structure, micronutrients and architecture of that flesh. Meat provides wholesome nourishment of which protein is only part. So do soybeans when eaten in whole form. Vegetarians can successfully replace meat in their diet with soybeans and other legumes. The effect of replacing meat in the diet with the textured soy protein has not been studied in depth. Short-term studies by Professor G. Debry of the University of Nancy, France, for example, show that one half of the meat of school children can be replaced with TVP for one week without changing gross nutritional parameters.[8] Professor Debry notes that the TVP has 72 per cent the quality of casein. The ersatz product furnishes protein of lowered quality, yet because people generally eat more protein than their basic requirement, the lowered quality of the product is submerged from view. Nevertheless, for athletes, eating such products could substantially subtract from their optimum nutrition.

The question of the protein quality of the chemically-processed soy product is important enough but the question of the quality of your nourishment is much broader. In the reshuffling of the soybean molecules many of the vitamins are partially destroyed or lost and some of the minerals are washed out.[24] There are data for the known vitamins, but what of the unknown ones? More importantly, the essential balances of nutrients in the original soybeans have all been destroyed and because we don't know exactly what the balances critical for optimum nourishment should be, it is impossible to reconstruct them by adding selected nutrients. Dr George M. Briggs, Department of Nutritional Sciences, University of California, Berkeley, feels that the textured soy proteins represent 'a nutritional step backwards' because they dilute the diet with a substance lacking a broad spectrum of vitamins and minerals.[4]

The textured soy product is currently used as a partial replacer of meat in stews, sauces, hamburgers, sausages and ground meat dishes of various kinds. The fact that the synthetic product comes in a final form familiar to the consumer masks its true nature. This is true for all fabricated foods; they are sold as familiar forms. North Americans now obtain almost 60 per cent of their daily calories from refined foods. Nutrition science possesses neither the experimental tools nor the fundamental knowledge to assess the effects of eating such products. Knowledge is sufficient however to tell us of the deficiencies in these products compared to the original whole food.

I have used the textured vegetable protein to illustrate the detrimental nutritional effects of chemical processing. The other classes of foodstuffs are similarly treated. Vegetable oils are subjected to harsh chemical refining and carbohydrates are refined through milling and chemical treatment to give refined flour, chemically modified starches and purified sugar. I will not give any more technical details of chemical food processing but I would like to discuss the topic of sugar because it plays such a major role in the diet of the average person and because this role has been criticised by many medical authorities.

Sugar

Persons eating a typical western diet obtain about half their carbohydrates in the highly refined form of sugar (about 20 per cent of daily calories). The nutrition tables do not separate sugar out from carbohydrates, they include sugar under the carbohydrate heading. The word sugar needs to be understood. Its chemical use refers to a class of compounds of which table sugar (sucrose) is only one. Blood sugar is not sucrose, it is another molecule, glucose. Sucrose, glucose and many other simple carbohydrates occur in relatively low amounts in all plant foods, so in a diet of natural foods one eats a certain amount of these substances. But the bulk of the carbohydrates in natural foods is found in a complex form composed of an aggregate glucose. Thus when you eat starch (a complex carbohydrate) your digestive system breaks it down into the individual glucose molecules which are readily absorbed into the system. The human body, through evolution, was designed to handle large quantities of starch and other complex carbohydrates in the diet.

Much controversy has arisen over the fact that the western diet has changed from one low in the refined simple carbohydrates (sugars), to one high in these substances. Many authorities attribute major diseases to the highly refined sugar content of the western diet. Surgeon-Captain T.L. Cleave has assembled a massive amount of evidence indicting the high consumption of sugar as a major contributor to heart disease, diabetes and digestion disorders.[5] Cleave points out that not only does sugar cause harm but in eating this refined product you deny your body the fibre that would normally be present in an unrefined product. In Cleave's opinion it is the double-barrelled blows of high sugar and low fibre that cause these diseases.

What can we learn from this evidence? That dietary imbalances cause derangement of the body biochemistry that ultimately leads to major degradation. Diabetes and heart disease are serious and final manifestations of a slow biochemical deterioration that has been occurring for years. It stands to reason that young athletic people, although fit, if eating a diet high in refined sugar are already compromising the potential of their own body biochemistry. I should point out that the evidence doesn't suggest a simple cause and effect relation. There are other factors contributing to these diseases. The diet high in sugar also contains other refined products (you don't eat sugar by itself) that could contribute. The important feature to consider is that eating large quantities of refined foods can derange your body biochemistry.

Adding chemicals to food

3500 chemicals added
The chemically altered proteins, refined fats and carbohydrates are the raw materials engineered into the fabricated foods found in the supermarket. Such foods, however, could not be manufactured from the basic ingredients without the addition of thousands of chemicals. It has been estimated that a person eating a typical American diet consisting mostly of fabricated foods consumes 3500 different chemicals. We can ask what are the effects of eating this mass of chemicals. The food and drug bureaus of each country ask the same questions but their concern lies only in safety. Will the chemical additives make people sick? And, consequently, they design their testing and control procedures to ensure that people don't become ill from eating modern food. The question we pose is quite different. First it is important to recognise that your body must process everything you eat, it cannot ignore anything. If a substance is not a nutrient it is a toxin, there is no neutrality. In other words, the 3500 food additives act as drugs on your body and burden its biochemistry. Perhaps the person engaged in light activity can tolerate a diminished biochemical capacity but the high performance athlete cannot.

To illustrate, BHA and BHT are initials that stand for butylated hydroxyanisole and butylated hydroxytoluene, both widely incorporated into fabricated foods in order to extend shelf life. Both substances, however, interfere with the respiratory process of the heart muscle, presumably cutting down the efficiency of the contractile process.[17] It so happens there is useful information concerning these particular food additives, but for most additives experiments have not been performed except those concerned with gross toxicity. The amount of any one food additive in a food may seem tiny but in adding up all their effects the total result could be appreciable diminution of peak biochemical performance.

Enriched foods
Food scientists, aware of the loss of many of the nutrient substances during fabrication of foods, now recommend the addition of vitamins and some minerals to the products. The problem in this approach of trying to restore a lost nutritional balance is that of the unknowns that have vanished. Further, among the known vitamins and minerals only some are replaced because in many cases the added nutrients interfere with the manufacturing processes. When flour is milled it loses up to 80 per cent of each of twenty-four known vitamins and minerals[1]. The manufacturers add back three vitamins and one mineral. The product called enriched flour is used in all commercial baked goods and breakfast cereals. The breakfast cereals may be fortified with additional vitamins but that still does not restore the lost balance. Dr Briggs comments: 'We are still a long way, knowledge-wise, from being able to balance the diet of the American public to any large extent by enrichment....'[4]

The term 'vitamin' is used too loosely. It confers all the biological properties on the chemical. For example, vitamin C refers to the chemical, ascorbic acid. In actual

9

fact, the scientific concept of vitamin is that of a biological function. Ascorbic acid has no vitamin activity until it is placed in its cellular milieu, in which it can function. In other words, a vitamin has no function until all the other components in its cellular systems are present. For this reason it is dangerous to rely on such statements as: 'this particular product has 50 per cent of RDA of Vitamin B_1.' The chemical thiamine has no B_1 activity until it is integrated into the body metabolism, and the efficiency of that integration depends a great deal on everything else being eaten.

Vitamin supplementation

I have spoken rather negatively of the trend to fortify fabricated food with vitamins, but that does not mean vitamin supplementation will not be helpful. There are two principles. First, the superior way to obtain vitamins and minerals is in whole foods because the vitamins and minerals often exist in forms better utilised by the body and the natural balances of all the nutrients are present. Second, vitamin supplementation may be helpful but it should be done in moderation and in a manner complementary to what you eat. For example, if your diet includes a lot of citrus fruits then your need for vitamin C supplementation would be minimal, for others extra vitamin C could be useful. Keep in mind the fact that athletes tend to eat large quantities of food and obviously the extra food, especially if they are whole foods, will supply additional vitamins and minerals.

No-one can be sure if they are eating an optimal diet, and even with the very best of intentions the quality will vary from day to day. For this reason vitamin supplementation with a balanced vitamin mixture will be good insurance. This supplementation is in addition to good food selection. Don't make the mistake of believing that eating vitamins will make up for poor food choices.

Proteins for strength

How much protein is good

What is the importance, to exercise, of the quantity and quality of protein in the diet? The available information is scanty and imprecise. Dr R.C. Darling and co-workers of the Fatigue Laboratory, Harvard University, Boston, Mass., studied three groups of men engaged in heavy physical work. The subjects ate a normal diet but varied the proportions in order to vary the amount of protein. One group eating mainly potatoes, grains and vegetables had a protein intake of 50 g per day. A second group eating mostly meat and high protein foods consumed between 157 and 192 g per day. A third group fell in between with 95–113 g of protein. These investigators could detect no difference in physical performance or health of the men.[7]

Protein differs from both fat and carbohydrate in that it contains nitrogen. Proteins cannot be stored by the body so that any protein consumed over the body's basic needs is metabolised for energy and the excess nitrogen excreted. For a male engaged in light activity 0·35 g of protein per kg of body weight suffices. However, when the body is physically stressed the demand for protein increases. Men doing heavy physical work and eating a low protein diet suffer decreases in their haemoglobin and proteins circulating in the blood.[13] The National Academy of Sciences (U.S.) has established an allowance of 0·6 g/kg/day for adults if the protein is of animal origin. For a standard mixed diet they recommend 0·8 g/kg/day. For a 70 kg man that is 56 g.[19]

Some recent experiments carried out by Dr N.S. Scrimshaw and Dr V.R. Young show that individuals eating a diet for three months providing just that recommended amount of protein, suffered decreases in lean body and muscle mass and sometimes changes in liver metabolism.[20] Thus we are left in a quandary. The National Academy of Sciences' figures were established for adults engaged in light activity (and for males) that would represent the burning of about 3000 Cal (kilocalories) per day. Persons exercising strenuously will burn more than 5000 Cal per day so that their protein consumption will rise automatically unless they make the mistake of getting those extra calories through sugary foods. Dr Darling pointed out his middle group of exercising men, eating a normal mixed diet furnishing about 5000 Cal, consumed 95–113 g of protein a day. The conclusion we can draw is that the physical demand of athletics requires more protein than the bare amount suggested by the National Academy of Sciences, and that a normal diet of non-fabricated foods will automatically provide much more than the base line, which should be adequate.

Protein quality

I would like to comment on some basic protein biochemistry because readers may ask how much additional protein is required. First, with respect to protein quality, scientists use a measure of net protein utilisation (NPU), which refers to the percentage of the protein eaten that could be converted into body protein. For example, egg protein has an NPU of about 95 per cent which means 95 per cent of the egg protein could be converted into human protein. Brown rice has an NPU of about 68 per cent and beef steak about 68 per cent ([20]). Protein consists of amino acids of which some cannot be made by the human body and must be consumed in the dietary protein. The amino acid balances of plant protein have NPUs ranging from about 30 per cent (lentils) to the 68 per cent of brown rice. Because of this, people concerned about getting adequate protein sometimes neglect plant sources. Don't be misled by the tables of NPU values, however, because they only have significance if you eat the single food. Proteins from different sources complement each other. A cup of cooked dried beans (200 g) with five slices of whole wheat bread (115 g) has as much protein as a six ounce (155 g) lean steak and an NPU of 83 per cent compared to the beef steak's 68 per cent. Thus, in a properly mixed diet, single protein quality is not such a critical factor.

The body cannot store surplus protein

The body can store surplus fat and carbohydrates. It cannot store surplus protein. Any protein consumed above the body's basal requirements will be metabolised to yield energy. Your muscles represent a form of protein storage but your body biochemistry is constituted in such a way that there is no protein gain in the absence of exercise. This is not true of carbohydrates and fats, because your body lays down fat even if you remain in bed. Thus, only during actual muscle building is there net retention of protein, and for an athlete building muscles the extra demand would only be a few g a day which can be easily accommodated by the extra protein normally eaten in the average mixed diet.

Nevertheless, the exact protein requirements for humans, outside of our knowing the bare minimum, remain hazy. The available evidence would suggest that an intake of 1·5–2 g/kg/day of mixed proteins should suffice for any athlete engaged in strenuous activity. If you strive for more protein in your diet you risk unbalancing your body biochemistry and that might negate any value from the extra protein. As it is, to get 2 g of protein per kilogram of body weight, a 100 kg person would have to eat 1 kg of beef steak. All foods, however, contain protein and even eating a vegetarian diet it is possible to consume an amount of protein far above the base line. A high meat consumption may provide a psychological lift but it has no bearing on increasing muscle performance and if it distorts a balanced body biochemistry then the total effect is negative.

To get the most out of the proteins in your diet pay attention to quality. Although you may eat meat I would suggest you balance your vegetable protein as vegetarians do. In the later section on specific dietary suggestions I give more information.

Fatty proteins

Meat was once the flesh of a living animal, and it supplies many nutrients other than protein. The trace minerals and vitamins it supplies are desirable, but commercial meat supplies another nutrient much less desirable — fat. Under conditions of intensive raising of chickens, pigs and cattle, the animals lay down large quantities of fat interspersed throughout the muscle flesh. It is the fat content which makes a beef steak tender. Dr M. Crawford of the Nuffield Institute of Comparative Medicine, London, England, has done studies that show the beef steaks obtained from intensively raised cattle have an abnormal type of fat. Dr Crawford notes that a certain amount of fat is normal. All cells contain fat molecules, which integrate with proteins to form essential cellular structures. These fats consist of mostly unsaturated fats, some of which the human body cannot make and must, therefore, be derived from a plant source or the flesh of animals that have eaten plants. The fat marbled throughout beef muscle is not this type of essential fat but is a storage fat consisting of saturated fatty acids. Dr Crawford finds that the muscle of intensively raised cattle contain 15 g of fat per 100 g of flesh weight compared to 2 g/100 g from cattle which grazed on the open range. The fat composition of the free range animals is similar to that of wild animals.[6] Nature intended man to eat meat but not necessarily the fatty type of meat sold commercially.

The unnaturally high fat content of commercial beef for example yields a disproportionate amount of fat calories. One hundred g of so-called lean commercial beef steak yields 80 Cal of energy from protein and 135 Cal from its fat. The high consumption of animal fat in general has raised much concern among medical scientists and they now feel that it is a contributory cause of heart disease. Dr Crawford has refined that concern by distinguishing the type of fat laid down in commercially raised animals. The more youthful athletes may not be concerned about middle age heart problems but those same problems start early in life. One change that occurs is a gradual narrowing by fatty deposits of the arteries that supply the heart muscle with nutrients and these changes have been found in teenagers and young men. Heart disease is a complex issue and no one factor should be damned exclusively. The fatty deposits in the arteries however, are an expression of a deranged body biochemistry and probably could be avoided by striving for a balanced body biochemistry through judicious selection of foods.

The case for whole nourishment

Four principles
In this article I have stressed that you should strive for optimum body biochemistry because only through achieving peak body biochemistry can you hope to achieve peak physical performance. And the foundation to achieving top biochemical performance is achieving a sound nutritional programme. But when it comes to designing such a programme we find that the art of nutritional science is still underdeveloped and at best can only provide general guidelines. However, we can seek additional guidance from the more recent knowledge of biology and through using some sense. After all, the human race has flourished for some millions of years without the direction of nutrition scientists. Thus, in selecting food to achieve maximum biochemical potential I recommend the following principles.

1 *Everything you eat should be as whole as possible.*
A corollary of this principle is that everything you eat should be as nourishing as possible. There is no place for the naked calories of refined foods in your programme. The high energy yield required by athletes requires an intricate metabolic network powered by the entire spectrum of nutrients.

It is practical to eat whole wheat products but perhaps it is not practical to eat olives when it is the olive oil you really want, but don't eat olive oil that has been refined. Eat vegetables and fruit raw when practical instead of cooked. Any kind of heat treatment reduces the nutritional quality of a food. However, many valuable foods require cooking to make them palatable. Potatoes need cooking, wheat needs cooking although if you sprout it first it can be eaten·raw. Beans and other legumes may contain harmful substances that are destroyed only by cooking. So one needs to be realistic. It is beneficial, however, to include some raw food with every meal.

To follow this principle is to exclude all fabricated foods and commercially baked goods.

2 *You should eat a wide variety of foods every day.*
We know the human body requires a wide spectrum of nutrients but we don't know exactly in what quantities and in what balances. If you choose from whole foods according to the schedule below, your balances of protein, fats, carbohydrates and accessory factors will work out almost automatically. Because of the growing dominance of fabricated foods in supermarkets it is getting more difficult to find the variety of foods your body needs. Many fruits and vegetables available a generation ago have disappeared. You will, therefore, have to seek out a supplemental or even alternative source of food from the large commercial supermarket. Athletes who are prepared to invest large amounts of time in training should not begrudge the relatively small amount of time to develop their nutritional foundation.

3 *Everything interacts with everything else.*
This principle means that every nutrient, every food you consume, affects the metabolism of all the other foods being eaten. This principle stresses the importance of nutritional teamwork. In practical terms this principle also suggests that you don't rely on a few foods for optimum nourishment. Strive for that balanced variety

of foods. It is true that some cultures exist on rice and a few vegetables. There is, however, a long way between subsistence and peak body performance. In the 1920s Sir Robert McCarrison studied the diets of various ethnic groups in India. He fed typical diets to groups of rats and found that the health and the physique of the rats correlated exactly with those of the particular ethnic groups. Those Indians with robust health and splendid physiques were those who ate a wide variety of vegetables, nuts and grains, although not necessarily much meat or eggs. Those Indians eating white bread, margarine, cheap jam, canned vegetables and sugar, like the corresponding rats, were of poor physique and generally sickly.[16]

You should strive for whole nourishment. I talk of whole foods but your real goal is whole nourishment which can only be achieved through combining all your foods in an appropriate way.

4 *You are extraordinary.*

Your particular body biochemistry is unique so that your nutritional requirements are unique. Science, however, provides no help in tailoring the diet to a person. So the best you can do is to work out your diet according to the first three principles, keeping in mind that a particular dietary regime may give your neighbour excellent results but won't be entirely satisfactory for you.

Specific dietary recommendations

Nutritional advice is generally given in terms of specific nutrients with the objective of showing how you are to obtain the recommended daily allowance (RDA) of that nutrient. If you added up all this information, theoretically you could be well fed, but as I have already pointed out the RDAs are minimal values, and then only for the nutrients known.

In designing your own dietary schedule think in terms of foodstuffs, and if you choose whole foods in suitable combinations the vitamins, minerals and other essential nutrients will take care of themselves. You should choose a combination of foods. Below I list categories of foods with specific advice. The actual selection will vary according to your ethnic and personal preferences but the guidelines should serve everyone.

Grains

The common grains, wheat, rice, corn and oats, should be supplemented with millet, sorgham, triticale, rye and others. Grains and grain products will be your major source of carbohydrate and you would be wise to eat a variety of grains. Always eat the grain unrefined, i.e. brown rice, whole wheat flour. The polishing of rice and refining of wheat flour removes a major amount of vitamins and minerals.

Avoid commercially baked products because they are made from refined flour and in addition contain sugar, refined fat and various chemical additives.

Sprouted grains can be added to salads. They can be a source of vitamins and proteins superior to the unsprouted grain because of the metabolic conversions occurring during sprouting. Analysis shows, for example, that sprouted wheat has significantly higher protein content, thiamine and riboflavin.[15] Flour can be ground from sprouted grain and made into bread.

Vegetables and fruits

Fresh vegetables and fruits should be part of the daily diet; include at least two vegetables in addition to potatoes or grains at main meals. In addition, a fresh salad made from a green leafy vegetable should be eaten every day. Salad dressing should be simple unrefined oil and vinegar or good quality mayonnaise made from un-refined oil. Avoid commercially prepared dressings because they are concocted from refined oils and contain many chemicals. The sprouts of many legumes can be eaten directly. This avoids cooking and you get a very nutritious food.

Vegetables, if possible, should be eaten raw but for aesthetic reasons you may wish to cook them. If so, cook minimally and eat immediately. The Chinese stir fry method is good. If you boil the vegetables save the water for other cooking purposes because it will contain the minerals and some vitamins from the vegetables.

Fresh vegetables are preferable to frozen which in turn are preferable to canned. Fruits should always be eaten fresh; they make good 'in between meal' snacks.

Dried legumes

Dried beans, peas and lentils are good sources of balancing proteins. Eaten together with grains the combined protein is the equivalent of high quality animal protein. If one has a minimal source of animal protein in the diet the quantity of legumes should be increased.

Because some dried beans and other legumes contain harmful substances they have to be cooked before eating. Heat destroys these substances. Nearly all dried beans can be prepared at home by soaking in water and cooking for one half to one hour or more to soften them. The beans may be mashed, cooked and dried to form the grams of India. Also in India, legumes are ground into a powder called dahl.

Dairy products

With the exception of eggs the protein of cow's milk gives the highest net protein utilization (NPU). Whole milk is very close to a whole food in itself but many adults cannot tolerate it because they cannot digest the milk sugar, lactose. It is probably better to eat milk in the form of yogurt (unsweetened). Cheese is rich in milk protein and butter fat.

Butter should be eaten in moderation; it is preferred to margarine. At least butter is a natural product whereas margarine is prepared (by a harsh chemical process) from vegetable oils, and the molecular architecture of the natural fats is sub-stantially modified. Experimental evidence suggests that the synthetic fats of mar-garine are metabolised differently.[10].

For cooking purposes use unrefined vegetable oils.

Meats

The superior source of meat is from animals raised in a free-ranged manner, or from wild animals (including fish). Meat obtained from commercial animals has an unnaturally high content of fat. In North America about 90 per cent of beef and 100 per cent of chickens are raised under the intensive conditions that give rise to the unnatural muscle structure.

In selecting the amount of meat you wish to eat every day, keep in mind that muscle meat contains about 20 per cent by weight protein. Thus a 200 g steak yields 40 g of protein worth 160 Cal. You would be wise to divide your meat allowance and eat some at every meal. Of course, I have emphasised it is possible to get large amounts of protein in a balanced form even if meat is excluded from the diet. But I suspect most athletes would prefer to include meat in their diet. However, do not eat muscle meat to excess because you will deprive yourself of other needed nutrients.

Include organ meat in your meat diet. If you don't like the idea, grind it up and add to good quality hamburger. Liver, heart, kidney, brain and pancreas (sweet breads) are all good. Races that thrived on an all meat diet (such as the Eskimos) ate everything except the fur.

Avoid processed meats, sausages, frankfurters. All these products are high in fat and high in added chemicals.

Sweeteners
Avoid table sugar (sucrose), corn syrup, and any food to which they are added. Sucrose occurs naturally in small amounts in most fruits and vegetables and within this context it is supplied with the vitamins and minerals necessary for its digestion and assimilation. It is the refined sugar that is to be struck out of your diet. Brown sugar is white sugar dyed brown so is no less naked than white.

Soft drinks have a high sugar content (up to 15 per cent) and contain many artificial chemicals. Drink fruit juices or milk instead.

Do not take a chemical sweetener such as saccharin. It has a drug-like action on your body. Besides, fabricated foods containing artificial sweeteners contain many undesirable chemicals.

Natural sweeteners such as dates, raisins and honey are preferable. Honey is a mixture of sugars including sucrose. In a strict chemical sense honey would be considered to be identical with sucrose. In a biological sense it is very different because it is a natural substance containing a number of accessory substances. In cooking, because honey is sweeter than sucrose, use less.

Nuts and seeds
Nuts and seeds are good sources of protein, unsaturated oils, minerals and vitamins. Include them in your daily diet. Eat as snacks. Avoid the commercially roasted nuts, high in salt, chemical additives, added fat and often dyes.

Supplements and protein balancing
1 *Proteins*. Although athletes on a meat diet will get more protein than the bare minimum recommended by the National Academy of Sciences (U.S.), I suggest that the protein quality of the entire diet be balanced. Thus take a tip from the vegetarians and balance your vegetable proteins the way they do. The rules are simple. To balance you must eat the foods at the same time. The body cannot store protein, so the protein you eat in the morning has been metabolised by the middle of the day.

A more detailed description of how to balance vegetable proteins is contained in such books as *Diet for a Small Planet* by Francis Moore Lappe (1971, New York: Ballantine).

A convenient source of soy protein (legume) is a supplement prepared from soy flour. Choose a product made from full fat flour. This flour has undergone the minimal processing and retains most of the vitamins and minerals compared to the

16

more refined flours.[4] Keep in mind principle one, that everything you eat should be as nutritious as possible. The vitamin and mineral content of the soy flour is essential to the digestion and assimilation of the protein.

Try the following combinations:

grains	— legumes
eggs	— legumes
eggs	— grains; pasta
cottage cheese	
cheese	— grains
milk	
cottage cheese	
cheese	— nuts and seeds (peanuts and peanut butter are the most deficient of the common nuts — try other nut butters)
milk	
eggs	

2 *Vitamins and minerals.* The superior way to obtain your vitamins and minerals is through the whole foods you eat. Realistically, the vitamin and mineral levels of foods vary. The vitamin C content of different varieties of tomatoes, for example, can vary five fold.[11] The mineral content of plants reflects to a large extent the mineral content of the soil. Moreover, the plant's peculiar needs for minerals may not match human needs. Thus the plant may flourish yet be deficient in the minerals you require. Many areas which are farmed intensively have become deficient in magnesium, manganese and zinc. If your dietary selection is sufficiently varied the natural fluctuations of vitamins and mineral content of foods should even out. Nevertheless, because you can never be sure of the amount of vitamins you are taking, a balanced vitamin supplement is good insurance.

Table 1.1 Daily vitamin and mineral supplement according to Dr R.J. Williams

Vitamins		*Minerals*	
Vitamin A	10 000 units	Calcium	300·0 mg
Vitamin D	500 units	Phosphate	250·0 mg
Ascorbic acid (E)	100 mg	Magnesium	100·0 mg
Thiamine (B1)	2 mg	Cobalt	0·1 mg
Riboflavin	2 mg	Copper	1·0 mg
Pyridoxine (B6)	3 mg	Iodine	0·1 mg
Niacinamide	20 mg	Iron	10·0 mg
Pantothenate	20 mg	Manganese	1·0 mg
Vitamin B12	5 mcg	Molybdenum	0·2 mg
Tocopherols (E)	5 mg	Zinc	5·0 mg
Inositol	100 mg		
Choline	100 mg		

There is much talk these days of mega vitamin supplementation. In particular Professor L. Pauling has presented a strong case for supplementing your diet with up to a gram a day of vitamin C.[18] Other authorities have suggested large amounts of one or more vitamins to treat a disease. Athletes are not sickly, however, so I recommend a modest supplementation and suggest you use as a guide the above vitamin and mineral supplementation worked out by Dr Roger Williams. The only change I would make would be to increase the vitamin C to 500 mg and vitamin E to 100 mg (100–150 I.U. depending on the form of a-tocopherol). The figures in this table are for people expending 2500–3000 Cal per day, so as your daily calorie expenditure goes up increase accordingly.

Remember that all the vitamins have not necessarily been discovered so that the best this list can do is to indicate the known ones. For this reason you might be wise to seek some of your vitamin supplements from traditional natural sources — wheat germ, fish oils, yeast.

References

[1]Akroyd, W.R. and Doughty, J. (1970). *Wheat in Human Nutrition*. Rome: Food and Agriculture Organisation of the United Nations.

[2]Astrand, P.O. and Rodahl, K. (1970). *Textbook of Work Physiology*. New York: McGraw-Hill.

[3]Bergstrom, J. and Hultman, E. (1972). 'Nutrition for Maximal Sports Performance.' *JAMA*, 221 (9), pp. 999–1006.

[4]Briggs, G.M. (1975). 'Nutritional Aspects of Fabricated Foods.' *Fabricated Foods*, ed. G.E. Inglett. Westport: AVI Publishing Co.

[5]Cleave, T.L. (1975). *The Saccharine Disease*. New Canaan, Conn.: Keats Publishing Co.

[6]Crawford, M.A. (1974). 'The Relationship of Dietary Fats to the Chemistry and Morphologic Development of Muscle Liver and Brain.' *La Rivista Italiana Delle Sostanze Grasse*, 51 (Sept.), pp. 302–309.

[7]Darling, R.C., Johnson, R.E., Pitts, G.C., Consolazio, F.C. and Robinson, P.F. (1944). 'Effects of Variations in Dietary Protein on the Physical Well Being of Men Doing Manual Work.' *J. Nutr.*, 28, pp. 273–281.

[8]Debry, G., Poullain, B. and Bleyer, R.-E. (1974). 'Valeur Nutritionelle et Acceptabilité des Protéines de Soja en Alimentation Humaine.' *Alimentation et Travail*. (Deuxiéme Symposium International 15–18 Mai, 1974), ed. G. Debry and R. Bleyer (La Société du Nutrition et de Dietetique de la Langue Francaise), pp. 361–372.

[9]'Influence of Body Intake'. (1971). *Encyclopaedia of Sport Sciences and Medicine*, pp. 1124–1134.

[10]Hall, R.H. (1976). *Food for Nought. The Decline in Nutrition*. New York: Vintage Books, Random House.

[11]Harris, R.S. (1975). 'Effects of Agricultural Practices on Foods of Plant Origin' *Nutritional Evaluation of Food Processing*, 2nd edition, ed. R.S. Harris and E. Karmas. Westport, Conn.: AVI Publishing Co., pp. 33–57.

[12]Karlsson, J. and Saltin, B. (1971). 'Diet, Muscle Glycogen and Endurance Performance.' *J. Applied Physiology*, 31, pp. 203–206.

[13]Karvonen, M.J. (1967). 'Nutrition in Heavy Manual Labour'. *Nutrition and Physical Activity*, ed. for the Swedish Nutritional Foundation by Gunnar Blix. Uppsala: Almquist and Wiksells, pp. 59–63.

[14]Lockmiller, N.R. (1972). 'What are Textured Protein Products?' *Food Technology*, 26 (5), pp. 56–58.

[15]Lemar, L.E. and Swanson, B.G. (1976). 'Nutritive Value of Sprouted Wheat Flour.' *Journal of Food Science*, 41, pp. 719–720.

[16]McCarrison, R. (1921). *Studies in Deficiency Disease*. London: Henry Froude, Hodder and Stoughton.

[17]Pascal, G. (1974). 'Physiological and Metabolic Effects of Antioxidant Food Additives.' *World Review of Nutrition and Dietetics*, 19, ed. G.H. Bourne. New York: Karger, pp. 237–299.

[18]Pauling, L. (1971). 'The Significance of the Evidence about Ascorbic Acid and the Common Cold.' *Proc. Nat. Acad. Sci.*, USA, 68 (11), pp. 2678–2681.

[19]*Recommended Dietary Allowances*. (1974). 8th revised edition. Washington, D.C.: National Academy of Sciences.

[20]Scrimshaw, N.S. and Young, V.R. (1976). 'The Requirements of Human Nutrition.' *Scientific American*, (Sept.), pp. 51–64.

[21]Sinclair, H. (1971). 'Modern Diet and Degenerative Diseases.' *Just Consequences*, ed. R. Waller. London: Charles Knight, pp. 85–95.

[22]Williams, R.J. (1958). *Biochemical Individuality*. New York: John Wiley & Sons.

[23]Williams, R.J. (1971). *Nutrition Against Disease*. New York: Pitman.

[24]Wolf, W.J. (1975). 'Effects of Refining Operations on Legumes' *Nutritional Evaluation of Food Processing*, 2nd edition, ed. R.S. Harris and E. Karmas. Westport, Conn.: AVI Publishing Co., pp. 158–187.

Athletes and their coaches, no matter how primitive their methods, have been remembered throughout history for their efforts to improve athletic performance. Much of the credit for the continuous breaking of athletic records can be attributed to the constant improvement in training methods, techniques in performance, facilities and diets. In this continual effort to attain athletic excellence, the emphasis placed on the importance of proper diets for athletes should not be subordinated to the other factors credited as important to athletic success.

Although there may be general agreement that an athlete must have a good diet in order to perform at his best, there is far from general agreement as to what constitutes such a good diet. Much has been written on this subject, and the views expressed have differed so vehemently that athletes and coaches are faced with a mass of conflicting information. These differences have reached a state where the subject of special foods and diets has become the most prominent of the many idiosyncracies which are still associated with training for athletics.

Of the many aspects of an athlete's diet, one of the most controversial relates to the meal just prior to the athletic event, which is normally referred to as the pre-game meal. In New Zealand, for example, the common practice is to provide those engaged in an endurance-type event such as rugby with a 'steak meal' before the game. Many, however, are changing to what is termed a 'liquid meal' prior to participation in such a sports event.

Pre-game emotional tension, gastrointestinal motility and the feeding of athletes

Dr K.D. Rose and Dr S.I. Fuenning

This paper was first published in the *Nebraska State Medical Association Journal* (December 1960), vol. 45, no. 12, pp. 575–79.

It is the practice of many colleges and universities to feed their football players a rather heavy pre-game meal. This is true at our university. A training-table meal consisting of steak, potatoes, vegetables, and so forth is offered at 9.00 to 9.30 a.m. on the day of the game. This presumably serves two purposes:
1 The voracious hunger of these healthy young males is satisfied.
2 They can go into the game with the feeling that they are supplied with the needed energy to fulfill the requirements.

The meal time is supposedly far enough in advance of the game to assure complete digestion before game time. However, a certain degree of first-half sluggishness suggested that the validity of this feeding regimen should be investigated.

Recitation of a few common analogies will refresh your memory on the relationship between eating and physical and mental activity.
1 All of you who have eaten a good holiday meal recall only too vividly what you most liked to do immediately afterwards.
2 Although subject to some question at the present time, the old adage of 'an hour or two after eating before swimming to prevent cramps' is well known.
3 The phenomenal drowsiness of students in the one o'clock lecture class needs no elaboration.

If we accept the fact, then, that the post-prandial interval is attended by mental and physical sluggishness, what relationship has that to a football player fed four and a half to five hours before game time? For a partial understanding of the relationship, let us turn to the effect of emotions on digestion. All of you have heard the reminder not to argue at mealtime, it interferes with digestion. May I quote from Cecil and Loeb's *Textbook of Medicine*?[1]: 'The symptoms of the psychophysiological disturbance in the gastrointestinal tract are the consequence of anxiety in interpersonal affairs. They may take the form of anorexia, nausea, nervous indigestion, vomiting, belching, distress from gas, and epigastric pain resulting from diarrhea and constipation.' What could cause more 'anxiety in interpersonal affairs' than the week to week need to be up for the big game, particularly in a relatively young man not yet accustomed to the emotional vicissitudes of this modern life as exemplified by present day college or varsity competition? The correlation between pre-game tension and digestion needs no further elaboration.

In order that we not be complacent in the knowledge that our players are fed at least four hours before game time, let us examine the matter of gastrointestinal motility. Best and Taylor[2] in the sixth edition of their book *Physiological Basis of Medical Practice* state this concerning the emptying time of the stomach: 'In normal young males, the test meal is evacuated (from the stomach) in about two hours.'

Referring to intestinal motility, they have this to say: 'The material (barium meal) commences to leave the stomach almost immediately after it has been swallowed; it moves steadily and at a fairly rapid rate through the duodenum and very rapidly through the jejunum. Its progress through the ileum becomes progressively slower as the ileocecal opening is approached, and in the lower part of the ileum the material tends to accumulate before it is passed into the cecum. It commences to enter the latter in about two and a half hours on the average. In four hours or so, the material arrives at the hepatic flexure and in about six hours at the splenic flexure.'

In the spring of this year, four of our football players volunteered to serve as test subjects in an analysis of gastrointestinal motility before and after a football game. The game chosen was the annual Varsity-Alumni Game, one most likely to simulate actual varsity competition. It was our hypothesis that pre-game tension would be sufficient to affect digestion of a pre-game meal. It is the custom, as stated above, to feed our football players a heavy meal consisting of steak (8 oz), potatoes, vegetables, and so forth at 9.00 to 9.30 a.m. in the hope that it would be digested by game time. This procedure was followed, but with a small glass of barium sulphate added. About two and a half to three hours later, just before suiting up for the game, flat film X-rays were taken of their abdomens. These X-rays were then repeated after the game, and after the boys had showered, changed clothes, and walked or driven to the Health Service. On the average this was seven to seven and a half hours after eating. By this procedure, it was hoped that some information might be obtained on rate of passage of a pre-game meal.

The results obtained were surprising but not unexpected.

Only one case has been chosen to demonstrate the delay in gastrointestinal motility brought about by pre-game tension. A film taken two and a half hours after eating showed that about 90 per cent of the subject's meal was retained within his stomach. After the game, and six hours and forty-five minutes after eating, he still had the meal in his jejunum and it was only just entering the large bowel. He was over four hours behind in his digestive schedule. The other three boys retained 25 per cent to 50 per cent of their meals in their stomachs at two and a half to three hours after eating, and were from two to three hours behind on their digestive schedule.

We do not believe that these cases represent physiological variations but rather examples of reduced gastrointestinal motility secondary to pre-game emotional tension. The net result was that these four players were simultaneously playing football and digesting a meal.

Assuming, therefore, that these players were digesting while playing, let us examine what effect that might have on their physical and mental aptitude. First and most important is the reminder that it takes blood to digest food. Under normal circumstances, such as after that Thanksgiving meal, one becomes sluggish and lies down 'to let his food digest'. This is only a manifestation of the fact that the bulk of his blood supply is being pooled in his visceral organs for the purpose of digestion. If one chooses to be physically active after eating, the situation then resolves into a conflict between one's digestive and muscular systems for the available blood pool. I do not know which one wins in any given case, but I strongly suspect both suffer. In muscular activity, glucose, as the energy source, is burned to lactic acid in an oxygen-free environment, giving about 0.16 calories per gram. Were this lactic acid to accumulate in the muscles, cramps would ensue. This is, in part, what is presumed to occur when a person undertakes too strenuous activity after eating. Our bodies, however, are endowed with a mechanism to prevent this and to obtain more energy. In the presence of oxygen, as furnished by the blood, lactic acid is burned to carbon dioxide and water, releasing 3·8 calories per gram of original glucose. This is twenty-five times the energy released by the oxygen-free mechanism. One can thus see the importance of oxygen in muscular function, i.e., to further oxidize the lactic acid to produce the major part of the needed energy. Since blood is the oxygen transporter in our system, one can immediately recognize the detrimental effect a conflict between digestion and muscular activity would have on physical stamina. Bullen and co-workers stated, in a recent article on 'Athletics and Nutrition',[3] that: 'Availability of oxygen and its efficient use can become the limiting factor in performance.'

Next, we must remember that the mere act of digestion is a complex process. First of all, ingested food must be broken down into molecular-sized particles before it can be transported across the intestinal membrane into the circulation. From there it must be transported to the liver and muscles to be so altered as to be available for use. In other words, one is not sustained at the moment by what is in the process of digestion but what has been stored in the past. Bullen has stated: 'In sports which demand endurance and prolonged activity, there is evidence that performance is better maintained if the person is on a high carbohydrate diet ... if these diets have been consumed for several days prior to the event.' And again: 'Available evidence indicates that the relative composition or size of the meal preceding an athletic event of short duration is generally unimportant to the performance of the athlete.'

It is easy to pose a problem, but less easy to offer a solution. Should you feed or not feed an athlete? If not, as do most track men, how are you going to appease that huge, hungry football player? We believe that there is a satisfactory solution to the problem.

'The degree to which the gastric contents have been reduced to fluid or semifluid consistency appears to be an important factor determining the rate of emptying of the stomach.' 'Solid particles act as mechanical stimuli which, coming into contact with the pylorus, cause pyloric closure' and prevent emptying of the stomach until the food mass is fluid or semifluid. 'Fluids and semifluids commence to leave the stomach almost immediately after being swallowed.'[2]

Steak and potatoes should be taboo, but there are, on the market, certain protein hydrolysate mixtures with added carbohydrates and vitamins which, when mixed with milk as a milk shake, produce a palatable cold drink containing about 2400 calories per quart. The mixture is liquid and would be expected to leave the stomach at once; it is predigested so that absorption should be rapid; a high caloric intake is concentrated in a relatively small volume; an immediate but not sustained energy source should be readily available; the finished product can be made quite palatable and in a form acceptable to the young adult, namely, as a chocolate milk shake. One should be cautioned that not all protein hydrolysates are palatable. Two, marketed under the trade names of Sustagen and Meritene, are in the acceptable group. In any event, feeding should be early in the day of the game.

Acceptance of such a programme of pre-game feeding depends, of course, on the acceptance of the rationale behind it by the coaching and training staff, because they are the ones who must convince the players that this is a basically sound method of preparing them to be in peak physical state when the whistle sounds. We hope that this paper will stimulate some of you to give consideration to the rationality of proper pre-game feeding.

References

[1]Cecil, R.L. and Loeb, R.F. (1959). *A Textbook of Medicine*, 10th edition. Philadelphia: W.B. Saunders & Co.
[2]Best, D.H. and Taylor, N.B. (1955). *The Physiological Basis of Medical Practice*, 6th edition. Baltimore, Md.: Williams and Wilkins Co.
[3]Bullen, B., Mayer, J., and Stare, F.J. (1959). 'Athletes and Nutrition in Sports Injuries.' *The American Journal of Surgery*, ed. Thomas B. Quigley.

A liquid pre-game meal for athletes

Dr K.D. Rose, P.J. Schneider and Dr G.F. Sullivan

In an effort to obviate vomiting in athletes before important competitive events, a liquid meal was devised, and its ingestion was so timed that the stomach would be empty at the beginning of the game. The volume of the liquid meal, served cold at 10.30 a.m., was 474 cc. It supplied 925 large calories; of these 68 per cent, 24 per cent, and 8 per cent were contributed respectively by carbohydrate, protein, and fat. It passed through the stomach in less than two hours. It did not differ from the conventional solid meal with respect to subsequent hunger, diarrhoea, or weight changes, but in those who took it dryness of the mouth was less frequent during the game, strength and endurance seemed to be improved, and both vomiting and muscular cramps were eliminated.

This paper was first published in the *Journal of the American Medical Association* (October 1961), vol. 178, pp. 30–33. Copyright 1961, American Medical Association.

Report on a field trial

The problem of physiological upsets attending stress-associated human endeavours is well known. Gastrointestinal counterparts of the traditional cardiopulmonary 'wind-up' are common in athletic endeavours.[1]

This fact was forcefully emphasised by our athletic director during one of the periodic meetings between the medical and coaching staff of our athletic department. His statement: 'Surely there must be something you can do to get rid of pre-game vomiting', led us to consider the entire problem of pre-game and game-time food and liquid ingestion. In an excellent review article, Bullen *et al.*[2] have discussed the field of athlete feeding. However, primary emphasis was placed on the effect of various feeding regimens on physical stamina, and no reference was made to our basic problem. This led to an investigation of the role of the pre-game meal in gastrointestinal disorders.

In a previous publication[3] some of the aspects of gastrointestinal motility in relation to pre-game feeding of athletes were discussed. Evidence presented indicated that ingestion of a solid pre-game meal by football players was attended by delayed gastric emptying time, such that food was still in the stomach or small bowel, or both, during the actual game. Assuming that such game time digestion compromised muscular blood supply and resulted in decreased physical capabilities, it appeared that some feeding regimen was needed which would assure an empty stomach and small bowel at game time. It was proposed that a liquid meal might answer the problem because of its rapid gastric emptying time. The present paper reports on our experiences with a liquid pre-game meal fed during fall practice and the varsity football season, 1960.

Methods and materials

A liquid surgical meal (Sustagen) formed the basic pre-game meal throughout the test season. During the fall practice session, a liquid meal was given upon arising. It was again offered at noon to those who wished not to eat the usual solid food. Most of the regular varsity players voluntarily chose the liquid meal. During the ten-game varsity season, the following feeding regimen was used on the road as well as at the home field. At 9.00 a.m., a light meal of toast, honey, and sliced peaches was offered. At 10.30 a.m., 8 to 16 oz of the liquid meal was taken during the taping and tactical conferences. No other food was consumed until after the game, at which time the traditional 12 oz steak dinner was eaten by all. During the game, cool 0.2 per cent sodium chloride solution was offered in moderate quantities, to replace salt lost by perspiration. Football players frequently lose 3 to 5 lb or more during a game, most of this in the form of perspiration which contains 0·2 to 0·5 per cent sodium chloride. Severe cramps can result from acute salt loss, and 0·2 per cent sodium chloride is recommended as the proper replacement.[4] When taken cool (but not cold) it can be consumed in moderate amounts without causing detrimental effects and is, in fact, quite refreshing to the hot, dry football player.

The fetish of water abstinence, as practised by most football teams, has no basis in physiological fact when such water is taken as 0·2 per cent sodium chloride. There were four heat exhaustion deaths in the school year 1960 to 1961 on the football fields of America. With such an etiology these deaths were preventable and therefore unnecessary and deplorable.

When prepared with plain water in cup for cup proportions, the liquid meal furnishes 1790 calories per quart (32 oz). To increase palatability, it must be served cold and with various flavouring agents added, such as chocolate, strawberry, and coffee syrups. It is then practically indistinguishable from a milk shake. This is not true when served warm or lukewarm; thus attention must be directed toward preparing and keeping it cool, even to the extent of icing the container if need be. Flavouring additives furnish calories themselves so that the final solution contains 1850 calories per quart or 925 calories per usual 'meal' of 16 oz.

Table 1.2 presents a comparison between the caloric value of the average solid pre-game meal consumed by our football team and staff and that of the liquid meal regimen. It will be observed that there is little difference in the total caloric value of both regimens.

Table 1.2 Comparison of calories and cost, 'solid' and 'liquid' pre-game meals

Food item	Calories Solid meal regimen	Liquid meal regimen
Broiled steak (8 oz)	770	
Eggs (2) fried or scrambled	220	
Oatmeal (236 g)	148	
Cream for above	300	
Orange juice (8 oz)	110	
Toast (2 slices)	125	125
Honey (42 g)	125	125
Coffee or tea (with cream and sugar)	60	60
Peaches in heavy syrup		355
Liquid surgical meal (16 oz)		925*
Total calories	**1858**	**1590**
Cost	**$3.50 to $10.00**	**$1.50**

*68% in form of carbohydrate, 24% in form of protein and 8% in form of fat.

Motility studies were carried out by feeding 2 oz of a moderately thick barium sulphate mixture simultaneously with the liquid meal. Posteroanterior 'flat' films of the abdomen were taken at two hours and six hours after ingestion of the liquid meal. These times correspond to the two-hour pre-game film and to the immediate post-game film, respectively.

Results

Football games are not won by any gimmick such as a liquid meal. The factors which determine whether a team will or will not win or lose a football game on any given Saturday are many, not the least of which is the current emotional state of the coaches and players. In approaching this problem we were interested solely in improving the total physical capabilities of the team as a whole. In keeping with that interest, we will evaluate our results in terms of observable changes in general physical state. Table 1.3 lists the seven physical symptoms and signs which were evaluated. They will be discussed individually.

Weight change. Bearing in mind that the team consumed the liquid meal only pre-game during the varsity season, no particular weight change was anticipated and none was noted. During the fall training period, when the liquid diet was consumed frequently as two of the three meals, weight loss was still only consistent with the expected loss attending physical conditioning.

Hunger. Initially there were numerous complaints about lack of bulk. This was resolved by (a) adding the early morning toast, honey, and peaches in heavy syrup, and (b) by time, i.e., as the players became acquainted with the diet they accepted it and, in fact, staunchly supported it. Complaints of hunger disappeared. As a concrete example, the evening before the fifth game, the players were polled to determine whether they wished to return to the solid pre-game meal. Of 52 players, 51 voted to stay with the liquid regimen, their reason being a general sense of improved well-being. This opinion was expressed in spite of some vicissitudes creat-

25

ing concern at the time. They went out and won their game the next day. Prior to the seventh game the first two varsity squads were again polled. Of 24 members voting, 20 favoured staying with the liquid regimen, the reason again being the general feeling of physical and mental alertness associated with pre-game ingestion of the light food.

Nausea and vomiting. Pre-game vomiting was completely eliminated. This was probably the most significant beneficial change noted. When the already observed delay in gastric emptying time attending the solid regimen[3] and rapid emptying time attending the liquid meal regimen (q.v.) is considered, this result was not surprising. Needless to say, it was a most welcome change both to players and trainers.

Table 1.3 Comparison of important symptoms, 'solid' and 'liquid' pre-game meals

Symptoms	*Presence of in*	
	Solid meal regimen	*Liquid meal regimen*
Hunger	None	None
Vomiting	Common	None
Diarrhoea	Occasional	Occasional
'Cotton mouth'	Common	Rare
Muscular cramps	Occasional	None
Strength and endurance		Improved
Weight change	None	None

Diarrhoea. Some individuals exhibit intestinal hyperperistalsis under emotional stress. Thus, diarrhoea has always been a troublesome symptom with certain players. The liquid regimen did not eliminate this. However, there were only two players who seemed to have trouble with loose stools and only one of these to any degree. He was controlled by one dr. of paregoric after eating.

'Cotton mouth'. The term 'cotton mouth' describes a complaint of dry mouth with relative concentration of the saliva which is experienced by some players. Being a common trade complaint, it has been explained in various ways, all the way from altitude to diet. It appears to be, however, the result of a relatively complex neurohormonal reaction to nervous tension plus dehydration in which increased production of a more concentrated saliva occurs. We experienced 'cotton mouth' only once during the season and that was the first game, played in the south in the presence of high humidity and 80° (F) heat. Profuse perspiration was undoubtedly the cause here. Freedom from 'cotton mouth' can probably best be attributed to the freely allowed 0·2 per cent sodium chloride solution and not to the liquid diet itself.

Cramps. No complaint of either abdominal, generalised, or localised muscular cramp was encountered. This salutary effect of the liquid diet regimen can be attributed to two facts:

1 Digestion and absorption having been completed, all of the available blood pool was being used for muscular activity.

2 Salt replacement during the game obviated gross electrolyte disturbances.[4]

Strength and endurance. 'Fought in 80° heat, it was Nebraska which showed the greater strength at the finish.' This quote from the wire services of the day probably most clearly expresses the effect of the liquid diet regimen on the general stamina of the team throughout the year. Even in defeat they were the first ones off the ground after the play. This was particularly noticeable during the final quarter of the games. Of more importance to our study, however, was the simple observation that ingestion of the recommended pre-game meal did not compromise the physical stamina of the players. In fact, they felt better.

Gastrointestinal motility. Three to four hour delays in gastric and small bowel emptying times have been shown in varsity players consuming a solid pre-game meal.[3] During the regular 1960 football season, four first-string freshman football players volunteered to participate in a similar motility study with the liquid diet. Prior to their most important game they were given 2 oz of barium sulphate mixture along with the liquid meal. Two hours and six hours later they were X-rayed. Of most significance was the consistent observation that the stomach was empty at two hours. Frequently the meal had traversed a large portion of the small bowel also and was into the colon. Having evacuated the stomach and traversed a large portion of the small bowel two hours before game time, it is reasonable to assume that at game time the meal had completely evacuated the small bowel. In other words, the meal had undoubtedly been digested and absorbed by game time, four hours after eating.

Comment
The recommended use of a liquid pre-game meal is based on several sound physiological principles. They are:
1 Solid foods must be converted to a liquid or semi-liquid state before they are evacuated from the stomach.[5] Emotional tension can further delay that emptying time.[1, 3]
2 Liquid foods leave the stomach immediately.[5]
3 Simultaneous demands upon the general blood pool by digestion and muscular activity compromise either one or both functions.[1] Either digestion is decreased or halted, or muscular efficiency is decreased. In either event, the presence of food in the stomach or small bowel is of no use to the player. It is, in fact, detrimental.

X-ray studies of gastrointestinal motility have shown that a solid pre-game meal eaten the traditional 4 hours before game time has not passed through the small bowel by game time (i.e., is still in the process of digestion).[3] Present studies have shown that a liquid pre-game meal has evacuated the stomach and has largely traversed the small bowel in two hours after ingestion. It is safe to assume it has traversed the small bowel completely two hours later at game time.

An average-sized young male adult will require about 72 calories per hour for his basal metabolic requirements. Athletes require an additional 3·5 to 10·6 calories per minute while in active competition.[2] Assuming the maximum calorie requirement, a 60-minute football game would require 708 calories. The liquid diet regimen recommended furnishes 1590 calories, or twice as much as is needed. In fact, the liquid portion of the regimen itself, furnishing 925 calories, would be adequate for the task. The bulk of the energy is in the form of carbohydrate (Table 1.2), a form most desirable for contests requiring sustained effort.[2] Absence of hunger symptoms and maintenance of strength and endurance reflect this caloric adequacy. Muscular cramps, particularly those involving the muscles of the calf, are usually common.

The fact that none were encountered during this field trial attests, again, to the value of the liquid diet regimen.

The most significant effect of the liquid diet was the elimination of pre-game nausea. With the stomach empty, nausea and vomiting cease. The relief of the trainers and the boys beset by this problem is sufficient to make it all worthwhile, not to mention the increase in player morale and efficiency.

Summary

The entire coaching staff, training staff, and squad of a varsity football team participated in a field trial of a liquid pre-game feeding regimen during the fall training and football season of 1960. A calorie-rich liquid meal replaced the solid food pre-game meal, and cool 0·2 per cent sodium chloride solution was allowed when desired, with some moderation, during practice and during varsity games. Gastrointestinal motility studies by X-ray indicated that the liquid meal had traversed the stomach and small bowel by game time. Hence, muscular activity was not in conflict with digestion. Muscular cramps and pre-game and game time vomiting were eliminated. Weight remained constant; strength and endurance were improved. It appears that a liquid, calorie-rich pre-game meal is physiologically and practically sound, and it is recommended for use by all athletes.

Sustagen was supplied through the courtesy of Mead Johnson and Company, Evansville, Ind.

References

[1]Upjohn, H.L., *et al.* (1953). 'Nutrition of Athletes.' *JAMA*, 151 (March), pp. 818–19.

[2]Bullen, B., Mayer, J., and Stare, F.J. (1959). 'Athletics and Nutrition.' *Amer. J. Surg.*, 98 (Sept.), pp. 343–352.

[3]Rose, K.D., and Fuenning, S.I. (1960). 'Pre-Game Emotional Tension, Gastrointestinal Motility and the Feeding of Athletes. *Nebr. State Med. Jour.* 45 (Dec.), pp. 575–579.

[4]Best, C.H. and Taylor, N.B. (1955), *Physiological Basis of Medical Practice*, 6th edition. Baltimore: Williams and Wilkins Co., p. 734.

[5]Ibid., p. 567.

The liquid pre-game meal three years later

Dr K.D. Rose *et al.*

First published in the *Journal of the National Athletic Trainers Association* (1963).

The concept of preparticipation emotional tension and its effect on the gastrointestinal tract is certainly not new, the problem having been with mankind since the beginning of time. In spite of recent idealistic comments[1] in regard to a game being only a game, wishing tension away will not dispose of it. In fact, tension is the stuff from which good competitors are made. It is part of man's make-up, but some of its less desirable side effects can be ameliorated in the same preventive spirit that an ankle is taped to prevent its being resprained.

In recent years occasional reference has been made to this subject in relationship to sports. Billick in 1948, for instance, mentions the need to consider pre-game emotional strain in planning what to feed an athlete prior to the game.[2] Bogert, in 1949, called specific attention to the suppressive action of strong emotions on gastrointestinal motility in athletes.[3] In 1951 Bensley stated specifically in regard to the pre-game meal: 'The chief consideration to be borne in mind in planning the meal is the emotional stress which the athlete may experience on the day of the event. This may lead to loss of appetite, abdominal discomfort, and even nausea, vomiting and diarrhoea.'[4]

Various authors have recommended certain pre-game diet schedules, apparently based on the knowledge that digestion and absorption, *under normal conditions*, are complete by four hours. Thus we find Morehouse and Rasch recommending bouillon, broiled steak, peas, toast, tea and fruit as a 10 a.m. pre-game meal in preparation for a 2 p.m. contest.[5] Dayton, in his book *Athletic Training and Conditioning* makes similar recommendations, the meal to be eaten between 8.30 and 10 a.m. with supplemental bouillon and melba toast at about 11.30 a.m.[6] Upjohn *et al.* lists essentially the same diet and time of eating (*viz.* 10 a.m.) but does admit that game tension might delay gastric emptying as long as six hours.[7] These recommendations, however, are made on the basis of the expected normal gastrointestinal motility, but there are several factors which modify this normal pattern. One is the physical consistency of the food; another is the emotional state of the individual in whom this meal has been placed.

Our University of Nebraska football team was in the habit of eating this recommended pre-game meal between 8 and 10 a.m., but had experienced a considerable amount of pre-game nausea and vomiting, a not uncommon phenomenon across the country. Our experience with this digestive malfunction had extended also to fall camp practice sessions. At the fall camp of 1959 a record was kept of the incidence of gastric upsets. The practice day began at 7 a.m. with a regular balanced breakfast; noon lunch was served at twelve and dinner at 6.30 p.m. The mean ambient morning temperature was 73°F and the average humidity was 62 per cent, in other words ideal practice weather. Practice was held for two hours in the morning and two hours in the afternoon. On the four recorded days of observation an average of nineteen men a day became nauseated and lost their breakfast during morning practice. Very few of the team ate lunch, consuming mostly liquids.

As a result of these and similar experiences on game days during the regular playing session our then Director of Athletics requested that consideration be given to a solution to this problem, since it appeared to be compromising the well-being of the team. As newcomers to the field of athletic nutrition and blissfully ignorant of the esoteric studies which had been published in this area of athletic medicine, it seemed perfectly obvious to us that our players were vomiting because of gastric

29

retention secondary to emotional tension and a too heavy meal. We set about to prove this.

At spring practice in 1960, at the Annual Varsity-Alumni football game, four men were selected as candidates for a gastrointestinal motility study. Simultaneous with the traditional pre-game meal between 9.30 and 10.00 a.m., they were given 1 oz of thick barium sulphate suspension. Between two and a half and two hours forty-five minutes later, just before suiting up, a prone film of the abdomen was taken. After the game, or from six and a half to seven and a half hours after eating, and after they had showered, changed into their street clothes and walked the four blocks to the Health Centre, they were again X-rayed. All of them had a decided gastric retention at two and a half hours. After the game there was still a considerable portion of the meal in the terminal jejunum and ileum. In other words, this meal was being digested and absorbed during the football game. It is a well accepted theory that digestion or muscular activity or both are compromised under such conditions.

The results of this study were made available to the general public at the National Athletic Trainers meeting in Kansas City in June, 1960 and published in the *Nebraska State Medical Journal*.[8] Based on the knowledge that solid food must be rendered liquid or semi-liquid before it is evacuated from the stomach,[9] it was suggested that a high calorie liquid meal, such as that used in post-surgical cases, might be the answer to this problem. These liquid diets are highly nutritious, well-balanced, and are readily digested and absorbed.

At the fall camp of 1960, following a schedule similar to that of 1959, 16 oz of a liquid surgical meal was fed each player at 6.45 a.m. and at noon for those who requested it. The morning ambient temperature averaged 84°F and the humidity was 69 per cent, almost unbearable for practice, yet not a single case of nausea or vomiting occurred during fall camp. The results were so spectacular the coaches and players were convinced immediately, and it became a part of our regular football routine.

The question was asked whether the liquid meal did in fact leave the stomach and small bowel in the accepted length of time. This question was resolved by testing four freshmen players similarly at one of their inter-school games. In all instances the results confirmed our expectation, the meal had passed through the small bowel by two to two and a half hours, and digestion and absorption were essentially complete by game time. The results of our experiences during the Varsity season 1961 have been published along with further discussion of the physiological basis of this feeding technique.[10]

As a result of these studies, the University of Nebraska has since offered the liquid pre-game meal routinely to all its athletes. To say it has met with unqualified success would be an erroneous statement, much depending on what is expected of it, but it has met with an unusual reception both on our campus and elsewhere in all sports.[11,13] Most of the criticism has come from those who misunderstand its purpose, which is to circumvent the problem of pre-game nausea and vomiting. The secondary gain, namely the improved sense of well-being, is taken as the primary goal. An example is a high school in California who had their boys drink the liquid the night before a game as well as on the day of the game but found they played no better. Clearly they misunderstood the purpose and were seeking some mysterious source of super muscular power not inherent in any extra-corporeal substance. Having been closely associated with this subject for three years we feel we are qualified to render an educated opinion on its value, and we would like to pass some of it on to you.

In the words of Dr Warren Guild of Harvard University,[14] who I think has made the best analysis to date of pre-event nutrition: 'Loose bowel movements with abdominal cramps and weakness, metabolic acidosis, dehydration, impaired emptying of gastric contents, low salt syndrome and inadequate energy supplies can be expected to impair the athlete's performance. If these can be avoided or minimised, the athlete can exert himself closer to his full potential.' He further states that the meal should not be high in protein to prevent enhancing the metabolic acidosis of muscular activity by the addition of exogenous acid from a high protein diet. (He is speaking now only of a pre-game meal.) Thus meat, eggs and fish should be eliminated. The pre-event meal 'should be easily digestible since the implications of competing "on a full stomach" are well known'. Since fat slows gastric emptying already compromised by tension, he recommends that fat be severely restricted: 'Carbohydrate, the most readily available and quantitatively significant source of calories in athletics ... is pre-eminent.'

The pre-game meal we have been using consists of 1590 calories of which only 104 are in the form of fat, 254 in the form of protein and 1232 in the form of carbohydrate, largely dextro-maltose and sugar. Toast, honey and peaches in heavy syrup are fed early, seven hours before the event. The liquid meal is fed four hours before game time. It is easily digestible and assimilable, passes readily into the small intestine and does not remain in the stomach. It thus appears ideally suited for the pre-event meal, and far superior to the present solid-type meal, if we can accept the suggestions and interpretations of Dr Guild.

Athletic hydrophobia is a word popularised, if not actually coined, by Dr J. Jay Keegan of the University of Nebraska College of Medicine. It refers to rigid liquid abstinence by players during an athletic contest for fear of suffering stomach cramps. This erroneous philosophy is still perpetuated by many coaches and trainers, but international publicity on heat exhaustion deaths on the fields of athletic contest is beginning to erode this bad training practice. Before a national TV audience watching the Orange Bowl game of 1961 the cameras showed a close-up of players as they came off the field to receive a transient spray of water in their mouth, only to spit it dutifully out on the ground after a brief mouth wash. This need not be so. At every contest our athletes have available a palatable, cool 0.2 per cent sodium chloride solution, and they may have as much of it as they desire within reason. It is not expected that all fluids lost during contest will be replaced, but by drinking water which is essentially isotonic with perspiration, body stores of salt are conserved and the dangers of heat exhaustion minimised. Undoubtedly this fact also contributes to the freedom from painful abdominal and leg cramps we have experienced since the inception of this regimen.

Does the liquid meal win games? After reviewing our football won and lost record for '60 and '61 the answer is obvious, it doesn't. Yet we have been accused of implying that this regimen will furnish a mysterious source of energy, and we have been cast with the lot of proponents of Royal Jelly, Vitamin E. protein pills and gelatine, to name only a few. It is not and has never been intended as a gimmick to supplant good coaching and motivation. Our present coach carved out a 9 to 2 record this past season, the best since 1904, and he did it with essentially the same team that the year before had suffered one of our most disastrous seasons. But again to paraphrase Dr Guild, if gastrointestinal symptoms can be avoided or minimised, the athlete can exert himself closer to his full potential. We think the liquid pre-game regimen has helped in this regard.

Do all athletes like it? The answer here is definitely not, nor do all require it. Some can play just as well on an empty stomach. Certain ethnic groups reject it almost entirely, preferring to have a full stomach before going into battle. But after three years trial, 29 of the 36 members of the varsity football squad still use the liquid meal voluntarily.

The most enthusiastic supporters are the members of the wrestling team, who found early that by going on a controlled Sustagen or Nutramen diet they could achieve weight levels easily and without the detrimental effects attending starvation diets or steam bath dehydration. Our wrestling team has had its best seasons in the past three years, since 1929. Mike Nissen, who wrestles at 137 lbs and has not lost a match in two years, including national matches, says it is 'the best thing since the wheel was invented.' Ray Knaub, one of our outstanding dash men, had trouble maintaining weight and stamina before supplementing his regular diet with the liquid diet before track meets. Mike Flemming, who doubles in the mile and two mile run, is a slightly built lad who had trouble running out of steam in the second event because he could hold no food on his stomach on meet days. Now he not only doubles but occasionally triples in the 880.

One must bear in mind that we are dealing with young men not yet accustomed to handling the tension of competition. In the pro ranks the story is different. Dr Nellen, team physician for the Green Bay Packers, has spoken to us on his experiences with the World Champions. When asked about the liquid diet he reported that they tried it in 1961. The team ate their usual pre-game meal and then the liquid meal, too, apparently just to please the 'Doc.' In 1962 it was not offered and no one asked for it. The obvious conclusion was that they could take it or leave it alone and still play championship ball. Yet there are athletes in the professional ranks who are bothered by pre-event vomiting. It seems reasonable that they could be helped by some friendly advice, antispasmatics and the liquid meal.

There are a few boys who state that the liquid meal makes them sick, largely due to the taste, which is not to their liking. But these are boys who have never held anything easily. On a questionnaire completed at the end of this last season some stated they ran out of energy, *but twice as many who were eating the regular diet had the same complaint.* One out of every three on the liquid regimen stated they felt hungry sometime during the game or immediately after, *but one out of every two on the regular meal had the same complaint.* It appears, therefore, that the liquid meal has not enhanced the normal subjective complaints referrable to hunger and energy.

In summary, after three seasons' use of the liquid pre-game feeding regimen we at the University of Nebraska remain convinced that it is a useful adjunct to the field of athletic nutrition. It unquestionably eliminates pre-game nausea and vomiting in the susceptible individual. Strength and endurance are not compromised, but in most instances seem to be improved; abdominal cramps and 'charley horses' have been essentially eliminated. This is not all dietary and fluid balance but probably reflects good training, too. Although I have not mentioned 'cotton mouth,' this symptom has also been essentially eliminated, probably as a result of freely offered 0·2 per cent salt solution.

The liquid pre-event meal has become established as a form of adjunctive nutritional therapy, applicable primarily to those athletes whose digestion is compromised by pre-game emotional tension, but useful for all. It is widely used, the degree of success experienced depending upon a thorough understanding of the rationale behind it and its expressed purpose. Although the technique of its use must be modified to meet the needs of the event, some form of the recommended regimen is applicable in all sports. An example is its use in the Pan-Am Games in Sao Paulo, Brazil, where one form of it was used in a variety of sports. In this instance its easy portability (twelve cases or 576 cans were carried as part of the standard equipment) and stability (no refrigeration needed) helped solve a knotty problem in feeding in an area where refrigeration was not available. In this situation it was fed warm instead of cold as has been previously recommended[10] without significant problems.

It appears that the liquid meal is here to stay. We admonish those who use it to do so wisely and where indicated, and it will add to their armamentaruim in preparing for peak physical fitness.

The co-operation of the University of Nebraska Department of Athletics in making this study possible is greatly appreciated.

References

[1]Quigley, T.B. (1963). *Medicine in Sports Newsletter*, 3(1).

[2]Billick, S.E. (1948). *The Trainer's Bible*, 8th edition. New York: T.J. Reed & Co., p. 106.

[3]Bogert, L.J. (1949). *Nutrition and Physical Fitness*, 5th edition. Philadelphia: W.B. Saunders Co., p. 323.

[4]Bensley, E.H. (1951). 'The Feeding of Athletes.' *Can. Med. Assn. Jour.*, 64, p. 503.

[5]Morehouse, L.E. and Rasch, P.J. (1958). *Scientific Basis of Athletic Training*. Philadelphia: W.B. Saunders Co., pp. 79–83.

[6]Dayton, O.W. (1960). *Athletic Training and Conditioning*. New York: The Roland Press Co., p. 37.

[7]Upjohn, H.L., Shea, J.A., Stare, F.J. and Little, L. 'Nutrition of Athletes.' *JAMA*, 151, p. 818.

[8]Rose, K.D. and Fuenning, S.I. (1960). 'Pre-Game Emotional Tension, Gastrointestinal Motility and the Feeding of Athletes.' *Nebr. State Med. Jour.*, 45, p. 575.

[9]Best, C.H. and Taylor, N.B. (1955). *Physiological Basis of Medical Practice*, 6th edition. Baltimore: Williams and Wilkins Co., p. 567.

[10]Rose, K.D., Schneider, P.J. and Sullivan, G.F. (1961). 'A Liquid Pre-Game Meal for Athletes. Report on a Field Trial.' *JAMA*, 178, p. 30.

[11]Cooper, D.L., Bird, B. and Blair, J. (1962). 'Use of a Liquid Meal in a Football Training Program.' *Jour. Okla. State Med. Assn.*, pp. 484–86.

[12]Thomas, D. (1963). 'A Report on Liquid Meal Diet for Weight Control.' *Amateur Wrestling News*, p. 9.

[13]Samka, Wm. (1963). 'Athletic Conditioning and the Liquid Meal.' Address presented at the all-American Clinic, Bemidjii, Minn., Aug., 1963.

[14]Guild, W. (1960). 'Pre-Event Nutrition with some Implications for Endurance of Athletes.' *'Exercise and Fitness': a Colloquium*. Univ. of Illinois College of Phys. Ed. and the Athletic Institute, pp. 135–37.

2 Replace that sweat — why?

Fluid balance and athletic performance

Dr R.B. Morrison

Dr R.B. (Bruce) Morrison, Member of the Australasian College of Physicians, has written this article on fluid (electrolyte) replacement specially for this book. This most important aspect of sports medicine is usually completely overlooked by participating athletes. ('Athlete' is used here in the broadest sense of the word, because sportsmen do not understand fluid replacement, nor its importance in body function and performance.)

The importance of normal salt and water balance in sustained athletic performance has taken a long time to become generally accepted. Most of our basic knowledge has come from physiological studies of animals and healthy human subjects, together with observation made on patients whose fluid balance is disordered. More recently, exercise physiologists have carried out detailed studies of highly trained athletes, the only 'experimental animal' in whom other athletes are likely to be interested. In fact all athletes should be encouraged to take part in well conceived experiments, preferably backed by the Sports Medicine Federation.

Body fluids and circulation of blood

Water accounts for approximately ⅔ of the body weight of the average lean athlete, e.g. 47 litres in a 70 kg person. Although much of this is contained within the body cells, a significant amount surrounds and bathes them (extra-cellular fluid). In addition there are 3 litres contained within the blood vessels. The water surrounding the cells and present in the blood stream has a high concentration of salt (sodium chloride).

Actively working muscle cells have a great demand for oxygen and glucose, most of the latter coming from glycogen stores within the cells. Of equal importance is the ready diffusion of carbon dioxide and other potentially harmful substances out of the cells; these substances are then carried away in the blood and eliminated by the lungs or the kidneys.

It is obvious that effective and sustained muscular activity requires both a good blood supply and an adequate cushion of fluid bathing the cells if substances are to be transported efficiently to and from the cells.

Water and salt balance
Water is lost via the kidneys and bowel as well as by evaporation from the skin and lungs. When muscle glycogen is burnt, water is released from the cells (metabolic water).

Table 2.1 An example of water balance in a normal sedentary subject

Urine	1400 ml
Stool	100 ml
Lungs and skin	800 ml
	2300 ml
Metabolic water	−300 ml
Total loss	2000 ml

During exercise, metabolic water production is increased, but the amount is greatly exceeded by losses due to sweating. The kidneys conserve salt very efficiently, and water less so, but if losses exceed intake, significant depletion soon occurs.

Control of body temperature
In addition to energy being supplied, a lot of heat is produced when glucose is burnt, and when the over-heated blood comes to the surface, sweating is stimulated. As sweat evaporates, the skin temperature falls, cooling the blood. Some heat is also lost by radiation. On hot humid days the water vapour content of the air is high, the rate of evaporation is reduced, and the athlete has to produce much more sweat to maintain a normal body temperature. Heavy people sweat more vigorously, but as we all know there is a marked individual variation in the rate of sweat formation. The body is rather like a car, with muscle cells as the cylinders and skin as the radiator.

Losses of salt and water
1 *Sweat*. Vigorous competition in hot humid conditions may cause losses of up to 3 litres an hour. Sweat contains about ⅓ of the concentration of salt found in extra-cellular fluid and results in a relatively greater loss of water from the body. Sweat losses are naturally more important in the tropics, and administrators should note there is no way of hurrying the body's adaptation to hot humid weather.
2 *Urine*. Drugs called diuretics, which cause a dramatic increase in the excretion of salt and water (plus potassium, magnesium and calcium) by the kidneys, are being used by athletes and jockeys to reduce weight before the 'weigh in' (Some take sauna baths for the same purpose).
3 *Diarrhoea and vomiting*. Fluid lost has the same composition as extra-cellular fluid. Many will have experienced the debilitating effects of diarrhoea and vomiting when touring overseas.

Salt and water depletion may develop insidiously when cumulative losses are associated with either several exhausting events during the day, or with strenuous daily activities, and they may not be recognised by the athlete. Unfortunately thirst is not a reliable guide for salt replacement.

The effects of salt and water depletion
Fluid lost through sweating seems to come mainly from the extra-cellular fluid whereas losses in the urine and from diarrhoea and vomiting reduce the blood volume as well. As a result, blood flow and muscle cell function are both impaired.

1 *Performance and stamina.* A trained athlete can tolerate some fluid loss without any obvious deterioration in performance. If more than 2 per cent of body weight is lost, e.g. 1·5 litres in a 70 kg person, there is a detectable fall off in the ability to carry out prolonged exhaustive exercise in the laboratory. Water loss exceeding 4 per cent will impair most people's performance during competition.

2 *Cramps.* The most striking effect of fluid loss is the precipitation of muscle cramps which are promptly relieved by replacing salt and water. Decreased blood levels of calcium and potassium may make a contribution in some circumstances but calcium levels do not change while levels of potassium tend to rise during sustained effort. The physiological disturbance which causes cramps is ill understood.

3 *Blood pressure.* Severe salt and water depletion leads to a drop in blood pressure. This is particularly likely to occur after taking diuretic drugs. (They are used to treat patients with high blood pressure.) Blood flow to the brain is reduced (as well as to other regions), leading to impaired mental function and dizziness. The tendency for weightlifters to black out is likely to be greatly increased.

4 *Impaired heat regulation.* This is particularly disastrous in endurance events. When more than 2 per cent of body weight is lost, blood flow and sweating are impaired and body temperature rises. If it goes beyond 40·5°C (105°F) the subject becomes lethargic and eventually collapses from heat exhaustion.

It is of great interest that many successful marathon runners appear to tolerate body temperatures which would cause great distress in others.

Absorption of fluid and glucose from the gut

It is impossible to separate fluid balance from food intake, and some understanding of the principles of nutrition and digestion is necessary before treatment is prescribed.

The average athlete expends 3000 to 5000 calories daily during training and a further 500 to 1500 calories on the day of competition. The energy is best provided by a balanced diet (e.g. carbohydrates 55 per cent, fat 30 per cent, protein 15 per cent), which will supply in addition all the necessary trace elements and vitamins. Glucose, the main fuel for prolonged muscular effort, is made available from stores within the cells, but the blood glucose, some of which is used by the muscles, is maintained by the liver and ingested glucose.

A little digestion takes place within the stomach, its main function being to mix and break up food. After an hour or so the stomach contents pass into the small bowel where the digestive process is completed and absorption into the blood stream takes place.

Anything which delays stomach emptying delays the availability of food, water and salts. The most striking delays are caused by fat. It may take up to six hours for the stomach to become empty after a meal containing an appreciable amount of fat. Strenuous exercise and emotional strain induce some delays, while strong glucose solutions not only slow down stomach activity, but also attract sufficient fluid back into the stomach to induce an unpleasant sense of fullness.

Water and dilute solutions containing glucose and salt pass rapidly through into the small bowel. Even so, it may be thirty minutes before the full benefits are obtained, and there is no need to drink during an event which takes less time.

Treatment

Those who tend to sweat profusely should weigh themselves before and immediately after events to get some idea of the volume of sweat they lose. Fluid drunk during competition must be taken into account (1000 ml of sweat weighs 1 kg or 2·2lb).

Dietary principles

During training the athlete must have a balanced diet, and in most instances should choose items of food with a high salt content or add salt after the food is served. On the day of competition a bland, non-greasy meal high in carbohydrate is most suitable. A liquid meal high in carbohydrate is relatively easy to prepare and it may be more convenient. At least five hours must elapse after a normal meal to ensure complete stomach emptying before competition. At the end of the day a good three course meal should be served. I cannot stress strongly enough the importance of both coaches and athletes asking the advice of a trained dietitian.

Salt and glucose solutions

Athletes should ensure they do not dehydrate themselves on the morning of competition. Conversely there is certainly no advantage in starting out in a water-logged state; it's not always easy to pass urine once underway!

Suggested solutions (flavouring added if preferred) are:

1 Glucose 25 g and sodium chloride 1 g (18 mmol) to 1 litre of water. This could be made up in large quantities and provided by race or tournament organisers. N.B. Stronger glucose solutions delay stomach emptying.

2 Glucose 5 g (level teaspoon) added to 200 ml water (large tumbler). A salt tablet 0·3 g (5 mmol) may be crushed and dissolved or taken separately. A slow release tablet, Slow Sodium (10 mmol), manufactured by Ciba-Geigy, is in my experience totally non-nauseating. It is also very useful for the rapid correction of salt losses caused by gastroenteritis. Unfortunately it is rather difficult to obtain.

The solutions may be cooled to further aid temperature control.

Potassium blood levels tend to rise and replacement during competition is unnecessary. Although blood levels of magnesium fall slightly, there are such large body stores that supplements are probably unnecessary. Commercially available solutions seem unnecessarily complex.

Suggested plan for fluid replacement

400–500 ml taken 10–15 minutes before competing. For events less than 30 minutes duration nothing further is needed. For events which last between 30 and 60 minutes, 500 mls after 30 minutes. For longer events it is most important to drink small amounts at frequent intervals to prevent serious fluid depletion later, e.g. 200 ml every 15 minutes. If a large volume is drunk at once, an unpleasant sense of fullness is produced. Despite the most enthusiastic replacement, marathon runners cannot keep pace with the production of sweat and some weight loss during the race is inevitable.

Solutions containing salt should be used after the event to repair deficits, as pure water passes rapidly out in the urine. Fruit juice is a pleasant source of potassium.

The after-race meal should complete the process of repletion.

During lengthy competition it is important to keep a daily record of weight to detect any tendency for chronic fluid depletion to develop. Remember that thirst is not a reliable guide to the need for fluid replacement.

The above suggestions are intended as a guide and must be modified according to individual preference, taking into account temperature and humidity.

During hot humid weather the prevention of fluid depletion is of more importance than carbohydrate supplements. There is now very good evidence that adequate salt and water replacement enables the endurance athlete to maintain a high level of performance as well as reducing the risk of muscle cramps and heat exhaustion. The Scottish Harriers in Wellington co-operated in a study in which the effects of salt and dummy tablets were compared in a series of relatively short races. When we broke the code it was significant that those who took the salt supplements reported a marked reduction in after-race stiffness.

Summary

During prolonged heavy exercise it is important to maintain a near-normal circulation of blood and volume of body fluids, to allow for efficient muscle function and the control of body temperature by sweating. The use of diuretic drugs and saunas, in an attempt to lose several kilograms suddenly, is to be deplored.

It is relatively simple to provide adequate salt and water replacement which, in addition to maintaining a high level of performance, reduces the risk of muscle cramps and collapse from heat stroke.

3 Climatic extremes and their possible effects on the body

Heat exhaustion

Dr A. Puskas

Dr Albert Puskas is a specialist in internal medicine in Los Angeles, California, and the following paper on heat exhaustion (hyperthermia), its effects and prevention, was written in 1976.

Thermal control

1 *Temperature regulation*.
  a The human body is a low-grade furnace:

fuel	oxidiser		work
+		combustion ⟶	+ heat
food	oxygen		energy

  b Temperature of the body is maintained at 98·6°F (37°C)
  c Heat loss
    i) Conduction: direct molecule to molecule transfer of heat from warmer to cooler object (e.g. upon touching ice).
    ii) Convection: the air next to the skin is heated by the body and expands as its density is reduced. The heated air rises and is displaced by heavier, cooler air adjacent to it. Air movement can be aided by a breeze or a fan.
    iii) Radiation: heat lost by transfer from a hot body (e.g. the sun) to a cooler body (e.g. human) and vice versa. Majority of heat loss from a nude resting person is by this mechanism.
    iv) Evaporation: the major method of heat loss during exercise. Involves changing of a fluid (e.g. water) from its liquid to its gaseous state. Liquid (water from sweat and lungs) must increase its heat content in order to evaporate. The liquid to vapour transformation requires heat which is extracted from the immediate surroundings. Mechanism less operative when high humidity (saturated air) prevents sweat from evaporating.
2 *Body adaptation to heat stress*.
  a Vascular: internal body heat produced by liver and muscle metabolism is carried by blood to the surface. The superficial blood vessels of the skin dilate, resulting in 'flushing'. Heat is lost by conduction, convection and radiation. The cooled blood then returns to the warmer body core and the cycle is repeated. Heart rate is increased.
  b Sweating: this occurs when more heat must be dissipated than can be done by conduction and radiation, resulting in greater loss of water than salt. In order to maintain osmotic equilibrium, water flows out of the cell leaving salt behind.

Heat exhaustion

1 *Most common heat injury*. (Others are heat cramps and heat stroke.)

2 *Causes*. Exertion in hot and humid environment, excessive salt and water loss, inability to dissipate body heat.

3 *Mechanism*. As the body loses more water than salt, the water must move from the blood thus decreasing the blood volume. A high concentration of salt will remain behind in the blood. If the athlete continues to sweat without replacing water he becomes dehydrated and the sweating mechanism is turned off to maintain blood volume. If it progresses further, the internal body heat increases, injuring the brain, and the high salt content of the blood will interfere with the electrical rhythm of the heart resulting in heart failure and death (heat stroke).

4 *Complaints*. Gradual development of fatigue, faintness, dizziness; progressing to mental confusion, inco-ordination, restlessness, sensation of prickling or burning. Nausea, vomiting and occasionally cramping of extremity and abdominal muscles occur in later stages.

5 *Findings*. Skin *cool* and *clammy* with sweating present.

(N.B. Skin is hot and dry with *no sweating* in **heat stroke**.)

Ashen-grey skin caused by low blood pressure.

Rapid pulse (approx. 100).

Body temperature *normal* or slightly elevated (99°–101°F).

6 *Treatment*. Respond IMMEDIATELY!

Replace *fluids* and salt.

Remove clothing.

Lie down.

Cool with water (shower, sponge, wet towels).

Cool by rubbing extremeties and trunk with ice.

Fan with towels.

Medical assistance as needed.

Prevention of heat disorders

1 *Salt and water*. Replace water and salt before, during and after work in heat. Far more water than salt is lost with exertion in heat. Keep daily weight records before and after practice sessions. Replace hour by hour the water lost by perspiration — hold intake at one-half glass of iced water or less at any one time. Water breaks should be frequent. Takes approx. fifteen minutes for water to be absorbed, large volumes at one time will feel 'uncomfortable'.

Most salt loss can be met by normal diet. Extra salt need decreases as athlete becomes acclimatised to heat. Salt tablets on an empty stomach can be irritating and poorly absorbed, and taking salt tablets without large amounts of water aggravates the imbalance by causing more water to be removed from the blood. Usually there is no need for supplemental salt provided not more than 6 lb or 6 pints of water have been lost.

Table 3.1 Salt and water

Water loss (lb or pints)	Salt tablets (7 grain) taken per pint water replaced	
	Acclimatised	*Non-acclimatised*
Up to 6	diet adequate	
8	2	1
10	4	3
12	6	5

Salt tablets usually come in 7 and 10 grain sizes. Salt tablets must be taken with an adequate amount of water — at least 1 pint of water with each 7 grain tablet. One teaspoon of salt may be added to six quarts of water for drinking during hot weather workouts.

2 *Acclimatisation to heat.*

a Carefully graduated practice schedules can result in improved circulatory and sweating responses in one to two weeks.

b Major changes occur in one week as the blood vessels develop the ability to meet the demand for greatly increased cutaneous blood flow and the pulse rate becomes more stable.

c By the second week of progressive exercise the athlete perspires more freely (dissipating body heat) and excretes a more dilute sweat (thus conserving salt).

d Good pre-season physical condition promotes more rapid acclimatisation.

e Adequate hydration by voluntary intake via thirst mechanism takes several days.

f Initial workouts should be in shorts — the approx. 13 lb weight of a football uniform increases the work load and interferes with heat dissipation.

3 *Clothing.* Padding of a football uniform covers 50 per cent of the body, limiting heat loss through evaporative cooling.

To aid in heat dissipation:

1 clothing should be loose fitting and light in colour.

2 sleeves should be short to allow for increased surface area for heat loss.

3 conservative taping should be used on exposed skin surfaces.

4 clothes should be permeable to moisture (i.e. netted jerseys), to allow heat loss via sweating.

5 during rest periods, remove as much clothing as feasible to expose skin surfaces.

6 change soaked T-shirts during practice.

4 *Environment.* Air temperature and relative humidity, not the sun, are the important factors likely to cause heat problems. Heat illnesses can occur in the shade. Schedule workouts during cooler morning and early evening hours in hot weather. Provide frequent rest periods in hot weather.

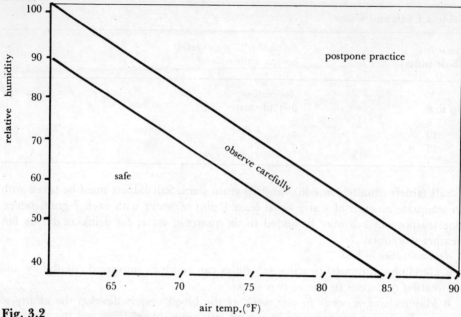

Fig. 3.2

Exposure

National Mountain Safety Council

The following paper presents the opposite extreme: exposure (hypothermia), and its possible deadly effects, and has been extracted from the *Mountaincraft* manual published by the National Mountain Safety Council (1975).

Basically, exposure is a lowering of body temperature caused by wearing clothing that is inadequate for wet, cold, and windy conditions, combined with over-exertion and lack of food. The exposure victim is exhausted, lags behind, stumbles, is reluctant to carry on, and is not 'with it' mentally. He may be difficult to convince that there is any danger. The signs and symptoms are frequently mistaken for simple fatigue and the victim and his companions may not realise the need for remedial action. His condition must be recognised and treated urgently. People have died of exposure without even complaining of the cold. Indeed, the real danger lies in this lack of recognition of the condition by either the victim or his companions, since frequently the whole party is affected by varying stages of exposure.
Exposure, or hypothermia, is defined as the general lowering of the central body temperature caused by greater body heat loss than body heat production.

The sources of body heat that provide normal body temperature are muscular activity and basal metabolism, both of which are dependent on an adequate food (energy) supply.

Causes

When a man is walking, muscular activity generates body heat that is about three to four times greater than that generated when his body is resting. While he continues to move, he will generate some heat provided he does not continue to the point of exhaustion. He should, of course, be adequately clothed to prevent excessive heat loss. While resting or on nearing the point of complete exhaustion, however, the heat loss may exceed heat production unless his body is well insulated by clothes or sheltered against the cold, wind and rain, and food is eaten to restore his 'energy' level and maintain his basal metabolism.

Body heat loss occurs at all times, and although clothing helps control it, there are factors which cause it to be accelerated. These are:

1 Increasing wind speed which causes increased heat loss from bare skin, especially if skin is wet, even if air temperature remains the same.
2 Wet clothing and wet skin, which greatly increase the heat loss, especially if the wind speed increases.
3 Insulating (or protective) effect of clothing, which depends to some extent on its 'windproofness'.

The ability of a climber to complete a particular trip without risk of exposure depends on:

1 The physical fitness of the person, relative to the trip he plans to do.
2 The capability to follow the planned or escape routes.
3 The quantity and quality of food carried to provide energy to do the trip.
4 The protective clothing carried.

When there is a large number in the party, a pace that is within the capacity of the less fit members will be set. In these circumstances the fastest members of the party then may not be travelling at their usual speed and may not be able to maintain their optimum body temperature in exposure conditions. On the other hand, the least fit may need to travel faster than their fitness allows, and become exhausted more quickly. For this reason, large parties should be discouraged when adverse weather conditions are likely to occur. However, the minimum number in a party should always be four for an adequate safety margin.

It is unlikely that a person's body temperature will begin to drop within a few hours of beginning the day's activities and after having a substantial meal. However, as a person becomes tired and weary his muscular activity slows down, and this source of heat, needed to maintain body temperatures, decreases.

Additional factors such as decreasing air temperatures, increasing wind speed, and/or rain, will also increase the heat loss from the body.

Unless adequate protective clothing is put on and food eaten to maintain an adequate energy level, or the work load curtailed (i.e. by stopping and setting up camp), the body temperature may continue to fall.

Symptoms

The stage has now been set for exposure (hypothermia). The sequence may follow the following pattern:

1 Weariness and reluctance to continue moving.

2 Unawareness of any danger to life and false feeling of well-being.
3 Clumsiness and loss of judgement.
4 Collapse and unconsciousness.
5 Death.

The period of time from the first symptoms to unconsciousness may be as short as thirty minutes. The symptoms of exposure may be felt, to a greater or lesser degree, by all members of the party who may have been lulled also into a false sense of security.

Prevention of exposure

Equipment. It is important that whatever the length of trip you undertake, whether it is an afternoon rock scramble a short distance away from a hut, a long day's climb, or a three weeks' transalpine journey, you must be prepared for deterioration in weather conditions.

1 For a short climb a spare pair of socks, windproof over-mitts, spare jersey and windproof trousers are sufficient.

2 For a long day's climb a spare pair of socks, windproof over-mitts, spare jersey, parka, windproof trousers, and a sleeping bag cover or a survival tube in addition are required.

3 Food must also be taken, even on a day's climb, so that in the event of a 'night out' it can partly restore the energy level of the body and contribute some body heat during the night. A deterioration in the weather the following day may demand substantial effort that uses considerable body resources before the safety of the hut or camp can be reached.

During a climbing day. Have a substantial meal the evening before, and before you begin the day's climbing, depending on the hour of departure, have a reasonable breakfast.

1 Have frequent short stops during the day for rest and intake of quick energy food.

2 Endeavour to drink some liquid during the day as dehydration can contribute to exhaustion. A thermos of hot liquid is the ultimate in self-preservation but is not always practical.

3 If there is a strong wind and the temperature is fairly low, e.g. 40°F, you may lose one-half of your body's total heat production through your uncovered head, therefore wear a woollen cap or balaclava, or pull up your parka hood.

During a travelling day. When travelling above the bushline with a full pack, it is wise to anticipate any possible exposure situation.

1 Have a good breakfast before leaving camp.

2 Even if the weather is not bad enough to wear your mitts (gloves), windproof trousers and parka, keep them ready for use at the top of your pack.

3 Keep some quick energy food in your shirt or parka pockets, or in the back pocket of your pack for quick access.

4 Have frequent short stops during the day, to eat quick energy food, and at the same time check the physical state of all members of the party.

5 As soon as the weather 'packs up' get on your storm gear, have some food, and make a quick decision whether to turn back, go on along your planned route, or drop off to shelter.

6 The leader of the party should consider any complaint of tiredness, cold or exhaustion, because, if these factors are allowed to continue and the person has inadequate storm gear, an exposure situation can easily develop when the victim may collapse and die.

7 If the situation has been allowed to deteriorate beyond the point where shelter and safety can be reached easily and quickly, quick and decisive action is required.

Treatment of exposure

1 Stop and quickly pitch the tent on the spot or at some convenient site, and give the whole party shelter from the wind.

2 If the patient must be carried a short distance, do so with his head down.

3 Dress the patient in dry clothing and place him in a dry sleeping bag.

4 If he is very cold, let a warmer person get in with him to warm him gradually.

5 Be careful not to overheat him, e.g. by standing him in front of a roaring fire.

6 Try to get the patient to eat some quick energy food or hot drink, but not if he is in a state of collapse as he may vomit and choke.

7 If his breathing should falter and/or stop, use mouth-to-mouth resuscitation immediately and continue until deep regular breathing has begun again.

8 If the patient is or has been in a state near to collapse, do not move him for at least a day.

9 If he is to be moved on a stretcher, do so only if his body temperature can be maintained at a safe level during the carryout.

10 All the party should try to maintain a cheerful disposition in difficult situations, as a high morale may mean the difference between life and death to one or more of the party.

Deaths from exposure on Four Inns walking competition, March 14–15, 1964

L.G.C. Pugh

The following paper is a report to the Medical Commission on Accident Prevention by L.G.C. Pugh, MA, BM, Oxon, formerly of the Division of Human Physiology, National Institute for Medical Research, London, and was first published in *The Lancet* (May 1964), pp. 1210–1212.

This report is based on evidence heard at the inquest held at Glossop on 8 April, and on the written reports of members of the Glossop District Rover Crew Mountain Rescue Team.

Organisation
The Four Inns walking competition has been held annually for the last seven years

and is organised by the 51st Derby (St. Luke's) California Rover Crew. It is very popular in the Scouting movement. This year eighty 3-man teams started; a further forty teams applied to enter but were turned down for lack of accommodation. The age-range of the participants is from 17½ to 24 years. There are both team and individual trophies. The course involves a forty-five-mile walk over the moors at altitudes ranging from 650 ft to 2000 ft and a total ascent and descent of about 4500 ft. The record time is 7½ hours. However, competitors usually take from 9½ to 22 hours. I understand that up to a third of the competitors give up, most of them after the toughest sections, either at Snake Inn (sixteen miles) or Edale (twenty-four miles). There have been cases of fatigue but no accidents or fatalities.

Precautions
Preliminary and final information sheets are circulated which contain details of the course, the system of tallies, the kit required, and so on. A pamphlet containing advice about clothing is also issued. There are check-points at intervals of three to eight miles along the route and a rescue team is on call. From reading the information sheets it is clear that the organisers have taken great care to safeguard the participants. They also follow the weather forecasts for several days before the race. The reason given for holding the competition so early in the year is that March is the most convenient month from the point of view of school and university examinations.

The 1964 event
The eighty 3-men teams started at two-minute intervals beginning at 06.00 hours. The weather forecast that morning was that there would be showers with fine intervals. Actually there was drizzle and a light wind at the start, and the weather deteriorated all day with heavy rain and strong winds. During the night there was sleet and snow (from 04.30 hours). Temperatures recorded by four meteorological stations in the area (supplied by the Meteorological Office) ranged between 4°C and 7°C during the day with a night minimum of 3°C on 14–15 March. Temperatures on the moors at 2000 ft would be about 3°C lower than these readings. Winds near sea-level were up to 25 knots in velocity, but were probably much stronger on the moors.

Of the 240 competitors only ninety were competing for the first time. This year only twenty-two competitors finished. Usually only a third drop out: one year 85 per cent finished.

At about 13.15 hours the check-point at Snake Inn, about sixteen miles from the start, received word that some competitors were in difficulties, and the Glossop Mountain Rescue Team began rescue operations. (The section before Snake Inn is the most difficult part of the route and contains a long ascent of 1300 ft over boggy ground.) They brought down five exhausted walkers (two in a state of collapse) and escorted a number of others who had retired. They got to Gordon Withers at about 14.00 hours. He was then conscious and able to walk with assistance, but he later collapsed and was transported on a stretcher. The rescue took five hours altogether.

Later in the afternoon a search was started for two competitors who were stated to be sheltering about half a mile off course near the River Alport. The rescuers never made contact with these men, and their bodies were found two days later.

Witnesses at the inquest said that the weather conditions were severe but they were accustomed to such conditions, although not for so long.

Over 800 persons took part in the the two-day search for the missing competitors, i.e. Welby and Butterfield.

Case histories

1 *G. Withers*

Student. Aged 19. Eleven years a Scout; took part in the Four Inns Walk in 1962 and 1963. Severe attack of influenza three weeks previously.

According to his team-mates, Withers began to flag around midday after the long climb to Bleaklow (2000 ft) which they all found very tiring. By this time they had been out some five-and-a-half hours and had covered about twelve miles. They were wet and cold. Withers began to fall down frequently and his companions had to walk one on each side of him. Shortly afterwards, they sat down and one of them went for help, which arrived within two hours. Withers was then conscious and able to walk with assistance. At about 16.15 hours rescuer Dean stated that he was semiconscious and incoherent. By this time he was being carried by three rescuers. While they were carrying him along a narrow steep slope he had a convulsion which threw the rescuers off their balance, and one of them fell 20 ft and hurt his chest. Eventually they were met by a stretcher party, and Withers was carried on the stretcher in a thick kapok sleeping-bag with waterproof cover. It was reported that, on arrival at Alport Farm at 19.15 hours, Withers's body was rigid and he had become very pale. A pulse was detectable at his temple. It was not stated whether he was conscious or not. An hour later, at 20.15 hours, he was admitted to Glossop Hospital apparently dead. Artificial respiration and oxygen were given for three hours without success.

Necropsy. Average build, abrasions of knees and wrists Lungs, liver, and kidneys congested. Heart enlarged and congested; right ventricle distended and wall 'thinned out'. Cause of death: acute myocardial failure after extreme exposure to cold. The pathologist thought that the attack of influenza might have contributed.

2 *L. Butterfield and M. Welby*

Students, both aged 21, and members of the same team. They were experienced hikers and Welby had taken part in the Four Inns Walk in 1962. The third member of the team was R. Kydd, aged 19, and he gave evidence at the inquest.

The team started at 07.45 hours. Near Bleaklow, Butterfield complained of cramp and kept stopping. He was going more and more slowly. They were all very wet; at this stage they lost their way and went about a mile off course. The time was not stated but it was probably early afternoon. Butterfield became unsteady and his companions had to urge him on. In the words of Kydd: 'Butterfield was slowly tiring and getting unsteady. We had to help him although I was not much good because I was stumbling too.' They helped him by walking on each side. He did not say much, but when he did speak his voice was normal. When he could go no further they sat down, and Welby, who was the fittest, went to reconnoitre. When he returned, Kydd went to fetch help while Welby stayed with Butterfield. Kydd met a rescue party and was assisted down to Alport Farm, suffering from exposure. Two parties searched for Welby and Butterfield but failed to find them.

It is thought that Welby may have stayed with Butterfield until he died, and started back perhaps in the dark, when his torch may have given out. Their bodies were found two days later. Butterfield's body was in a stream bed, partly in the water. Welby's body was lying covered with snow about a mile to the west.

Necropsy. The findings were essentially similar to the findings on Withers, except that the organs were less congested.

3 D. Rhead

Sometime between 15.30 and 16.00 hours this competitor was found sheltering under the wall of a sheep pen. Rescuer Davies stated he was semiconscious. He was carried down on a stretcher to Snake Inn and later admitted to Glossop Hospital where he recovered.

4 R. Kydd

Kydd was the third member of the team to which Butterfield and Welby belonged. When Rescuer Simm met him on the way to the Snake Inn he was exhausted. To quote Rescuer Simm: 'He was able to inform me that he had had to leave two of his team-mates up the valley ... but due to his condition he could not give me the exact location.' Kydd was accompanied down to the Snake Inn by two rescuers. There he recovered, and later he was transported to Buxton base camp.

Comments

Weather. Weather conditions were severe but not exceptional. The official forecast was wrong. Temperatures on the moors would have between + 1°C and + 4°C, which, in the presence of strong winds and rain, is a typical wet-cold situation. It would clearly be safer to postpone the annual race until later in the season when the weather is warmer and the days longer.

Clothing. The clothing of the dead boys was produced in court. Each outfit consisted of:

1 An anorak: two were of poor quality and one satisfactory.
2 A jersey: one light-weight, others medium.
3 A shirt and singlet.
4 Trousers: one jeans, one 33 per cent terylene-wool mixture; one corduroy.
5 Socks: two to three pairs each.
6 Climbing boots: of good quality.

The trousers afforded little protection against wind and rain. Anoraks, however good, will not keep a man dry for more than two-three hours; for, to avoid condensation, they have to be made of permeable cloth. Witnesses did not seem to appreciate this. All competitors who gave evidence said they were wet through and very cold. A patrol warden for the Peaks National Park said he always wore an oilskin on the moors in wet weather.

Public attention needs to be called to the dangers of the wet-cold environment. These boys would have been all right if they had not been wet through. They were lightly clad because it was a race. The organisers might consider making it compulsory to carry spare clothing and a plastic rainproof coat.

Food. All the witnesses said they had enough food with them in the form of chocolate and raisins, and coffee and soup was issued at the check-points. I should not expect a calorie intake of more than 1000–1500 Cal on an exercise of this kind, although the total energy expenditure may be over 6000 Cal.

Heat balance. The oxygen consumption of men walking in mountains at a pace they can maintain over many hours has been measured in various parts of the world and is generally about 2·0 litres per minute for a 75 kg man in good training (Table

3.3). The record-holders on the Four Inns Walk have been long-distance runners, and can probably maintain an oxygen consumption of at least 3·0 litres per minute. For the average competitor a figure of 1·5–2·0 litres is likely. The corresponding heat production values are 900 Cal per hour and 450–600 Cal per hour.

These values are similar to the values observed in cross-Channel swimming races. Channel swimming is in some respects similar to hill walking in that it involves a high rate of energy expenditure over a very long period. Some years ago it was found (Pugh and Edholm 1955, Pugh *et al.* 1960) that fast swimmers maintained normal rectal temperatures after nine to ten hours in water at 15°C, although they were relatively thin. Slow swimmers became hypothermic unless they were fat. Fast relatively thin swimmers became hypothermic if they got tired and slowed down. In hill walking under conditions of wet-cold the situation may be much the same. The stronger teams who can maintain a fast pace produce heat at a high enough rate to keep themselves warm in spite of the low insulation value of wet clothing. Slower walkers, or fast walkers slowed down by fatigue, may not have a high enough heat production for thermal equilibrium, in which case they will cool slowly over a period of hours until a state is reached where balance and muscular control are impaired. At this stage their pace begins to fall off, and owing to the associated decline in heat production, the rate of body cooling may be expected to accelerate.

According to the above case histories, the onset of collapse follows within one to two hours after a person begins to slow down. Once serious body cooling has occurred, warming by natural means takes many hours. In the case of Withers, the kapok sleeping bag and cover used by the rescuers were ineffective. On the other hand, if a man is only moderately impaired, whether by fatigue or cold, he may recover rapidly with rest in a warm environment.

Table 3.3 Determination of oxygen intake and heat production in eight subjects during steady prolonged climbing at the subject's habitual pace

Adjusted to equal body-weight of 75 kg (Durnin 1955, Pugh 1958)

Subject	Altitude	Oxygen consumption (litres per min.)	Heat production (Cal per hour)	Locality
G.P.	1000	1·88	565	North Wales
G.P.	3500	2·00	600	Swiss Alps
G.P.	6000	2·18	654	Himalaya
M.W.	6000	1·89	567	Himalaya
A.S.	2000	2·32	700	Scotland
J.B.	2000	2·53	757	Scotland
J.B.	2000	2·03	608	Scotland
M.W.	2000	2·30	689	Scotland
Mean		2·14	641	

Signs and symptoms. In these cases the signs of impairment, whether through cold or fatigue, were slowing (followed by clumsiness and stumbling), falling, and finally collapse. Mental symptoms were not apparent until a late stage.

Table 3.4 Theoretical estimate of minimum insulation value of clothing worn on Four Inns walking competition, when wet through

Heat production	500 Cal per hour
Body-surface area	2·0 sq. metres
Body weight	75 kg
Heat production/sq. metre body surface (M)	250 Cal, h^{-1}
Evaporative heat loss (E) from lungs and skin at 20% of M	50 Cal, h^{-1}
Heat loss through clothing and exposed skin (H)	200 Cal, m^{-2}, h^{-1}.
Ambient air temperature (t_a)	+2°C
Mean skin temperature (t_s)	30°C
Thermal gradient $t_s — t_a$	28

Total insulation — i.e. clothing (I_{cl}) and air (I_a) $\dfrac{28}{200} = \dfrac{0·14°C}{Cal, m^{-2}, h^{-1}}$

$= 0·78$ clo units

The insulation value of the surrounding air in winds of 25-knot velocity and over is nearly constant at around 0·1 clo units (Burton and Edholm 1955). Hence the insulation value of the average competitor's clothing on the Four Inns Competition in wet stormy weather at a temperature of 2°C would be $0·78 - 0·1 = 0·68$ clo units. When dry the same outfit would have an insulation value of not less than 1·5 clo units.

Clothing insulation. The clothing worn by the dead boys was brought back to Hampstead. The thermal insulation of the three sets of clothes, both wet and dry, will be determined in our climatic chamber. Meanwhile it is possible to make an approximate assessment, based on certain assumptions (Tables 3.3 and 3.4). Inspection of the clothing suggests a value of about 1·5 clo units for the dry state.[1] If one assumes a mean rate of heat production of 500 Cal per hour, the minimum clothing insulation for thermal balance works out at 0·68 clo units. This seems a likely value for the clothing when wet through. It would mean that competitors unable to maintain a heat production of 500 Cal per hour would gradually cool down, whereas in dry clothing they could just keep warm with a heat production of 330 Cal per hour. This is equivalent to an oxygen consumption of 1·1 litres per minute, which is the oxygen consumption required for walking on level ground at three miles an hour.

The calculations are as follows (symbols as in Table 3.4):

The minimum heat production for warmth with dry clothing is 1·5 clo (Table 3.4). Let

$$I_a + I_{cl} = 1·5 + 0·1 = 1·6 \text{ clo} = 1·6 \times 0·18 = 0·288 \frac{°C}{Cal,} m^{-2}, h^{-1}.$$

For warmth, t_s will be not less than 32·5°C and

$$t_s - t_a = 30·5°C.$$

Hence heat loss through clothing and exposed skin (H) is

$$\frac{30·5}{0·288} = 106 \text{ Cal}, m^{-2}, h^{-1}$$

and $M = H + E = 106 + 50 = 165$ Cal, m^{-2}, h^{-1}.

Hence metabolism for a 75 kg man is 330 Cal per hour, and oxygen consumption is

$$\frac{330}{300} = 1·1 \text{ litres per min.}$$

This is the oxygen requirement for level walking at 3 m.p.h.

Conclusions and suggested recommendations

1 The risk of casualties from exposure could be avoided by holding the competition later in the year, when the weather is warmer and the days are longer.

2 Competitors should not be allowed to start unless they are carrying spare clothing, a plastic mackintosh (or other waterproof outer garment) and waterproof trousers (i.e. plastic impregnated nylon as used in sailing).

3 Anoraks have to be made of permeable materials, to avoid condensation. Chemical proofing and fine weave gives partial protection against wetting but no anorak can be expected to keep a man dry all day. Jeans, or trousers of terylene-wool mixture, are neither windproof nor waterproof, and are unsuitable at temperatures near freezing-point in the presence of strong winds, except for walks of less than two to three hours' duration.

4 In view of the relatively short period between the onset of symptoms and collapse, early symptoms such as slowing and inco-ordination call for urgent action (dry clothing; shelter; get off the mountain).

5 As long as a man can walk, evacuation is quick. Once he is a stretcher case it is dangerously slow.

6 In view of (5) methods of on-the-spot resuscitation of stretcher cases require urgent development.

Summary

1 The 8th Annual Four Inns walking competition (forty-five miles) took place in wet-cold conditions, the air temperatures on the moors being 2–3°C. There was heavy rain most of the day, and a strong wind. The official weather report was misleading.

2 From the fifth hour some competitors began to get into difficulties. Three Scouts lost their lives and at least four others had narrow escapes.

3 The clothing of the dead men was not waterproof, and the trousers were not windproof.

4 The cause of death was given as exposure to prolonged cold. In one of three cases a severe attack of influenza three weeks previously was thought to have been contributory. There were no significant necropsy findings other than terminal congestion.

5 Symptoms of exposure, in order of development, were:
  a slowing of the rate of progress, clumsiness, and stumbling
  b repeated falling
  c inability to continue
  d incoherence, impairment of consciousness
  e unconsciousness, extreme pallor, and in one case what happens to have been a convulsion.

In these cases mental symptoms were late in appearance.

6 Only about two hours elapsed between first symptoms and collapse.

7 Evacuation of one of the fatal cases took five hours.

8 Mild cases recovered with rest and warmth.

9 The race was well organised and all recognised safety precautions were taken.

References

[1] A clo unit is the amount of insulation required for thermal equilibrium in an environment of 21°C (70°F) with minimal air movement and 50 per cent humidity. This is the insulation afforded by the clothing worn in summer by the average business man.

1 clo = 0·18°C/Cal, m⁻²; h⁻¹.

Other reading

Burton, A.C. and Edholm, O.G. (1955). *Man in a Cold Environment*. London, p. 50.
Durnin, J.V.G.A. (1955). *J. Physiol.*, 128, p. 294.
Pugh, L.G.C. (1958). *J. Physiol.*, 141, p. 233.
Pugh, L.G.C. and Edholm, O.G. (1955). *The Lancet*, ii, 761.
Pugh, L.G.C., Fox, R.H., Wolff, H.S. Harvey, G.R. Hammond, W.H., Tanner, J.M. and Whitehouse, R.H. (1960). *Chem. Sci.*, 19.

Exposure, frostbite and mountain sickness

Dr R.J. Stewart and Dr P.J. Strang

This paper was written in 1969 for the Canterbury Mountain Safety Committee, and the authors, of Christchurch Hospital, acknowledge the assistance of the following in its preparation: Dr G.C. Riley, Dr D.W. Beaven and Mr J.W. Ardagh, Christchurch; Dr D.U. Strang, Dunedin; and Dr L.R. Stewart, Invercargill.

The harsh environment of our mountains is the major health hazard to the mountaineer. The most obvious dangers are those of avalanche, rock-fall, rivers, crevasses, falling-off, and even lightning. But less obvious and often more dangerous are the problems of cold, wind, moisture and altitude. We propose to outline in brief, the essentials of three increasingly important resultant conditions: *exposure, frostbite* and the *mountain sicknesses*, and we will also touch on a miscellany of other peculiar environmental hazards.

Exposure

Exposure is not a strict medical term, but in general usage it describes the serious effects which may result from exposure to a chilling environment. More precisely, it is a form of accidental hypothermia, which is the condition seen when the whole body becomes abnormally cold. For efficient functioning, the vital organs of the body must be maintained at a relatively constant temperature (circa 37°C or 98·4°F). A marked drop in this temperature leads to mental deterioration and loss of muscular co-ordination, and eventually to unconsciousness, circulatory and respiratory failure, and death. This dangerous situation is insidious in onset and therefore it is paramount for the climber to understand the causes and to recognise the early signs and symptoms of exposure.

Causes. The primary causes are those which lead to loss of body heat. Cold climatic conditions are basic, especially the triad of high wind, cold, and wetness which leads to maximum chill at body surfaces. Therefore, setting out in extreme conditions, being overtaken by bad weather, and unexpected benightment are all fraught with danger. In these circumstances, insufficient, wet, or poor quality clothing will facilitate the loss of heat. In addition, hunger and dehydration, poor psychological stamina, lack of fitness, and exhaustion are important contributing factors to final collapse. Clearly, however, there is great variation in individual susceptibility. It is said that people with more fatty insulation (e.g. women) survive longer. Also, there is evidence to suggest that cooling of the active muscles leads to local weakness.

Signs. The signs of hypothermia in others are variable and it is not easy to decide if you have an early case in your party. However, the following is a probable sequence:

1 Abnormal behaviour (at first aggressive and irrational actions, finally apathy and indifference).
2 Slowing of movements.
3 Slurring of speech.
4 Stumbling.
5 Weakness.
6 Repeated falling.
7 Collapse.

Although shivering is not prominent in serious cases, it may be seen in early or mild episodes, for it is known experimentally that shivering stops when the central body temperature is below 34^0 to 35^0C, and is replaced by generalised muscular rigidity. After collapse, the situation is very serious, for death usually ensues in one to two hours.

Symptoms. These are also variable and depend on the individual, but may include loss of sensation, muscle cramps, lethargy, poor vision, anxiety and feelings of unreality.

Prevention. As always, this is better than cure. Always watch the weather for signs of change. Good windproof clothing is essential to trap body heat and reserve garments should be carried. Avoid exhaustion — parties should be carefully balanced with regard to experience and fitness, should attempt reasonable objectives and carry moderate loads. Breakfast, often missed, is of great value, as is the carrying of adequate supplies of food and water.

Treatment. When evidence of exposure is established, good shelter should be sought and treatment proceeded with. Further exertion, such as forcing the victim to go on walking, may be dangerous and should be avoided. The essential aims of treatment are to prevent further cooling and encourage rewarming. In a *mild or early case*, a change to warm, dry clothing and the provision of food and hot drinks is valuable. In addition, mild muscular activity should be encouraged. *If the case is severe*, with immobility and semi-consciousness, the patient should be well insulated in a dry sleeping-bag, preferably with a fit companion alongside to provide warmth. Warm, sweet drinks should be taken liberally. Also, the head-down position may be helpful in preventing convulsions, which occur occasionally. **Do not** administer alcohol at any stage, since this promotes loss of body heat and may lead to a drop in blood pressure. Over-enthusiastic heating may also result in a lowered blood pressure. Rapid rewarming in a hot bath is the most effective method of treatment, but should only be carried out under medical guidance.

Only when the patient's condition has been reasonably stablised, should he be moved any distance. If being carried on a litter, great care must be taken to prevent further cooling.

Shock and trauma. These, combined with exposure, may present a formidable problem. In these cases, it is important to first stablise the patient's general state by arresting haemorrhage, establishing a clear airway and treating the exposure and shock as outlined above. Only then should the treatment of specific injuries, e.g. fractures, be initiated. The reader is referred to one of the numerous publications detailing the management of the injured patient.

Frostbite

Cold injury is peripheral tissue damage resulting from low temperatures. It may be found in association with exposure. Frostbite is the most important type and occurs when the temperature is at or below freezing. In our circumstances, it principally affects the toes and feet, less frequently the fingers and hands, and only occasionally the nose, cheeks, ears, knees, etc. The other principal types of cold injury include the related disorders of *immersion foot*, *trench foot* and *seaboot foot*, all caused by prolonged exposure to moisture and cold when the temperatures are above freezing point.

Frostbite. This appears to be increasing in incidence in New Zealand, and is a very real danger in winter climbing. Two other conditions should, however, be differentiated at the outset. Firstly, it is common when climbing in cold conditions to develop numb feet, which may persist for several hours but with no tissue damage. This is not frostbite. Secondly, a mild form of trench foot is occasionally seen, especially when one has been wearing the same dirty, moist socks and boots for several days in freezing conditions. There is no significant tissue damage, but transient waxiness occurs, and sensitivity to cold and increased sweating may persist for many months.

Causes. In general, the causes of frostbite are similar to those in exposure: cold, wind, moisture, lack of protection, exhaustion, hunger, dehydration and hypoxia. In addition, local factors play a part, e.g. constricting clothing, tight crampon straps, ill-fitting boots, dirty wet socks and trauma. It is also alleged that there is a naturally predisposed group; on the other hand there is no good evidence that smokers are more susceptible. The exact mechanism of injury has been hotly debated in the past, but it now seems reasonable that both direct freezing of tissues and blood vessel changes play a part.

Most authorities now group frostbite as either *superficial*, involving skin only, or *deep*, involving deeper structures often with loss of tissue. The older U.S. Army classification into four gradings is too complicated for ordinary use. During the chilling phase, the patient may notice a sensation of cold progressing to numbness, with stinging or aching as variable accompaniments. There is little to see. When the part is frozen, it is numb and waxy-white in appearance. On rewarming, it looks red or purple and inflamed and becomes painful. This is followed in several hours by swelling, and, later still, blistering occurs. In an uncomplicated case the affected tissues become dry, hard and black, and eventually shell off; in severe frostbite this may amount to auto-amputation. The long-term effects are variable and may include sensitivity to cold, increased sweating, dermatitis, and local colour changes.

Prevention. The steps in prevention are similar to those for exposure, with the addition of the following hints: select boots and crampons carefully, wear an adequate number of warm socks and gloves, and keep these clean and dry as far as possible. The use of greasy ointments, e.g. lanolin or hydrous ointment, and solidus or unscoured woollen socks is also recommended. Overboots may also be necessary in some situations.

Treatment. Only very superficial 'frost-nip' can be properly treated on the march, this usually being achieved by gentle rewarming in an armpit or on a kind companion's abdomen. In most cases the following principles of management should be followed. If the part remains frozen, it is safe for the patient to walk as far as possible towards shelter. Once rewarming has occurred, however, the part must not be used. Therefore **do not** thaw in a situation from where the patient cannot be carried out. Re-warming may be achieved by:

1 Rapid rewarming in water at $42^0 - 44^0C$, approximately no hotter than a hot bath. This is the best method.

2 Spontaneous thawing in a warm atmosphere.

After rewarming, the patient should be rested, kept warm and well fed. The affected part should be immobilised, elevated to combat swelling, and covered with loose, clean, dry dressings. **Do not** tamper with the part, exercise it, smoke, take alcohol, use pharmaceutical vasodilators or rub with snow or vaseline. The patient should be transferred to a hospital as quickly as possible.

The mountain sicknesses

These are the clinical states caused by the low oxygen pressure at high altitudes. They may be aggravated by cold, exhaustion or dehydration, or themselves aggravate exposure or cold injury. In general these have been of little importance in New Zealand, but episodes have become increasingly frequent since the advent of the ski-plane. It is interesting to note that at 12 000 feet the mean atmospheric pressure has decreased from the sea-level figure of 760 mm of mercury, to 480 mm, and the mean arterial pressure of oxygen has decreased from 100 mm to 60 mm. (These are approximate figures.) Therefore, even at our range of altitudes, careful attention should be paid to acclimatisation. For instance, if one flies in to 6000 to 8000 feet, plan to spend the first few days in graded activity.

Acute mountain sickness. This is the most common form, occurring in poorly acclimatised individuals a few hours to a few days after arriving at altitude. It is a general term for a miscellany of variable symptoms, the most prominent of which are usually headache, loss of appetite, nausea and vomiting and lightheadedness. The patient may also suffer shortness of breath, waxing and waning breathing (Cheyne-Stokes respiration), irritating cough, palpitations, sleeplessness, dizziness and mental confusion. The condition eases in a few hours with rest.

High altitude pulmonary oedema. This is a more specialised and lethal form of acute mountain sickness and has only recently been documented. It has occurred mostly in the Andes and the Himalayas, but has been reported, though rarely, in poorly-acclimatised people as low as 8000 feet in the United States. The clinical picture grossly resembles a severe pneumonia or acute bouts of heart failure, with firstly a dry cough and extreme shortness of breath, and later, great distress, rattly respirations and blueness of the skin. The condition is a medical emergency and is treated by transport to lower altitudes, oxygen, digitalis preparations, diuretics and morphine. So far as is known it has not yet occurred in New Zealand.

Chronic mountain sicknesses. These represent breakdown of acclimatisation in permanent residents of high altitude, and do not occur in this country.

Other problems

We have discussed the principal effects of cold and hypoxia, but other important features of the high altitude environment deserve brief mention. *Dehydration* is frequently noticed; it is due to the low water-vapour pressure at altitude, combined with increased loss of fluid by overbreathing and excessive sweating. It is aggravated by vomiting and loss of appetite. Overheating may be a problem in sheltered glacial basins or on long hot ridges, resulting in heat exhaustion or glacier lassitude, or even significant loss of body salt. The increased concentration of ultra-violet wave-lengths at higher altitudes, combined with reflection off snow and prolonged exposure, results in severe sunburn and snow-blindness.

These then are some of the more important environmental peculiarities we have to face in our mountains; knowledge of them and a healthy respect for the limitations they impose, make climbing more enjoyable and much safer.

We realise that many of the points discussed here are controversial, but we have attempted to present a balanced, yet brief, account. However, any comments or details of experiences would be most welcome, since it is our aim to accumulate more information on the New Zealand experience of these maladies.

Exposure: Reports

Federated Mountain Club of New Zealand

The following material is reprinted from the F.M.C. Bulletin published by the Federated Mountain Club of N.Z. (Inc.), 33, June 1969.

Report on the death of Martin Clyma (Taranaki)

The party of six Venturer Scouts and one friend embarked on Friday, 16 August 1968, on a journey as part of the Venturer Scouts Trampers Certificate. Their ages were between 15 and 16 years.

Although their Venturer leader had planned a route for them, David Maw, the party leader, stated that he did not particularly want to go via the Maude Peak route as the Pouakais were a bit too high for them — furthermore he had not covered that particular part of the route.

They left at 8.30 a.m. in gusty weather and drizzle. Martin Clyma was only wearing a cotton shirt, a jersey, raincoat, shorts, boots and socks. Some of the boys were feeling the cold as they reached the top of Maude Peak three hours later and shortly after as they re-entered the scrub some of them were complaining that this temperature drop was affecting them. They couldn't locate the track and when Clyma did not want to carry his pack, two boys carried it for him. Maw stated that he had to drive the boys as most of them wanted to sit down, and it was then that they decided to retreat back over the top of Maude Peak as they were not familiar with the planned route ahead. Some of the party were sent ahead by Maw and then both he and Dennis Johns found it necessary to practically carry Clyma over Maude Peak as his legs would not support him.

Later they tried to carry him but were unsuccessful so they had no alternative but to throw a tent over him and a groundsheet under him as well as covering him with a sleeping bag and a blanket. It was raining and sleeting and the trio were very cold. A solid fuel cooker could not be lit and Clyma was not able to take any food. Dennis Johns set out for help and at this stage Clyma was unconscious. At dusk Maw was able to contact David Rawson on the Citizen Band radio and he was told that help was on the way. Shortly afterwards, Dennis Johns arrived back with his brother and two farmers who laid Clyma on a groundsheet and put some blankets over him as well as massaging his arms and legs. Clyma was unconscious and was having difficulty with his breathing at this stage. All this time the boy had been lying in his cold, wet clothing and these garments were not removed until the main rescue party arrived and completely changed him into warm woollen clothing and warm, dry blankets, but it appeared that at this stage he was beyond human aid. He died in the New Plymouth Hospital six hours later.

Conclusions
1 The group lacked an experienced leader for the trip which was undertaken in winter conditions and in weather unsuitable for the proposed route.
2 Clyma was insufficiently clad for such a journey at that time of year.
3 None of the group or the farmers recognised early signs of exposure.
4 No remedial action was taken when Clyma showed signs of exposure — probably due to the inexperience of the party and because they were all suffering from varying degrees of exposure.
5 The very cold wind and prevailing conditions added greatly to the danger of the route over the tops.
6 Whenever signs of exposure become evident it is imperative to make camp and get the affected person into dry clothes at the earliest possible opportunity.

Report on the deaths of Christopher Thomas Stewart and James William Simister (Wangapeka Track)

Three Nelson College boys, Stewart, Simister and Mori left the Dart River at about 11 a.m. on 25 August 1968, for a six-day tramping trip on the Wangapeka Track. They were to stay each night in huts along the way and return to the road-head on the afternoon of 31 August 1968.

On 26 August the party spent the night at Stone Creek Hut, and on leaving next day left some food for the return journey. Their ultimate destination on the outward journey was the Stag Flat Hut, but on 28 August they arrived at Luna Hut on an off-shoot of the track. At 1 p.m. on 29 August, in conditions of low cloud and rain, the party left Luna Hut to return to the Stone Creek Hut via a track over Biggs' Tops, considered to be a short cut but traversing open sub-alpine tops.

In conditions of low visibility, rain, sleet and snow which prevailed on the tops, the boys lost their way. By 4.30 p.m. in falling darkness they bivouacked on the bushline. They were not equipped for such a night and all their gear and clothing became soaked. The evening meal consisted of 'Deb' potato mixed with cold water, some raisins, a little chocolate and a slice of raw bacon each. The bivouac was not an effective shelter under the conditions and although the boys' sleeping-bags were dry when they climbed into them that evening, no sleeping-bag covers were carried and their clothing and sleeping-bags quickly became saturated. In this way they crouched or sat the night out as far as the contour would allow.

Next morning, at about 8.30 a.m., after a small piece of chocolate each, they returned to the tops in blizzard conditions to retrace their steps by following the faint impressions left by the previous day's travel. At about 2 p.m. on 30 August, Simister, the party leader, died. He had for some time previous to this been having periods of hysteria alternating with near unconsciousness.

By this time Stewart was also exhibiting signs of exhaustion and exposure, but he and Mori eventually gained the bush again and the track back to Luna Hut, but at about 5.30 p.m. Stewart died.

Mori, the survivor, spent the night in a hollow log with his gear near the body of his companion, and next day after much travail reached Luna Hut where he was located on 3 September.

Conclusions
Contributing causes of death by exposure were:
1 Late start.
2 Change of plan from a bush route to an exposed high-level short cut.
3 Loss of route due to:
a Poor visibility.
b Inadequate map interpretation by the party.
4 Wrong type of clothing, i.e. cotton underclothes and cotton jeans.
5 Insufficient clothing worn. (Extra clothing was found in deceaseds' packs but was wet).
6 Spare clothing and sleeping-bags were permitted to become wet as they were not protected in waterproof bags.

7 A cold night was spent in the open with sleet, snow and strong winds in exposed, cramped conditions with only a limited attempt to prepare any form of survival shelter.

8 They had a survival kit but were probably too tired and confused to use the contents or to attempt to light a fire.

9 They were soaked to the skin and cold the following morning when they set off to struggle through deep snow and they were often entangled in sub-alpine scrub. The strong wind which frequently blew them over would also contribute to the acceleration of William Simister's death, which occurred after they had started, and to that of Christopher Stewart which occurred about three and a half hours later.

10 Unsuitable marching rations: they had only consumed some 'Deb' on a spoon and a slice of bacon, with six cubes of chocolate next morning.

Further information on exposure may be obtained from the National Mountain and Safety Council, Internal Affairs Dept., Private Bag, Wellington.

4 All teams fly these days

Medical aspects of air travel

Dr A. Turner

Dr A. Turner, Senior Medical Officer of British Airways, presented the following paper at the conference of the Association of Olympic Medical Officers at its second World Congress at Warwick University, England, in August 1974. It was first published in *The Travellers Health Guide* (Lascelles).

Let us look at it chronologically and first deal with the problem of pre-travel immunisation. There are two groups:
1 Those required by International Health Regulations and without which the passenger cannot travel to particular places.
2 Those which are medically recommended.

Immunisation: obligatory

Smallpox
There are now no countries in the world where smallpox is endemic. In fact, at the time of writing (July 1978), it is thirty-five weeks since a case has been recorded anywhere in the world.

The majority of countries, and all the countries to which New Zealanders normally travel, require vaccination against smallpox only for travellers who in the previous fourteen days have been in a country any part of which has an infected area — none at present. With Australia and Singapore now in this group the need for vaccination is much less. Many African, South American and Eastern European countries still require vaccination; the details can be obtained from local district health offices if necessary.

Contra-indications to smallpox vaccination are pregnancy, failure to thrive in infants, exposure to infectious disease, septic conditions, eczema, allergic skin disorders, deficient immune response syndromes such as leukaemia, lymphoma, Hodgkin's disease and related neoplastic diseases, hypogammaglabulinaemia, corticosteroid and immuno-suppressive drugs. In most cases travel can be arranged to avoid smallpox vaccination.

In the unlikely event of smallpox becoming endemic in a particular area again and a person with a contra-indication needing to travel there, then the risk of vaccination is probably less than risk of contracting smallpox. In this case vaccination should be done but it is advisable to do so in association with giving of vaccine immunoglobulin at the same time.

Cholera

Normally only one dose of cholera vaccine is required and this is the dose of 1 cc subcutaneously or 0·2 cc intradermally. However, many of the Muslem countries in the Middle East demand two injections at seven day intervals during the Haj Pilgrimmage, which is normally October to February. Classical cholera, caused by the *Vibrio cholerae* with its three strains Inaba, Ogawa and Hikojima, has always been an infective diarrhoea in China, India and Pakistan. However, during the last few years the El Tor variant has spread from South East Asia, where it originated, through the usual areas of the classical varieties in the Indian sub-continent to the Middle East. In 1970 it spread to Southern Russia, down through the Balkans and into Saudi Arabia. From the Arabian Peninsula it was introduced into Ethiopia through the French Territory of Affars and Issars at Djibouti, by smugglers crossing the strait of Bab el Mandeb by dhow and then carrying their goods by camel caravans to the interior of Ethiopia. From Ethiopia it spread North, West and South until in 1971 it was in North Africa and then briefly in Spain. In 1973 it reached Naples — see Naples and die. And the introduction of cholera to the Gilbert Islands in 1977 is of some concern.

The efficacy of cholera vacine is regrettably open to doubt. In December 1970 Doctor Jesse Steinfeld, Surgeon General of the United States Public Health Service, ruled that inoculation against cholera was not necessary for people entering the United States from cholera-infected countries on the grounds that cholera is only spread by lack of hygiene and faecal contamination of food. Inoculation is of no value in preventing spread of the disease across frontiers.

At the 26th World Health Assembly held in June 1973 it was recommended that vaccination should no longer be required as a condition of admission of any international traveller to any country. The great majority of countries have now accepted this recommendation.

It has further been found that sensitivity to the vaccine may develop. This has been noticed particularly in aircrew who have been inoculated against cholera every six months for over twenty-five years. Increasing local and general reactions may occur. When this happens the answer is to give maintenance doses by the intradermal method.

Validity is for six months after a six day waiting period.

Yellow fever

Inoculation against yellow fever is probably the most successful advance in preventive medicine there is. Recent inoculation against yellow fever prevents yellow fever. That is definite. It is a live vaccine and as such the contra-indications are as for other live vaccines. It consists of attenuated viruses grown on chicken embryo, hence egg allergy contra-indicates. With these people a test intradermal dose must be given first, but it is not always conclusive.

Encephalitis has been reported in infants inoculated under one year and hence the general policy is not to give it under this age.

It is preferable to give yellow fever inoculation at least three weeks before smallpox vaccination. If smallpox vaccination has been given first, at least three weeks must be left before yellow fever vaccination is given. If in fact it was a primary vaccination then the interval may have to be longer because the yellow fever must not be given until all signs of activity of the smallpox vaccination have cleared. If time is short then the two can be given at the same time, but at different sites.

The certificate is valid for ten years after a ten day waiting period. The inoculation can only be given at special centres.

Being a live vaccine there should if possible also be an interval of twenty-one days between the giving of this vaccine and any other live virus vaccine such as poliomyelitis. It should be avoided during pregnancy and on no account be given to anyone suffering from leukaemia, lymphoma, Hodgkin's disease and associated neoplastic diseases.

It is only required for travellers passing through the two yellow fever belts, in Central Africa and Central America: in Africa from 15⁰ North to 10⁰ South; in America from the northern border of the state of Panama, but excluding the Canal area, to 15⁰ South, excluding certain areas of Brazil. International airports in these areas are excluded.

Immunisation: medically recommended

Enteric group of diseases
Monovalent typhoid vaccine is best given without the paratyphoid A and B factions. It has been found that:
1 It has less side effects.
2 T.A.B. gives little immunity against paratyphoid A and B.

Work done in the R.A.F. suggests that if a full course has been followed by repeated regular boosters up to the age of 35 years, then there is no need to continue after this age. The antibodies do not increase.

It is not necessary to give it to the ordinary traveller on holiday, but only to those working in close contact with people in areas in which it is endemic. Sensible eating habits are more important than inoculations.

Given intradermally, a first dose followed 4–6 weeks later by a second dose with a third dose 6–12 months later. Boosters every three years.

Tetanus
It is more important for the traveller to be suitably inoculated against tetanus than it is for the person who never leaves the U.K. Firstly, because as a disease it is commoner in the tropics and sub-tropics, and secondly, because when people are travelling they are less likely to take their minor cuts to a doctor or local hospital.

Poliomyelitis
Poliomyelitis is basically a disease of warm climates. Because of the excellent campaign of poliomyelitis vaccine which has been carried out in countries like the U.K. we tend to forget what a problem it is in the developing countries. Although the risk for the average tourist is small, a full course or a booster every five years is essential for those working in close contact with people, particularly in rural areas of Asia and Africa.

Gregory and Spalding, writing recently in *The Lancet* from the respiratory unit in Oxford quoted two cases of businessmen who had contracted poliomyelitis whilst on brief business tours to the tropics. They were both over 30 years of age and both are in artificial respirators for the rest of their lives.

They further went on to say that although we look upon poliomyelitis as a disease of children and young people, as the old name of infantile paralysis infers, it can strike late in life and when it does do this it is likely to be more severe and so affect the respiratory system.

Diptheria
Diptheria is a disease practically unknown nowadays in the developed countries because of the excellent immunisation programmes which have been in action for over thirty-five years. In the developing countries where there have been no immunisation programmes it still exists. Although it tends to attack children, it can attack adults, and those of us over thirty-five years have probably never been immunised. Diptheria occurs throughout Africa, the Middle East and the Indian sub-continent. It is particularly prevalent in Nepal. Diptheria immunisation must therefore be seriously considered for travellers to these areas, especially if a Schick Test shows absence of immunity.

Plague
Very popular with the American tourist. The reaction is fairly severe and we in the U.K. believe it should only be given if going to the plague countries. Two injections at 10–20 days interval and a third six months later. Not at the same time as T.A.B. or Typhus.

Typhus
Again popular with the American tourist or perhaps with the doctor who is paid for giving it. Some protection against louse-borne and flea-borne, but practically nil against tick. Reaction can be severe and immune response can be variable. Again only for the areas where there is typhus. Two injections at 7–10 day intervals with a third six months later. Boosters annually. Not at the same time as T.A.B. or Plague.

Rabies
Even if a person is subjected to the whole course of prophylactic vaccination on being bitten by a possibly rabid animal he has to have the antiserum followed by the full course of vaccine.

Hence I feel the Canadian view is the best. Anyone working as a veterinarian or with veteriniarians should have prophylactic vaccine. Due to reactions from duck embryo vaccine its use is being discouraged and the Merieux vaccine is recommended.

Gammaglobulin for infective hepatitis
There is constant discussion over this inoculation — perhaps even argument over its efficacy and efficiency. The probable route of infection with infective hepatitis is faecal-borne. Hence a far higher incidence of this unpleasantly debilitating and sometimes fatal illness occurs in the developing countries with lower standards of sanitation. How effective is gammaglobulin? Woodson and Clinton in 1969 carried out a trial on American Peace Corps volunteers. They found the incidence of infec-

tive hepatitis in the first few months after inoculation was practically nil, but after four months the incidence rose. The survey was divided into eight geographical areas and the results were the same in each area.

Pollock and Reid carried out a survey with V.S.O. (Voluntary Service Overseas) in the U.K., an exactly similar group. They found the incidence was practically nil in the first six months after inoculation, but after that time the incidence was very similar in the inoculated and the uninoculated.

From these two trials it is obvious that immunoglobulin is very effective for preventing infective hepatitis for a comparative short period of 4–6 months. If protection is to be maintained it must be repeated every 4–6 months. It must not be given within three weeks of any live vaccine. I therefore feel it should be given to the business traveller to areas in which it is endemic.

We have now dealt with the pre-travel inoculations, and, I hope, in plenty of time before travel.

Flying

Next we are on our way, and many travellers take their holidays or do their business trips by air. One of the recent problems of high speed travel is the rapid crossing of time zones when flying East-West or West-East. For every fifteen degrees meridian of longitude that are crossed the time changes by one hour. When it is twelve noon G.M.T. in London, it is 4 a.m. in San Francisco, 7 a.m. in New York, 7.30 p.m. in Singapore and 10 p.m. in Sydney.

A mid-morning flight from London at present speeds arrives in New York shortly after lunch, and if not treated sensibly will make a very long day. These changes of time zones cause upset to several of one's physiological rhythms (which are now termed our circadian or diurnal rhythm). A lot of work has been done over the last ten years on these problems, both with long-distance flying and also with shift workers, and with long-term cave dwellers and pot-holers.

It has been shown that excretion of the seventeen keto-steroids in the urine, and normal sodium and potassium levels, take about nine days to re-establish after a flight from the U.S. to Japan. Hauty and Adams carried out tests on medical auxiliaries both young and middle-aged who were flown from Oklahoma City to Manila in a westerly direction (ten hours' time displacement), Oklahoma to Rome in an easterly direction (seven hours' time displacement) and Washington D.C. to Santiago in a southerly direction (one hour time displacement), though in this case assessments were kept to the same time. Three physiological factors with a circadian rhythm were checked, rectal temperature, palmar evaporative water loss and heart rate. All three were upset, an average of five days for East-West, seven days for West-East, but not at all for North-South. Subjective fatigue was the same in all directions, but, most important, reaction time and decision time were increased for two days with East-West and West-East but not North-South flight.

A further point was that with the older age group the subjective fatigue, the upset of circadian rhythms and the deterioration in psychological tests were all far more marked. Preston and Bateman of the British Airways Medical Service, in association with the M.R.C., carried out a study on the effects of flying and time changes on menstrual cycle length and on performance in airline stewardesses. Twenty-nine airline stewardesses were selected and from this group eight were picked for further study in an isolation chamber. Four were subjected to three time zone changes of eight hours, thus representing long easterly flights. Only one showed any change in menstrual cycle length but there was a significant impairment in efficiency over performance tasks and in particular in the ability to react quickly, memorise and search. For this work, tests of addition, reaction time, short-term memory, vigilance and visual search were included.

Colonel Adam of the British Army Medical Research Team flew a group of para-troopers to Singapore where there is a seven and a half hour time change on London G.M.T. He found that for the first three days they were passing urine according to English time. Instead of the urine being passed between the approximate hours of 6.30 a.m. to 11 p.m. he found that, decreasing over the first 72 hours, they were passing it between 2 p.m. and 6.30 a.m. In fact they were passing two-thirds during the night hours and one-third during the day. This led to disturbed sleep, increased fatigue and lowered efficiency. Shepherd and Barlow carried out further efficiency tests on another group of paratroopers with a similar flight which gave more confirmation.

As well as the problem over micturition, the bowel habit is also upset, so that a normal 'after breakfast' man when he flies West has the 'urge' in the night and when he flies East has it when he is busy in his day's work. Similarly of course the natural sleep cycle is upset. I therefore feel that all would-be time-zone breaking travellers should take a mild aperient and a short acting sleeping tablet with them. As far as airline scheduling will allow, travellers should try and arrive at their desti-nation in time to be able to go to bed at their point of departure.

Because of these upsets and the facts already mentioned, it is obviously quite wrong for business tycoons to fly the Atlantic and then go straight into an important meeting or reception. Wrong decisions may well be made — and this goes for the politicians as well. Why did Kruschev beat the table with his shoe when he met President Kennedy in New York? Was it just Kruschev? Or were his circadian rhythms upset? Of course there are those amongst us who feel most of the politicians would not be any better even if they did rest for the necessary twenty-four hours or even forty-eight hours before opening their mouths. At least it can be said that in March 1973 when Premier Heath flew to the U.S.A. to see President Nixon, he flew over on a Saturday to rest on Sunday and see the President on Monday. If common sense is coming even to the politicians, surely we must be able to persuade businessmen.

And so let me summarise a little pre-flight and in-flight advice before coming on to the real problem of maintenance of fitness after arrival.

1 Try to select a flight to arrive at your final destination — namely home or hotel, near your normal pre-departure bed time — and having arrived there go straight to bed. In this way you should sleep satisfactorily the first night which is most impor-tant.

2 Clothing for the climate to which you are going or through which you are passing (this is most important) should be readily available. Two points in particular with this are that:

a there can be far greater temperature variations in the 24 hours in the tropics or sub-tropics, so something light and warm for the evening, and b remember nylon is entirely non-absorbent and should not be worn in the tropics or sub-tropics. The wearing of nylon is a guarantee for developing prickly heat.

In flight

1 Smoking should be cut out or anyway reduced to help cut down the heavy smokers' carboxyhaemoglobin levels and so reduce the effect of relative in-flight hypoxia.

2 Alcohol should be kept to a minimum. It has adverse effects, of dehydration and fatigue, and on physiological adaptation on arrival.

3 In-flight feeding should be confined to a minimum and then to easily digestible foods. With the cabin pressure at approximately 6000 feet intestinal gases expand and distension occurs.

4 Because of the above, loose-fitting clothing in an aircraft is advisable.

5 With the comparatively dry atmosphere of the pressurised cabin, and the tendency not to drink a large amount of fluid, some dehydration occurs — so keep up your fluids, but no carbonated ones. It is interesting that BOAC fitted humidifiers to all their aircraft which the Americans will not do — presumably they are used to the horrible dry atmosphere of their intense central heating. By fitting these humidifiers we have cut down complaints from the crews of upper respiratory tract discomfort, and presumably the passengers feel better as well.

6 Due to the sitting in one position for such a long time, some venous congestion occurs in the legs, with frequent subclinical or even clinical swelling of the feet. A pair of loose-fitting slippers are therefore beneficial. The modern elastic-sided shoe and the ladies' popular boot are bad. At least with laces you can loosen them.

7 Motion sickness is a very rare occurrence in modern air travel when the aircraft is flying above the bad weather. One in a thousand is probably the incidence. Personally I recommend as prophylactics Phenergan syrup for children, Phenergan or Avomine for adults. For the severe sufferer who develops an anxiety state chlorpromazine or Largactil is the answer, and when vomiting is established, Hyoscine by injection.

On arrival — health maintenance

Acclimatisation

You have completed your journey and you have arrived in a tropical or sub-tropical climate. The most important point for visitors to all the hot weather areas is the encouragement of acclimatisation by the maintenance of fluids and to a lesser extent of salt. This is particularly so during the first six weeks — the period of full acclimatisation which normally covers the whole time of the holidaymaker or the business traveller. Once acclimatised, the amount of sweating decreases. The normal U.K. intake of salt is 10–15 g per day. The need in the tropics is 15–25 g per day. Therefore an extra 5–15 g per day is needed, dependent on temperature and physical load. The best way to take it is by additional salt on the food. Effervescent salt tablets can nauseate and enteric-coated pills can be passed unabsorbed, especially during an attack of diarrhoea when the need is even greater. More important than salt is the maintenance of fluids. One pint of fluid per 10^oF temperature per 24 hours is the level of fluid intake to try to maintain. In other words, 8 pints per 24 hours at 80°F. For those who agree with decimalisation I suggest two litres per 10°C for the first 20°C and an additional one litre for every 10°C thereafter, so taking 4 litres at 20°C and 5 litres at 30°C. Another check is to see that the urine remains nearly colourless as darkening of the urine means dehydration. Joseph Banks, the distinguished naturalist of the eighteenth century, who was subsequently President of the Royal Society, accompanied Captain Cook on his first visit to Tahiti in 1768–71. In his writings he described a dinner given by the Tahitians. Everyone was given one half coconut shell of ordinary water and one of salted water. The Tahitians obviously had the answer. On taking extra salt they doubled their fluid intake. Remember you must not increase your salt without increasing your fluid.

Regrettably most 'pale skins' in the world today like to take a holiday in hot spots and try to take on a sun tan. Presumably there must be something in the old saying 'All good looking men are slightly sunburnt', because the shores of the Mediterranean every summer are covered with the bodies of the frying bodies of Americans. Almost certainly the major problem is that the majority of the working community, hence their families as well, can only take a short holiday, probably about two weeks. Because of this they usually expose themselves far too much initially with dire results. For the traveller from a temperate climate to the Mediterranean, the Caribbean or similar shores, fifteen minutes of exposure of normally covered areas is plenty on the first day, subsequently thirty minutes on the second day, one hour on the third, two hours on the fourth and so on, until after 10–14 days the average person can lie out the whole day. Can one do anything to help the sun seeker? There are two ways. Firstly the use of a good moisturising cream or lotion to prevent drying out of the skin. Oils I do not personally recommend. They are not absorbed well and in intense heat can literally cause frying.

What of oral preparations? With exposure to sun, tyrosine in the skin is turned into melanin causing the tan and the pro-vitamin 7-dehydrocholesterol changes to vitamin D. Vitamin A is known to be antagonistic to vitamin D, and on the premise that excess vitamin D is laid down in the skin with its calcium-retaining effects during sunburn, the giving of vitamin A with calcium carbonate was suggested some years ago.

Since 1955 a preparation called Sylvasun has been on sale in South Africa. It became available in the U.K. in 1968. Each pill consists of 25 000 units of vitamin A and 120 mg of calcium carbonate as os sepia. These pills had a great reputation in South Africa and were in fact used with great success by the British Olympic Teams in Rome in 1960 and at Mexico in 1968. On the latter occasion they were put to the real test by the sailing team at Acapulco where with sea and sun the ultra-violet must have been excessive. None of the British team had any problems.

In 1970, in association with two of my colleagues I carried out a controlled trial on British Airways staff and families going on overseas holidays. Regrettably we could not make it double blind with a placebo because one was concerned lest staff on leave in Barbados might finish up in hospital burnt to a frizzle and send the bill to the airline. 1900 took part in the survey; 68 per cent travelled to the Mediterranean area, 7 per cent to the sub-tropics.

Before issue of the pills their previous burning history was taken and graded into severe, moderate, mild and nil. The dose was one pill twice daily, starting two days before sun exposure for not more than fourteen days. Out of the total, 630 were in the severe and moderate categories, the categories that need help — 163 severe, 467 moderate. After taking Sylvasun there were 15 in the severe and 44 in the moderate, 246 in the mild and 325 in the nil. Hence 90 per cent moved from severe or moderate to mild or nil. In other words Sylvasun appeared to be very beneficial in cutting down the pain in sunburn but in no way affected the tan.

To the truly sun-sensitive a barrier cream such as the benzophenones are advisable. One of these is mexenone (2-hydroxin-4-methaxy-4-methylbenzophenone) which is sold as a 4 per cent cream in an oil and water basis under the name of Uvistat (Ward Blenkinsop). But it is a barrier cream and if used liberally will stop tanning.

Diarrhoea

The next problem which we must consider chronologically is what we now call Traveller's Diarrhoea. Also known by various geographical names such as Gippy Tummy, Delhi Belly, Rangoon Runs, Ho Chi Minhs, Hong Kong Dog, Tokyo Trots, Montezuma's Revenge, Aztec Two Step or as in Mexico simply 'Turista'. This is almost certainly the best name because it is the tourist who is so frequently assaulted. Gordon described it as a notorious world-wide illness lasting one to three days after presenting, with a precipitous onset of loose stools and variable symptoms including nausea, vomiting and abdominal cramps. It often occurs sporadically as isolated cases though epidemics occur within families or groups of travellers of all ages.

Professor Kean of Cornell University and his co-workers carried out all the early work on the incidence, aetiology and possibly prophylaxis of this illness. The majority of this work was carried out in Mexico. Initially he found, in 1954, that the incidence was far higher in students visiting Southern Europe than those visiting Northern Europe. He next assessed two groups, one visiting Mexico and one visiting Hawaii: two areas with a similar climate. In Mexico the incidence was 33 per cent, in Hawaii 7·6 per cent. This, therefore, is against a climatic cause. In 63 per cent the attack occurred in the first week and in 32 per cent in the second week. In 57 per cent the attack lasted one day and in 32 per cent two or three days. In this third survey he looked into the aetiology. Here he found the incidence of pathogenic Escherichia coli far higher in those who had diarrhoea than those without. No cases showed Salmonella or Shigella.

In 1966 I carried out an extensive survey on the incidence of Traveller's Diarrhoea in BOAC staff and families travelling overseas on a world-wide basis using the cheap fares which are available if the seats have not been sold by the time of departure of the aircraft.

Nearly 1400 people took part in this trial. The incidence of diarrhoea was nearly 30 per cent amongst those visiting the African continent, 25 per cent among those visiting the Middle East, 17 per cent among those visiting Southern Europe and just over 20 per cent among those visiting around the entire Mediterranean littoral. Further I found that 35 per cent of the attacks lasted one day and 80 per cent not more than three days. This agrees with the findings of Kean and Gordon. More recently, the main work on the aetiology of the problem has been done by Rowe, Taylor and Bettelheim of the Colindale Reference Laboratory, in association with the Armed Forces.

Traveller's Diarrhoea can be a severe problem in the Army with a need to maintain a strategic force which is based in the U.K. and which is flown out suddenly to trouble spots for immediate service. The incidence of Traveller's Diarrhoea in 30 per cent of men in a battalion due for action could be extremely serious.

A very careful study was therefore carried out by Rowe and his fellow workers on a group of 540 British soldiers who had travelled by air from England to Aden. Of those who had diarrhoea, a new serotype of Escherichia coli with antigenic structure 0148K?H28 was found in 54·3 per cent. In a further 40 per cent of a number of different serotypes of E. coli were found including several which caused infantile diarrhoea. The peak incidence of diarrhoea was the tenth day and this was also the peak time for finding 0418.

Further, it was found that 0148K?H28 was enterotoxic. Normally adult organisms are invasive and only infantile organisms are enterotoxic. From all the above work there is very positive evidence that the majority of cases of Traveller's Diarrhoea are infective in origin and almost certainly due to pathogenic E. coli whose serotype varies around the world.

How are we therefore to prevent this annoying complaint which can upset a family holiday or, more importantly, a businessman's trip? There are two basic principles.
1 General preventive methods observing standards of food hygiene which are necessary in the prevention of all intestinal infections occurring in the tropics.
2 Providing anti-infective agents.

Although the first is the most important, as it covers all food poisoning, let us deal with the second first of all as it is a direct follow-up to Kean's, Rowe's and my own work.

Kean carried out two separate surveys with a placebo and with oikochlor-hydroxyquinaline or clioquinal, sold usually as Enterovioform but also as Entosan, Gedacol, Enterosan, Enteroquin and Mexoform. In his first trial, thirty-three taking a placebo had diarrhoea whilst 38 per cent taking clioquinal suffered. In the second trial 35 per cent in both groups had diarrhoea. From this he naturally assumed that clioquinal was valueless in preventing diarrhoea.

With the prolonged taking of clioquinal one must also consider the possible connection with sub-acute mylo-optico neuropathy known colloquially as SMON. In the work of Nakae, Yomomoto, Shigematsu and Kano, out of 1839 cases of SMON, 1381 or 75 per cent had received clioquinal. Spillane in Cardiff reported a probable case where the patient had taken two tablets of clioquinal, four times a day for five days. In a further double blind trial Kean and his co-workers found that phthalyl-sulphathiasole was more effective than neomycin, but surprisingly in clinically severe cases this was reversed. In the 1960 Olympic Games in Rome, D.J. Cussen, medical officer to the British Olympic team, gave the entire team one tablet of Streptotriad May and Baker twice daily. These tablets contain streptomycin 65 mg, sulphadimidine 100 mg, sulphathiazone 100 mg and sulphadiazine 100 mg. Although other teams in Rome had an appreciable amount of diarrhoea the British team had none.

In the survey which I carried out on BOAC staff and families, the 1400 participants were divided into three approximately equal groups who were given (1) an inert control, (2) neomycin sulphatriad and (3) streptomycin sulphatriad. In this way the difference in the active group was only between neomycin and streptomycin. The incidence of diarrhoea was slightly higher in those taking neomycin sulphatriad and those taking the placebo but not statistically so. The incidence of diarrhoea in the streptomycin/sulphatriad group was appreciably less than the other two groups. If in fact Traveller's Diarrhoea is usually infective in origin and carried by an Escherichia coli it is not surprising that a streptomycin/sulphatriad compound is effective. Based on Cussen's original work and my own work, Raymond Owen, medical adviser to the British Olympics team in Mexico City in 1968, gave the entire team and camp followers Streptotriad prophylactically. Out of the 300 athletes and camp followers there were only six who had to cease training for two days each. No one was confined to bed. Considering Kean's figures of 33 per cent, a figure of 2 per cent was very dramatic. Further, since 1966 all ground staff of British Airways Overseas Division going overseas on duty for periods of up to three weeks have been offered Streptotriad prophylactically. The incidence of Traveller's Diarrhoea has been cut drastically, and in seven years the absence of loss of effectiveness indicates that resistance to the drug has not developed.

It is therefore suggested that the taking of Streptotriad, one tablet twice daily for the period away (plus for two days after return to cover late infection) for a maximum of up to four weeks, is beneficial.

To turn next to the general preventative measures. The first we must consider are those concerned with water and milk. When one remembers the enormous population explosions which have occurred in the holiday resorts of the Mediterranean in the last few years one must realise that a stress can be put onto the public health services of these places. It is only necessary for the sewage system, swimming pool purification systems or the personal habits of the food handlers not to be above reproach and severe trouble is bound to occur. The only really satisfactory answer is to boil all drinking water and milk. This can be difficult in a hotel. There are three other methods which can be used instead of boiling, not as good but better than nothing.

The first is by drinking only mineral waters produced by a reputable firm — but this can be expensive. Coca Cola and Pepsi Cola are made world-wide under strict licence, and health inspectors travel from the U.S.A. to inspect the factories. Hence it is likely that other minerals made in these factories will be made under the same high standards of purity.

The second answer is the use of chlorination tablets such as Sterotabs or Halazone which can be obtained from most chemists.

The third method is for those staying in hotels where the boiling of water would be difficult. It is dependent on a satisfactory hot water system and is basically the same as pasteurisation of milk — the maintenance of a high temperature, but one below boiling, for a prolonged period. If the hot water system is maintaining the water at 140^0–160^0 or more, then it is most likely that most of the organisms are killed. On this basis the answer is to use water from the hot water tap as drinking water. Fill a container from the hot water tap and keep until cool for drinking, ensuring the container is covered.

Remember also that ice cubes should be made from boiled water. It is no good drinking only boiled water and then adding ice cubes which are from unboiled water and which dissolve in the drink in a matter of minutes.

One of the delicacies of many tropical, semi-tropical and Mediterranean hot spots which pull in the ever-increasing numbers of holidaymakers is shellfish. These we all know can be of very doubtful purity. They can cause the common and mild Traveller's Diarrhoea, the less common and less mild bacillary dysentery and also the severe typhoid. For the campers who are doing their own food purchasing it is sensible to only buy live shellfish.

The habit of eating underdone steaks is bad. Tapeworms are killed by satisfactory cooking. Steak tartare must be avoided in the Middle East. All meat must be well cooked, recently cooked and only once cooked. Uncooked food is another problem. All fruit which can be peeled should be peeled and this includes tomatoes. Fruit which cannot be peeled, such as strawberries, or salad vegetables such as lettuce, must be washed in a chlorinated solution such as a weak solution of Milton or Roccal. Watercress should be avoided.

The large Middle eastern watermelon is a problem because it is not unknown for the merchants of the markets to pump in dirty water to increase the weight and hence the price.

Great care must be taken with cold buffets which are frequently known as the 'Chef's special table'. If this refers to a specially high incidence of infection, it may be a good name. Regrettably, even in presumed high quality hotels one can see these dishes of cold meats, salads and cold sweets laid out uncovered on a table, with flies abounding and dive-bombing the food. This is also so with open-air cocktail parties and canapes. Ice-creams are very popular, but standards of production vary. Only buy ice-creams from large reputable firms — on no account should they or any other form of food be bought from street hawkers.

Finally, the avoidance of fly-infested restaurants is an essential. If one has any doubt as to the lack of cleanliness in a restaurant, take a quick look in the lavatory prior to entering the restaurant. If the lavatory is dirty then it is more than likely the kitchen will be dirty as well. Infective hepatitis is usually faecal spread so avoid bathing near harbours where there may be sewage effluent.

Schistosomiasis is spread by bathing in infected water as well as by drinking infected water. It occurs in Africa, all down the Nile Valley, right across Central Africa from West to East, and in Rhodesia and South Africa. Also in Zanzibar, Madagascar, Reunion and Mauritius, scattered areas in the Middle East and also in the Far East, and in the New World in Venezuela, Brazil and the holiday island of St Lucia. Wherever there is schistosomiasis there should be no fresh-water sailing or bathing. Also all drinking water must be boiled. And so I give you ten commandments for the avoidance of all intestinal and urinary tract infections including Traveller's Diarrhoea.

1 Boil all drinking water and milk.
2 Be very careful of shellfish — preferably see them alive before eating.
3 All cooked food to be well cooked and recently cooked.
4 All fruit including tomatoes peeled.
5 Lettuce and unpeeled fruit sterilised by chlorination — no watercress.
6 No leftovers or food on display.
7 Avoid local ice-creams — buy only from large firms.
8 Mineral waters from large firms only.
9 Avoid fly-infested restaurants.
10 Take one tablet of Streptotriad twice daily.

Having dealt with the common and minor ailments and problems of overseas travel, whether for businessman or holidaymaker, let us now move on to the more serious ones.

Malaria

By far the most important of the so-called tropical diseases is malaria. I say 'so-called' advisedly because many of them are not confined to the tropics. Malaria occurs along the North African coast in Tunisia and Morocco where the inclusive tour holidaymaker is a frequent visitor, but, I regret, an infrequent taker of antimalarial prophylactic tablets. Remember Falciparum. Malaria is a killer and as such must be prevented. It must be considered in the diagnosis of any illness in a patient of any race or colour who has been in an area in which it is endemic. It is the dominant illness in West, Central and East Africa. It occurs also in the Middle, Near and Far East, certain Pacific Islands, and Central and South America. For New Zealanders, malaria prophylaxis is essential for travellers to Papua New Guinea, the New Hebrides and the Solomon Islands. Remember one mosquito bite in a transit stop can give malaria. Vivax malaria is widespread in temperate subtropical and tropical climates. Ovale occurs in East, Central and West Africa. Finally, quartan is also widespread and rare, and the most difficult to eradicate.

In the U.K. in 1970 there were just over one hundred cases; in 1971, 269; and in 1972 there were 336. This surely shows it must be prevented, as it can be. General methods of eradication of the anopheline mosquito are the responsibility of local health authorities, but the visitor must take preventative measures as well, by wearing sensible clothes after dark and by chemoprophylactic substances.

The malaria-carrying anopheline mosquito bites from dusk to dawn, so arms and legs should be covered whenever possible after dark, and an insect repellent such as diethyl toluamide, which is contained in Flypel and Skeet-o-Stik, should be used. Dimethyl phthalate and Indalone are two other varieties. Repellent activity usually lasts for up to four hours, but this time is shortened by sweating. (Avoid eyes, lips, spectacle frames and rayon clothing.) See the bed and bedroom is mosquito-proofed with adequate netting and use an insecticidal spray in dark corners. Well-fitted air conditioning should be satisfactory but can be a snare and delusion.

There are at present three varieties of antimalarials:
1 Progunanil or Paludrine taken daily.
2 Pyremethamine or Daraprim taken weekly.
3 Chloroquine taken once or twice weekly.

In Britain we generally use Paludrine or Daraprim. In Canada and Holland, Paludrine. In New Zealand, Chloroquine for areas where there is no reported resistance to it (at present Africa only) and elsewhere Maloprim. In the U.S.A., France and Germany, Chloroquine.

The London and Liverpool Schools of Tropical Medicine support the Progunanil or Paludrine method. There are three good reasons for this:
1 It is an established fact that it is easier to remember to take a tablet every day rather than to take one twice a week or once a week.
2 If you do forget to take a daily tablet you go 48 hours, but if you forget to take a weekly tablet you go 14 days and the incubation period of malaria is 10–12 days. This could be disastrous.
3 Chloroquine is by far the best drug for treatment and should be kept for treatment so preventing resistant strains.

However, whichever drug is used the essential points are to start 24 hours before entering a malarious area, and take the drug regularly throughout the time in the malarious area and for 28 days after leaving the area.

Other diseases

Kala-Azar or visceral leismmaniasis does occur in pockets in the Mediterranean area, the Middle East, East and West Africa, India and South America. It can quite definitely be caught in Greece, the Greek Islands and parts of Yugoslavia, Sicily, Southern Italy, Corsica, the French Riviera, Southern Spain and Southern Portugal — all popular holiday resorts. A chronic, debilitating, intermittent febrile disease, it is spread by the sand fly, which gets through mosquito netting — another good reason for using repellent and an aerosol spray.

The safari holidays to the game park have become very popular during the last few years, and it is these areas that are inhabited by the tsetse fly, the spreader of that evil disease trypanosomiasis or sleeping sickness. A further reason for using netting and a repellent. For those spending a longer time in trypanosomal areas, the question of giving a prophylactic dose of 250 mg of Pentamidine, which should give protection for three to six months, should be considered. However, not everyone agrees with this policy, as if an infection occurs and breaks through despite the Pentamidine then the subsequent diagnosis can be more difficult.

One must mention typhoid once more. In the past we have had the periodic epidemic in this country: Croydon in the mid-thirties, Aberdeen in 1964. During the last few years we have had far more sporadic cases, quite a few after holidays in Tunisia. In 1969, thirty-eight cases were known to have occurred in holidaymakers staying in one hotel in Tunisia — eight from Britain, sixteen from Germany, thirteen from Switzerland and one from Holland. One British and one German patient died, but how many of these patients may have become carriers? There have also been further cases more recently.

Sun-glasses of a reputable make I do advise for all who are taking the tropical sun following residence in the U.K., especially with the reflection which occurs with sea and light sand, and also on snow.

Five final warnings.

1 No underdone steaks outside Western Europe, Canada, U.S.A., Australia and New Zealand.

2 Many swimming pools are of very doubtful hygiene standards with the result that a severe external otitis can develop. We have cut down the incidence of this with our flying staff by using spirit drops with mercuric chloride (1 in 1000) for use before and after swimming.

3 Fungal foot infections thrive in the humid heat, and use of a fungicidal powder prophylactically is beneficial — with a separate towel for the feet.

4 Walking in open sandals, and particularly with bare feet, can cause trouble. Hookworm, where the sanitation is earth closets; tetanus in tetanus-infected countries, and tick typhus in East and South Africa.

5 Cyprus is now a very popular holiday resort and the incidence of hydatid disease there is extremely high — higher than in the Brecon hills. And so to summarise I give you my ten commandments.

 a After a flight with a five-hour time change, rest for twenty-four hours.

 b See your foods are well cooked and recently cooked.

 c Peel all fruit and be careful with salads and ices.

 d Take two tablets of Streptotriad daily for up to four weeks.

 e Easy with the sun at first and take two tablets of Sylvasun daily for two weeks.

 f Maintain your fluids and salt.

g Take antimalarial drugs daily where necessary, and for twenty-eight days subsequently.

h Boil drinking water and milk.

i Never wear nylon in the heat.

j No bathing in unknown rivers, lakes or harbours.

5 Health, hygiene and the athlete

Health and hygiene

M. Oram

Mark Oram, a Member of the New Zealand Society of Physiotherapists, is a colleague of the author's at Palmerston North. He has written this paper specially for this book.

Medical check-up
No matter how fit the sportsman or woman think they are, a regular check-up is wise, as many problems may go undetected and then when noticed it may be too late. If a defect is found it doesn't necessarily mean that that person will have to give up his/her sport, because with treatment, and with a possible modification of training, he/she may well be able to continue.

Dental care
People may be reluctant to go to their doctor, but, for some reason, they are even more reluctant to visit their dentist. A mouth full of rotten teeth, for that matter any infection, will have a detrimental effect on training and competition. Frequent visits to your dentist are a must.

Immunisations
One of the problems of modern day medical science is that because certain diseases have become very rare, we are tending to forget about our immunisations. One of the most important of these, as far as sportsmen are concerned, is anti-tetanus. Is yours up-to-date?

Diet
This may vary along with the sportsman's needs, but the usual one tends to concentrate mainly on proteins at the beginning of the week, and then as the day of competition draws near, incorporates more carbohydrates, as these are easily broken down and stored as energy. Regular meals are a must and 'between-meal' pickings are to be avoided.

Fluid replacement
An electrolyte solution taken before and during the event will replace the electrolytes lost in perspiration. By replacing these the competitor will usually finish more strongly than someone not doing so. Failure to replace liquids over a long period may result in chronic dehydration, and poor performances.

Drugs
For maximum performance, the player should avoid all drugs except on the advice of his doctor. The most common of these are, of course, tobacco and alcohol. If a

person must drink alcohol, it must be in moderation, whereas smoking and active competitive sport definitely do not mix.

Smoking has a detrimental effect on the respiratory system. Briefly, the contents of the smoke irritate the lining of the airways in the lungs, and this causes an increase in the amount of normal secretions which keep the air moist and warm. This increase in secretions narrows the airways and decreases the efficiency of the gaseous exchange across the pulmonary membrane.

Adequate sleep
This, whatever your requirement, is a must. Not enough sleep, and you are not going to perform well the next day. Amongst other things, your reflexes will be slow. Too much sleep will not assist you either.

Baths and showers
Frequent baths or showers with soap, following training or competition, are necessary to wash away the harmful bacteria which could cause infection.

Frequent washing of playing and practice gear is necessary to remain friendly with your team-mates, but more importantly, is necessary to prevent infection. This is very important for touring teams who may have trouble finding washing facilities. That is no excuse — you must wash your gear regularly, especially underwear. Infected wounds, acne across the shoulders and chafing between the thighs can all be caused by dirty gear.

Adequate clothing
This is important for at least two reasons.
1 It is surprising how many people leaving a southern hemisphere summer do not realise that it will be winter in the northern hemisphere and do not include the necessary clothing.
2 Living in air-conditioned hotels, one tends to think the weather outside is as warm, and this can result in players dressing inadequately.

Lack of forethought can lead to colds which mean an unnecessary break in training.

Track-suits are not used as they should be. Often a player will start training in one then shed it when warmed. Later in training as it becomes a stop/start affair, he cools down but does not replace his track-suit. That is the time to put it on, to keep warm, and prevent injury and the common cold.

Treatment of abrasions and lacerations
Immediate attention and frequent follow-up treatment for abrasions and lacerations is most important in preventing infection. Most wounds are treated properly initially, but too many people then forget about them and don't bother to change dressings regularly, leaving the same blood-stained one on until it becomes infected. Injuries are mostly unavoidable; infection is unnecessary and to a large extent preventable.

Some sports, e.g. rugby, use grease on the knees to prevent grass burns. It may do this to a certain extent, but not completely. What it does do, however, is trap dirt in the grease over a wound, and unless cleaned off thoroughly after the match, will probably cause an infection.

80

Care of the hands and feet

Short clean nails assist in the care of the hands, similarly with the feet. The immediate treatment of tinea is most important in a team situation as this will spread quickly. Powders can be obtained for this, and the player concerned must not share bathing or shower facilities.

Blisters, which may form on the hands of feet, should be kept clean, punctured with a sterile needle, leaving the skin on, and then covered with a clean dressing.

Training

Do not overtrain, as this tends to reduce resistance to infection. On the other hand, a person who does just the right amount of training gains resistance and protection against infection. Training is an individual thing, and only you know how much you need to do.

Sports hygiene

International Cycling Federation of Rome

This paper on sports hygiene was originally published in the *International Manual of Cycling* in 1972, by the International Cycling Federation, Rome.

Hygiene is that branch of medicine which aims at maintaining the state of health. To attain this goal, two courses should be followed. The first consists of advising and applying all those rules which tend to increase the robustness of the organism in such a way as to render it more resistent to the action of harmful external factors. The second consists of studying and neutralising the exogenous morbid factors of all kinds (physical, chemical, biological, etc.) which may have a negative action on the state of health.

Within the framework of sports medicine, hygiene concerns all measures liable to safeguard the health of the athlete in the environment in which he carries out his activity and fights against easily diffused illnesses and harmful agents; lastly, attention is also paid to the rules of living to be followed in so far as sexual activity, pleasure-seeking habits, etc. are concerned.

Hygiene of the environment

Tracks and velodromes do not raise any great hygienic problems except for the elimination of those irregularities of the ground or potentially harmful objects (fragments of glass, etc.) which could easily cause accidents. It is hardly worth mentioning either the removal of tough grass and of any stagnant water present or of refuse at the sides or close to the track, which it is absolutely essential to have cleaned up.

Very much more important is the hygiene of the changing rooms, which should be properly lighted and aired; generally speaking, modern sports venues are built according to perfect rules from the point of view of hygiene, and therefore do not involve problems of this kind. However, they should be carefully kept up, both as regards daily cleaning and in respect of the need to undertake frequent disinfection of the floors and equipment with disinfectant solutions and detergents. The so-called 'athlete's foot', due to special fungi, is very often conditioned by the presence of the parasitic agent on the floors and benches of the changing rooms as well as by the habit, which should be strictly forbidden, of exchanging socks or shoes between one cyclist and another. An important item in the hygiene of changing rooms is represented by the fight against insects (flies and mosquitoes). The elimination of flies will obviously not be limited to the use of insecticides only, and should be based first and foremost on more thorough cleaning of hygienic installations, such as WCs and showers, and their maintenance in a perfect state of efficiency, as well as the necessary repairs in case of breakage.

Thus, besides being the responsibility of the concern which manages the sports venues, the hygiene of these quarters is based above all on the education of the athletes and all those who habitually use such installations; accordingly, it is absolutely necessary that the technician has recourse to all his authority in order to correct certain deplorable habits and render liable to disciplinary sanctions those athletes who, by declining to observe certain basic rules, cause damage or behave in an uncivil manner.

Reference should also be made to the need for the accurate maintenance of clothes and bicycles. It is up to the sports technician to make arrangements for clothing to be frequently washed and, as far as possible, not to allow replacements or exchange of such clothing between the various cyclists. The latter should be taught to lay out their clothes in an orderly manner.

Personal hygiene

Hygiene of the cyclist's person is essential in order to avoid contagion from illnesses, especially of the parasitic type. It should be borne in mind that the fact of living as a group vastly facilitates the transmission of such illnesses, and that accordingly the rules of personal hygiene should be much more severe than in the case of the individual. We have already stressed how essential it is to avoid any promiscuity of clothing; it is advisable that every cyclist be educated in this, and that he take the utmost care regarding personal washing, taking repeated baths and hot showers, and using disinfectant soaps. Steps should be taken to isolate those athletes who may be bearers of parasites of the skin and its annexes (hair of the head and of the pubis) until such time as a suitable cure has been effected.

The most frequent parasitic diseases in our climate are pediculosis of the head, of the clothing and of the pubis.

Infestation by lice (pediculus = louse or cockroach) causes a reaction of the skin, which becomes red and highly irritable; on the infested zone the typical small parasites may be noted (about 3–4 mm long, grey-brown in colour), together with their eggs laid at the base of the hair of the head or of the pubis. The cure for this condition consists in shaving the hair and in using anti-parasitic powders having a basis of mercury derivatives and DDT. Prophylaxis naturally consists in the utmost personal hygiene possible, especially in groups, and in avoiding the possibility of contagion.

We have already spoken of another illness of the skin known as 'athlete's foot' (interdigital epidermatophyzia), widespread especially in hot climates and seasons, and which consists of the blistering and fissuring of the skin of the toes, especially in the interdigital spaces. A similar parasitic disease is localised to the groin, and involves reddening and severe itching of the skin of the groin folds, of the pubis and at times of the scrotum.

All these affections are **contagious**, and accordingly recourse should be had to a prophylaxis consisting of eliminating all possibilities of contact either through clothing or direct, besides proceeding to a suitable therapy.

Thus it is very important for the athlete to take the utmost care in washing his skin, paying special attention to feet and the annexes of the skin (hair, nails), which should be cut frequently and worn short.

Living habits
The hygienic aspect and the influence of certain living habits should also be considered; this mainly regards the duration of rest and sleep and the use of pleasure items, such as the main stimulating beverages and the smoking of tobacco.

The duration of nightly sleep is of course very subjective; however, for those practising sports activity with a considerable expenditure of energy, the duration of compensating rest periods is obviously fundamental. Generally speaking, at least eight hours' rest period per night in addition to one hour's afternoon sleep, is considered necessary.

The rest period at night should begin no later than 10 p.m., so that the athlete can get up in the morning at 7 a.m. at the latest, and make full use of the hours of the day in accordance with the cycle of his training and meal times.

It is also advisable, as far as possible, to avoid lodging the athletes in common dormitories, thus helping to eliminate causes of disturbance during the rest period. The sports manager should undertake to advise quiet amusements such as reading or an evening stroll in the open air.

Coffee and tea (similar as regards chemical composition) may be allowed in small quantities, that is to say, two cups per day at the most. In fact, provided they are taken in small doses, these stimulating beverages exercise a tonic action on the organism; while if abused, especially in hypersensitive subjects, they cause psychic hyperexcitability and hypersensitivity of the cardiocirculatory and digestive systems, with the appearance of intermittent extrasystoles, palpitations of the heart, gastric hyperacidity, etc.

Smoking should be absolutely forbidden. In fact it is the opinion of all persons competent in this field that smoking harms the organism through various mechanisms, both on account of the substances it contains (nicotine and derivatives) and of its physical state (smoke, or dispersion in the air of carbonised corpuscles). The presence of nicotine carries out a pharmacodynamication on the heart and the peripheric region, to be avoided in subjects devoted to sports activities; whilst on account of its irritating action on the upper air passages and on the bronchia, smoke produces or maintains inflammation of the pharynx, the larynx and the bronchia themselves, the normality and soundness of which are essential conditions in the athlete. The chronic irritation by smoke of the air passages is moreover a predisposing cause for contracting illnesses of various sorts, especially when accompanied by other predisposing conditions which the athlete cannot avoid, such as damp, cold, etc. The athlete should therefore be convinced of the absolute danger of smoking and its negative influence on his sports performance.

Hygiene of the sexual functions

The male reaches sexual maturity around 15–16 years of age (puberty) when, besides being capable of reproducing, he is subject to physiological erotic stimuli.

The sexual function is largely under the control of the psyche, which translates and consciously elaborates sensations and determines attitudes; however, on the other hand, the psyche is also easily influenced by impressions, habits, environment, etc. Whence the need for the adolescent to be informed of all the so-called 'mystery of sex'.

The main problem of sexual hygiene in the sportsman is divided between two extremes: the supposed negative influence of sexual activity; and the supposed negative influence of abstinence. Obviously in medicine nothing is absolute; however, those prejudices which create extremely dangerous and harmful psychological complexes should be done away with. A sexual activity (without artifice and without excesses) not only does not have harmful consequences on the athlete's physique, but helps give him that sense of relaxation which is necessary if he is to devote himself to sport. In cycling, above all, there may in fact be a certain antagonism between intense athletic activity and sexual activity, but in this case too it is a question of not over-rating the problem and of sexual education.

It is well to clarify the repercussions which may be produced by natural sexual activity and by spontaneous nocturnal emission. The former, provided it takes place without artifices, excesses, or psychic commitment in periods of not excessive athletic and physical commitment at sufficient intervals, does not raise any problems of antagonism on the energetic plane.

In this connection, we would like to undramatise the erotic attention raised in certain individuals precisely as a result of the obligation to respect an abstinence which, in such cases, is shown to be more harmful than useful.

It should however be considered that, without attaching excessive importance to the problem, sports activity itself tends to unfocus the athlete's attention on sexual activity.

In fact, the psychic concentration of the subject committed to striving to attain sports goals is easily sufficient to distract him from erotic stimuli, providing however that excessive importance is not attached to the latter by prohibitions which have the effect of acting in a diametrically opposed way.

On the other hand, nocturnal emission is a purely mechanical and natural phenomenon which has no negative effect on the physical state of the subject and on his athletic performance, provided once more that a complex of culpability is not created in the athlete on account of such phenomenon, which would have the effect of convincing him of having been the victim of an impairment of his athletic capabilities.

In this latter case, a negative effect is obtained which has a consequent depressing effect on the young man's morale and performance.

By respecting such general hygienic advice, and above all by avoiding the excesses either of abstinence or of a sexual hyperactivity, the problem of sexual hygiene in athletes may be considered as solved. In addition, the prevention of contagious diseases should be considered.

Fight against doping

The taking of pharmaceutical products or the use of psychological methods (psychotherapy, hypnosis) tending to re-adjust a state of psycho-physical impairment, due to illness or to chronic fatigue (overtraining), should always be carefully considered and carried out under strict medical control. In fact it is up to the doctor, expert in the psycho-pathological problems which the cyclist may come up against, to decide on the means and best time for attempting to re-adjust the subject, bringing him back to his normal state of health and efficiency.

These treatments, which occupy an important place in medical therapy, are to be considered not only useful, but at times necessary, and should be carried out under the control of a doctor, after their exact prescriptions have been carefully worked out.

Any pharmacological or physical treatment, undertaken by the athlete on his own account and initiative should be excluded; in fact it is essential that any cure be applied only after ascertaining the conditions of the subject, in order not only to ensure that it carries out to the full its beneficial action, but above all that all those drawbacks or undesired secondary reactions which may be implicit in any therapy, may be avoided. Vice versa, the use by a healthy and efficient subject of substances or means aimed at artificially increasing psycho-physical efficiency, especially in athletes, should be forbidden, since these are included in the category of doping or drugging. In fact, by doping is meant:

'The use of substances whose aim is to artificially increase the efficiency of the athlete in competition, thereby altering his agonistic morality and psycho-physical efficiency; doping is an unfair practice in as much as it tends to place an athlete in conditions of advantage over the other competitors, which is not sportsman-like.'

If in fact there existed substances capable of increasing the muscular power of an athlete (which has not to date been scientifically proved) their use would constitute a sports fraud, since the morality of sport envisages competing loyally in natural conditions of parity.

The trainer also should consider doping as his potential enemy, even at the professional level. In fact, his ability and skill could be laid open to discussion by a victory or result obtained because of the decisive aid of pharmacological factors. In fact, in this last case it might be asked what part the ability of his trainer might have played in the preparation of the athlete.

However, the fundamental aspect of doping is of a toxicological nature, since the facts have by now proved that the substances commonly used by athletes for the purpose of artificially increasing their performance produce negative secondary effects, either acute or chronic, such as are liable to have pathological repercussions on the athlete's physique and mentality.

Of the various substances commonly used, the amphetamines are those which more than any others have toxic effects which may easily become manifest. In fact, these act exclusively as excitants of the central nervous system, giving a feeling of fallacious euphoria and strength such that the athlete, unconscious of fatigue, succeeds in producing an excessive effort, with all the consequences implied by physical strain. By removing the alarm bell of fatigue the athlete makes an excessive effort, and the accumulation of endogenous toxic substances and the exertion of the cardio-circulatory and respiratory systems added to the effects of the drug create dramatic pictures of cardio-circulatory deficiencies, which on occasion lead even to the death of the individual concerned.

In fact, in the case of the amphetamines, a mechanism of reciprocal strengthening exists between the drug and the product of fatigue, whereby while in a sedentary person an excessive dose of amphetamine only causes slight disturbances, in the case of an athlete already suffering from fatigue, it inevitably leads to a state of acute intoxication. In doping, the use of excitant drugs and the use of sedatives, inevitably taken to counter the excitant action of the former, can in the long run cause a toxic effect, with malfunctions of the various organs and above all of the liver, which constitutes an important stage in the metabolism of the athlete. In addition, it should be borne in mind that certain drugs, such as the amphetamines, are classified as para-narcotics since, in order to carry out their excitant action, they require, in the long run, progressively larger doses on account of increasing habituation to them; the consequent tendency to increase doses is extremely dangerous.

It is important for the technical experts also to appraise another aspect of doping, namely, its uselessness in so far as its effective action on athletic performance is concerned. In fact, recent experiments, severely controlled from the scientific point of view, have demonstrated that the amphetamines and many other substances used for doping purposes do not actually increase the sports efficiency of the athlete; indeed their administration leads to an increase in the energetic metabolism of the subject, who, however, arrives more rapidly at exhaustion of caloric reserves.

For all the above reasons, doping is a practice to be fought against not only by sports doctors, but also by the managers and technical experts, and should be replaced, through the intelligent education of the athletes, by the application of a rational sports preparation such as to prevent the basic psychological motive latent in the athlete from coming to the fore, namely, a would-be state of subjective or objective inferiority. Efforts to compensate this inferiority cannot be through recourse to doping, but through rational preparation (preventive action) or by means of cures capable of rapidly rehabilitating the athlete in cases of indisposition or environmental solidus psychological conflict.

6 Bike racing and sports medicine

Some thoughts on training for bike racing with a sports medicine slant

A.G. Haslett

Mr Alf. G. Haslett is the representative for cycling on the New Zealand Olympic and Commonwealth Games Association, and is also the representative of that association to the New Zealand Federation of Sports Medicine. The following article was written for use by coaches and racing cyclists.

You have chosen a tough sport, one of the hardest. Having been a racing cyclist and tried a few other sports, I have followed our sport for longer than I care to remember both here and abroad, and I consider the only harder sport is rowing. So, to perform well you must work hard. Your coaches have told you to put the miles into your legs and medical men have explained the cardio-respiratory needs to enable your coached muscles to perform. If you are to perform to the best of your ability you cannot skip the work but you can avoid wasting at least some of the graft by attention to the following.

Medical check-up
Before starting a season this is a must. If you are racing for fun (we should all do that) go to your GP for a physical to ensure that you are medically fit. If you are already a successful racer or have aspirations to make the big time, seek out the New Zealand Federation of Sports Medicine (N.Z.F.S.M.) doctor in your district. If you have difficulty and your club or centre cannot help, write to me and I will put you in touch with the secretary of your local branch of the N.Z.F.S.M. The N.Z.F.S.M. medic will doubtless tell you your pulse rate and your haemoglobin count. A low blood count could indicate an oxygen carrying deficiency/defect and is usually corrected with vitamin supplements and iron, or maybe a change of training. Make sure your doctor is familiar with the U.C.I. or rather the I.O.C. (International Olympic Committee)-F.I.A.C. list of prohibited drugs as even the most innocent of prescriptions such as a nasal spray could produce a positive if you are tested. There are alternatives to most medicants which will not offend, even for asthma.

Dope
The medical profession uses drugs to help sick people. If you are fit, drugs will not necessarily make you go faster; they may fight off nature's danger signals of exhaustion, but they can only adversely affect your health, if not now, in later life. There is no known drug which will give you more energy when the race is due to begin. You race for the sport but because of a few who are foolish you may compete in a race that is dope tested. If you do, be sure to tell the doctor at the briefing everything you have taken, whether it came from a doctor or was purchased from a chemist or whatever. Make sure that the people handling you fully understand what they are

about, and do not take anything before or during racing unless you know exactly what it is. Trainers and handlers are equally liable to penalty should you produce a positive test.

Hygiene

Probably the aspect of training that receives the least attention and this, strangely enough, includes keeping warm. I know that all I am recommending costs money but I assure you it's money well spent. Let's start at the bottom and deal with the feet. Get the best shoes you can afford and look after them — the bacteria formed from sweat has caused more discomfort and lost more races than you can imagine. See if you can get a physiotherapist to look over your shoes (while you are wearing them on the bike) to check for plate placement and toeclip pressure. Don't walk in your racing shoes, it strains the calf and thigh muscles, and never walk in bare feet. Never wear socks a second time between washes and make sure they are warm and comfortable. Use a good cream on your feet. Chemists have a good foot cream and I still have a few tubes of skin balm for the first ones that ask for it. Be most particular about toe nails.

Don't be deceived, New Zealand is not sub-tropical unless you live north of Whangarei, so always train in leg warmers unless it's really hot, and if you have any doubts at all, race in leg warmers and wash them every time you use them. Next to your bike, shorts are probably the most important part of your equipment, so get the best (and they might not be the most expensive). Remember that bacteria on leather also applies here, and wash your shorts in good mild soap, not detergent. Make sure the chamois is soft and pliable and use talcum powder or skin balm. In 1973 I saw Eddy Merckx lose a Paris-Nice with inflammation of the perineum.

Buy yourself a woollen vest that buttons to the neck and has short sleeves, and wear it racing or training. If in doubt wear arm warmers; remember it takes energy to keep those exposed parts warm, and wear a hat.

Bike racing all over the world is remarkable for its lack of washing facilities at the finish of road events, and in consequence, I note that even at track meets many of you neglect to use the showers. After racing or training wash off the sweat as soon as you can and change into fresh clothing to avoid the possibility of catching a chill. If there are changing rooms, sponge yourself down with a mixture of cologne, distilled water and surgical spirit in equal parts, but be careful in the region of the perineum or any open wounds. Once the area is clean use a lanolin-based skin balm.

Vitamins

A few weeks back I was privileged to attend the biennial conference of N.Z.F.S.M. and Dr K.D. Fitch of the Department of Physical Education, University of Western Australia, and a world name in sports medicine, said 'Australian and New Zealand athletes have the most expensive urine in the world' and Ken knows his bike riders. All excess vitamins come out immediately in the urine.

Some of you will have read the letters from Alan Dempsey, who is racing in Italy, in which he tells of all the vitamins his manager Bruno is pumping into him. Alan has jumped in at the deep end without the training that is the usual build-up for the sort of racing he is doing, and doing extra well at that, but he is suffering with his breathing, 'dilettantes' are expendable (there are 200 000 of them in Italy), and

Bruno has plenty of money to spend on the chosen few. Most of those vitamin capsules are just placebos, an expensive way to psyche him.

Providing you don't eat exclusively at the Burger Bar or Pizza Parlour, but eat normal New Zealand family food you will get all the vitamins your body requires for even the toughest racing, but if you want to be really sure, one Pluravit capsule a day will take care of anything you might miss. Providing the preparation is of pure vitamin-mineral content and is not a chemical stimulant it will ensure that you are not suffering a deficiency that prevents you from performing up to your capabilities, but it's better to be sure of your diet than depend on pills.

Just a few guide lines on vitamins:

Vitamin A. This helps to ward off early season colds and is essential for the mucuous membranes and the respiratory tract. It also has an effect on digestion. You will get all you need from milk, butter, eggs, liver, kidneys and fish liver oils.

Vitamin B. This is a complex group of sub-sections. B_1 or thiamine you need for the metabolism of carbohydrates, to break sugar down in the tissues to supply energy. You get B_1 in milk, lean meat, eggs, fruit, vegetables, liver, etc. B_2 or riboflavin also breaks down sugars and is good for nervous tissues and the skin; you will obtain all you need from meat and dairy products. Another vitamin in the B-complex group is niacin; for the skin, the digestive tract and the mucous membranes. This is present in foods as above but brewer's yeast is also a good source, as are oatmeal and rice. B_6 or pyradoxin breaks down protein and fats into amino acids, and if you have eaten the above you will get B_6. The B-complex group is water-soluble so that their effectiveness can be reduced in cooking. They are a chain so if you miss one, you soon affect the others. B_{12} is the vitamin that racing cyclists often take in excessive quantities even to the extreme of having it injected. Injection of B_{12} should be done by and under medical direction and never by an unqualified person. B_{12} is a metal-based vitamin and furnishes nutrition for the molecules in the blood stream. It reduces the symptoms of pernicious anaemia which results from the failure of your body to produce red blood cells in the bone marrow. B_{12} is present in the foods mentioned and really only needed as a supplement in extra hard long-distance stage races unless prescribed by a doctor. It is present especially in leafy greens.

Vitamin C. Also known as ascorbic acid, it makes collagen, a glue-like substance that joins the cells together in the bones, tissues, teeth and blood cells. Vitamin C is found in citrus fruits and fresh vegetables.

Vitamin D. This is derived by the exposure of the body to sunlight and is also present in fish liver oils. It is essential for the maintenance of the skeletal structure. The foregoing discourse on vitamins is basic and given to show that pretty well all you require can be obtained from a sensible diet.

Diet

I do not propose to tell you what you should eat; this depends on your own likes and dislikes, your weight and physical make up, etc. — suffice it to say that the normal New Zealand family food is more than adequate. Food is your race fuel and you will probably be eating larger portions than the man down the road who greatest exertion is to walk to the garage and climb into his car. Carbohydrate and fat are both sources of energy but it has been found that carbohydrate alone is the most efficient. Having this in mind you should raise your intake of carbohydrates during the two days before competition (potatoes, cereals, bread, treacle, etc.) and this will be converted into glycogen and stored in the liver and muscles ready for competition. A meal of steak or other high protein foods a few hours before a race will only tax the digestive process and decrease rather than improve performance. The glycogen store can be added to during racing by the use of glucose, preferably in liquid form (5 g per 100 ml) as powder glucose requires a lot of liquid, and powder glucose or glucose tablets dehydrate the body as they pull water into the intestines. Thirsty tiredness is best combated by the use of one of the proprietary preparations for the replacement of the mineral salts lost in sweat. Much work has been done in electrolyte replacement therapy. At one time it was the practice to take sodium chloride (salt tablets) but nowadays electrolyte replacement is effected more efficiently by known commercial preparations.

Well fellows if you have trained, eaten, clothed yourself right and attended to your hygiene the rest is up to your legs and your will. Best of luck.

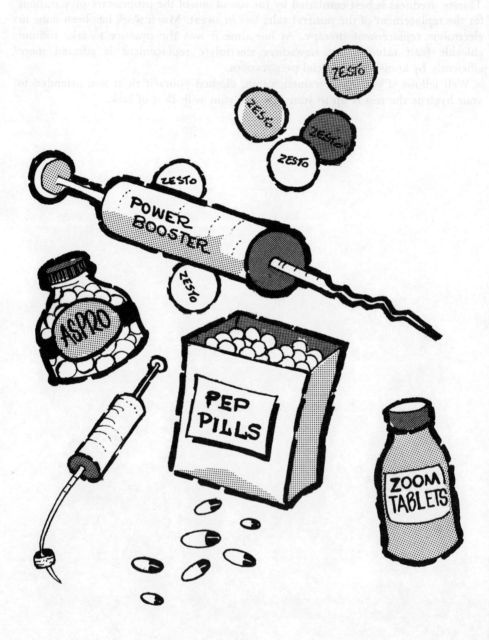

Anabolic steroid questionnaire

The following questionnaire was circulated among athletes at the Olympic village, Munich, in 1972. Its aim was to establish whether or not the athletes who were taking anabolic steroids were in possession of the facts relating to these substances and their effects on the athlete, both mental and physical.

The articles which follow are intended to clarify the situation with regard to these questions. It is the first time that these reasoned and authoritative papers have been published together. It is hoped that sportsmen and coaches will evaluate them and draw their own conclusions on the mental and physical effects doping may have on the athletes who strive to improve their performance by this method.

Answer all questions yes, no, *or no opinion* by placing X *in the appropriate column.*

	Yes	No	No opinion
1 Have you taken anabolic steroids within the last six months?			
2 Have you ever taken steroids?			
3 Ethically do you approve of anabolic steroid usage in athletics?			
4 If a test could be devised which could positively identify a person who had been using anabolic steroids, would you be in favour of total banishment of their use?			
5 With the knowledge you have at this time, are you aware of any specific reason why athletes who have not reached full maturity should avoid anabolic steroid usage?			
6 With the knowledge you have, if you were a coach would you recommend steroid usage to athletes in your event? (*Assume mature athletes.*)			
7 Do you feel that anabolic steroid usage has positively affected the performance of athletes in your event?			
8 Do you feel that anabolic steroid usage has negatively affected the performance of athletes in your event?			
9 Do you believe that use of anabolic steroids enables a person to gain strength at a rate faster than he could without using anabolic steroids?			

10 Do you believe that use of anabolic steroids enables a person to become stronger than he could otherwise become?

11 Do you believe that use of anabolic steroids enables a person to gain cardiorespiratory endurance at a rate faster than this endurance could be gained otherwise?

12 Do you believe that use of anabolic steroids enables a person to gain cardiorespiratory endurance beyond what could otherwise be gained?

13 In your opinion, is the rate at which you gain local-ised muscular endurance faster when taking anabolic steroids?

14 In your opinion, do you gain more localised muscular endurance than would otherwise be possible when taking anabolic steroids?

15 In your opinion, is your mental attitude enhanced when taking steroids? Do you feel more in control of your life? Do you feel that you will perform better in your event?

16 In your opinion, has steroid usage appeared to con-tribute to injury problems of athletes who take them?

17 Are you aware of the undesirable side effects which use of anabolic steroids may cause?

18 In your opinion, does steroid usage cause an increase in body weight?

19 In your opinion, is it difficult for athletes to obtain anabolic steroids?

20 In your opinion, does steroid usage affect other body functions?

a urine production	☐ increase	☐ decrease	☐ no change
b sexual activity/drive	☐ increase	☐ decrease	☐ no change
c body hair	☐ increase	☐ decrease	☐ no change
d low back pain	☐ increased incidence of pain	☐ decreased incidence of pain	☐ no change
e joint pain	☐ increased incidence of pain	☐ decreased incidence of pain	☐ no change

Anabolic substances and their use in sport

Dr J. Pelizza

This paper appeared originally in the *French Olympic Review*, February 1973.

For over ten years now, every time a record was beaten in a throwing or weight-lifting event, the question of anabolic substances was bound to be raised. But anabolic steroids, real muscle builders, or 'fertilisers' as they have been called, infest the field of light athletics just as much as heavy. Evading all analyses, all checks and tests (see the booklet *Doping* published by the Medical Commission of the I.O.C., presided over by the Prince of Merode), they have become products of current use in many physical activities quite outside the sphere of sports events based mainly on sheer strength. Dr Jacques Pellizza, a former French international athlete born at Pau on 29th October 1942 (Bronze medal for the javelin at the Abidjan Games of Friendship in 1961), recently presented a thesis on the subject — sponsored by Professors Paul Berthaux and Plas — to the Faculty of Medicine in Paris. He is the son of Henri Pellizza, who was for a long time one of France's best tennis players and is at present general commissioner of the Racing Club de France.

What follows is a selection of the most important passages from this thesis.

Nowadays competitive athletes are properly trained for performing great sporting achievements. However, some seek to do even better by calling on medical and pharmaceutical means for assistance — whether warranted or not — ranging from the simple taking of vitamins in normal doses during periods of fatigue to the use, or rather misuse, of amphetamine-based doping substances.

The latter are now subject to very strict laws governing their use in sports circles. But while a great deal has been said about doping, which has had certain tragic consequences in bike racing and athletics, very little has been said as yet regarding the part played by anabolic substances, which certain foreign athletes have been using for some time now.

These products, used daily in medical therapy under proper supervision for very definite indications, are also used by a number of athletes such as weightlifters, shotputters, discus, hammer and javelin throwers as well as boxers, and wrestlers. The following lines will be devoted to a study of these anabolic substances and their use in sports circles.

History

Since time immemorial, men have tried to develop their muscles with a view to increasing their strength and, for this purpose, even in the 6th century B.C., as Milo of Croton tells us:

'Athletes tried to increase their physical powers by eating meat that differed in quality depending on the event for which they were training. Thus, the meat of bulls was much prized by shotputters and boxers, while fat pork was reserved for the heavyweight wrestlers. As for the jumpers, they favoured goat's meat.'

Down through the centuries, meat-eating continued to be held in high esteem by athletes as a source of strength and stamina, in particular by the wrestlers and strong men of the Breton and Basque games.

Since the beginning of the century, it has been well known that in order to gain weight, shotputters, discus and javelin throwers, weightlifters and body-builders consumed whole quantities of dietetic products, in some cases even going so far as to 'feed' their muscles by rubbing in creams of varying degrees of efficacity in order to increase their bicep or thigh measurements.

'In 1955, Paul Anderson was the "strongest man in the world". His total for the three Olympic lifts in weightlifting was fabulous for the day: 533 kg (today's world champion out-lifts Anderson by over 100 kg). His measurements were impressive too. He weighed 152·5 kg for a height of 1·68 m, with a biceps measurement of 51 cm and a thigh measurement of 87 cm. This extraordinary athlete drank five litres (over one gallon) of milk a day but, on the other hand, ate comparatively little.'[2]

Since then we have seen aspiring champions go in for muscle-building sessions with a quart of milk at hand, attributing almost magical virtues to this beverage! During the last few years however, what was once merely a subject for anecdotes has become a science, and many countries have carried out exhaustive tests on products capable of enabling determined athletes to gain weight or build up their muscles with a view to improving their performances.

As Alberto Arcioni emphasizes: 'Russian athletes very probably used anabolic substances prior to 1960, but it was in that year that we received the first certain information of their use. At the same time, in the USA, Ziegler was using these substances on weightlifters in Pennsylvania.'[3]

But, before going any further and without taking sides for or against any particular method, we must join very many other authors in stressing the dangers inherent in the use of anabolic substances, these dangers being considerably increased by the ignorance — as a general rule — of those who take them regarding their harmful side-effects, and by the blameworthy behaviour of others who, under cover of medical supervision, falsely tranquilize athletes as to possible side-effects.

At present, there are very few doctors, anywhere in the world, capable of successfully carrying out a hormone treatment applied to the field of sport and, what is more, how many are there capable of predicting the individual reactions of each athlete to such treatment?

Definitions — general

For Garnier and Delamare, anabolism consists in the conversion of nutritive materials into living tissue inside the human organism.[4]

An anabolic substance favours this phenomenon by simplifying the absorption of elements necessary for cellular life, in particular amino acids, at the level of the cells of the muscular fibre.

It is this effect that has led to these substances being called — somewhat over-simply —real muscle 'fertilizers'. In other words, anabolic substances produce an increase in weight by positive action on the muscular mass.

Hormonal steroids related to testosterone or even androgenoproteinic hormones have a very marked anabolic effect and originally were used for this property (for therapeutic purposes). ... Let us consider first of all the study of the androgenoproteinic hormones, since these are the ones used almost exclusively by athletes up till now.

Androgenoproteinic hormones are a group of substances secreted partly by the testicle (one-third) and partly by the cortex of the suprarenal gland (two-thirds), which possess an androgenic action and are capable of stimulating the proteinic anabolism. This group comprises mainly:

1 Androsterone
2 Actiocholanone
3 Isoandrosterone
4 Dehydroisoandrosterone
5 Androstene
6 Androstadiene.

... Among the known androgenic steroids secreted by the testicles, the ovary and the suprarenal cortex, three especially are important from the quantitative point of view:

1 Testosterone
2 Androstenedione
3 Dehydroepiandrosterone.

Released into the main circulation, these steroids perfuse the 'target organs', on which they sometimes exert their biological activity, before reaching the liver ....

Physiological action of the androgens

This takes the form first of all of morphological effects on the primary and secondary sexual characteristics, and second, of metabolic effects; the various actions seem to be triggered off by the increased synthesis of proteins at the cellular level.

Morphological effects
Primary sexual characteristics. At the level of the male genital system, the absorption of androgens leads in theory to an increase in the size of the testicle and in the formation of spermatozoids. In actual fact, there is an indirect effect cancelling out this mechanism and even reversing it, leading in the end to an atrophy of the testicles and a decrease in spermatogenesis and in the function of Leydig's cells .... This complex and fragile mechanism can be completely disturbed when there is any additional outside contribution of male hormones (in other words when an athlete takes anabolic hormones). What happens then under these circumstances? The androgen content of the blood is artifically increased. The regulating centre is 'misled' and reacts by causing a decrease in gonadotrophins, which results in the testicle being set to rest with a consequent drop in spermatogenesis and an atrophy of the interstitial tissue leading in its turn to a wasting away of the testicle which then becomes incapable of producing spermatozoids or hormones.

Usual indications for hormonal anabolic substances
... What on the whole are the indications justifying the use of androgenic steroids in therapy?

In the first place, the powerful anabolic effect is sought after in cachectic states: malnutrition, anorexia, loss of weight due to cancers, chronic diseases, proteinic catabolism, long-term corticotherapy.

To a lesser extent, states of depression, asthenia in all its forms but particularly in old people, overwork, and andropause symptoms are favourably affected by these substances and by their psychotonic, or mood-elevating, effect.

The effect of fixing the calcium of the bones is used in the after-effects of fractures (especially in older patients), in pseudoarthroses and in cases of delayed consolidation, in all decalcification phenomena, in particular osteoporosis ....

Non-hormonal anabolic substances

They have a chemical structure completely different from the above and are completely unrelated to them. Furthermore, they produce none of their side-effects (nevertheless certain reservations need to be made here).

Dibencozide is the fundamental molecule of the two main products of this class used at present.

... The indications for these non-hormonal anabolic substances are mainly protidic disorders, states of asthenia, anorexia.

... The laboratories producing these new substances stress the fact that there are no contra-indications to the use of these molecules. In actual fact, the major disadvantages produced by the androgenic steroids do not exist. The virilising effects are nil. There is no hormonal interference, no mechanism of inhibition of the gonadotrophins. However the myotrophic effect and the gaining of weight can sometimes have a harmful effect on athletes, as we shall see in the next section....

Use of anabolic substances in sport

Anabolic substances started to be used in sports circles about the year 1960. At this date, only the androgenic steroids were known. They were used first of all in events where pure strength had to be developed (shotputting, discus, hammer and javelin throwing, weightlifting). Today these substances are used much more widely and, for this reason, we distinguish two quite distinct non-restrictive categories:

1 Sports requiring an overall increase in strength
Weightlifting
Athletics: Throwing events
Shot
Discus
Hammer
Javelin
Decathlon and pole-vaulting
Boxing
Wrestling (in the 'heavy' categories)
Judo
Ice hockey
American football
Body-building (it should be pointed out however that those going in for this are aiming much more at building their muscles for show than at increasing their strength)

2 Sports requiring the strengthening of one or more groups of muscles

Athletics: Sprints (100 and 200 m)

Jumping (high, long, triple), 110 m hurdles

To a lesser extent: 400 m hurdles, 800 m

Cycling
Rowing
Skating

Very probably other sports like rugby (the forwards), skiing, gymnastics and even swimming have been the object of similar experiments. These observations call for certain remarks.

Athletes belonging to the first category (with the exception perhaps of the body-builders) have to submit their bodies to intensive efforts while developing their muscles through the action of the anabolic substance, otherwise their strength will increase but little.

... In all dynamic physical exercise there is an element of speed, and therefore the higher the weight, the greater the muscle power required to ensure that the speed does not suffer. In other words, the muscular efficiency will have to increase with the myothrophic effect, in spite of an increase in the weight of the muscle, which partly offsets this action.

... As for athletes coming under the second category, in addition to taking anabolic substances they must also perform specific work aimed at strengthening one or several groups of muscles. Thus sprinters practise the weightlifter's squats as well as jumping up and down with heavily laden bars on their shoulders in order to increase the strength of their legs and thighs. Exercises are also done for strengthening the lumbar, gluteal and abdominal muscles....

Study of anabolic substances in sports circles

(Main studies carried out on androgenic steroids and their application in sports circles.)

... A significant study of the use of anabolic steroids is that of Johnson and O'Shea published in the magazine *Science*: twenty-four subjects kept on a diet with a high protein content and practising weightlifting for six weeks were examined. At the end of the third week, twelve subjects were given 5 mg of Dianabol per day, twelve subjects received nothing. Records were kept for all, concerning weight and strength, as well as a number of anthropometric and serological factors. This study enabled the authors to conclude that the injection of Dianabol had the effect of definitely, even if not excessively, increasing weight and muscular strength.

However the same authors concluded that very little is known concerning the collateral effects of anabolic substances on adults, and that in the case of individuals not yet fully formed physically (youths under 20 years of age) the consequences may be dangerous for the genital organs and the skeleton.

Another interesting study is the one carried out by West Germany's former long jump champion, Steinbach, of Mainz University. 125 young athletes were placed under observation for a period of three months with a check kept on their weight and the increase in their muscular strength; during this period some were given a daily dose of 10 mg of Dianabol, while others received only a placebo instead of the anabolic substance, with or without simultaneous training. The results showed a minimum increase in muscular strength in those taking Dianabol and training at the same time; the same author reports the possibility of side-effects caused by prolonged treatment.

... The Swiss Weiss and Muller (*Revue de Medecine Sportive Suisse*) have also carried out studies on a certain number of subjects receiving 10 mg of Dianabol per day and another group receiving only placebos. In this experiment too, the difference between the two groups examined was only negligible, which, in the authors' opinion, must be considered as a mere matter of chance.

Kereszki administered an androgenic steroid to a group of tired athletes for a period of three weeks and noted a return to their previous efficiency. As a result of these studies Arcioni thinks that substances like this with anabolic effects prove effective when the athlete's organism shows loss of weight and a negative nitrogen balance.

... Arkadi Vorobiev, five times world champion, ex-trainer of the Soviet weightlifting team, 'agrégé' of medicine, head of the Department of Scientific Research and Instruction, and a member of the Committee for Physical Education and Sport of the Council of Ministers of the USSR, expressed his opinion on androgenic proteins in a famous French daily (*Le Monde*, 3 July 1970). This trainer-cum-doctor pointed out that the increase in weight, the artificial 'inflation', so to speak, of a weightlifter's body exerts no decisive role in his athletic preparation. Being overweight can in fact have a negative effect on his locomotor activity and, consequently, on his performances.

There is a clearcut biological law: as the weight of the body increases, the locomotor powers decrease. All living beings expend part of their energy in overcoming the force of gravity, and the heavier the weight of their body, the more energy they expend. In this connection, Vorobiev quotes Soukhanov's formula (1968):

Lc = relative force, i.e.:

$$N = \frac{Lc - 3}{\dfrac{3(0.45 \cdot G60)}{900}}$$

$$\frac{\text{results of the three lifts}}{\text{weight}}$$

G = weight of the weightlifter

This formula enables us to calculate the approximate expenditure of muscular force needed to overcome gravity in terms of the weight of the body.

Vorobiev carries out an analysis of the world records where the N of Soukhanov's formula represents what he calls an 'index of mastery', and he goes on to prove that this index is higher in the bantamweight weightlifter Kourentsov (75 kg) than in the super-heavyweight parameters, e.g. Zhabotinsky (163 kg — see Table 7.1). Therefore, in the opinion of the ex-trainer of the Russian team, anabolic substances, which increase the muscular mass of the athlete do not — and precisely because of this fact — help to raise the level of the weightlifter's performances. He asserts, moreover, that anabolic substances are not used in the athletic preparation of Russian champions.... The 'secret' of their success lies in rational training and in a scientific observation of the recovery of the organism after effort.

The method of training is described as an alternation of intense effort (catabolic phase) and prolonged rest (anabolic phase), the first stage stimulating the second.

For Vorobiev, the supply of amino-acids, vitamins, mineral substances and micro-elements is vital and he concludes by calling attention to the efforts made with regard to general physical and psychological preparation as well as to the tailoring of training to each individual's requirements.

Table 7.1 Vorobiev's table

Weight athlete G	Results in the three lifts	Relative force Lc	Index of mastery N
56	367·5	6·56	7·01
60	397·5	6·62	7·13
67·5	440	6·52	7·18
75	482·5	6·43	7·25
82·5	487·5	5·91	6·99
90	522·5	5·80	7·04
163	590	3·62	6·58

Among the studies we have had an opportunity of examining, we were particularly struck by that of Fowler, Gardner and Egstrom of the University of Los Angeles. The performances and certain biological parameters of forty-seven adults were recorded over a period of sixteen weeks:

1 Eight were given placebos.
2 Nine were given 1 methyl[1] androstenolone acetate (Nibal) 20 mg daily.
3 Fifteen were given placebos and made to follow a course of strengthening exercises at the same time.

These forty-seven subjects were all men in good health, between 18 and 25 years old. Ten played American football, while the others trained regularly in their colleges.

...*Results*. Many parameters remained unchanged throughout the course of this study. Their height, thigh circumference, panniculus adiposus, and suppleness, for example, did not vary.

As for the serious enzyme content, the changes occurring in the 16 week period were not significant for any of them. The variations in weight and vital capacity were hardly any more conclusive. Finally, with regard to physical performances, the only improvements noted were among those belonging to the groups doing thirty minutes training every day, but there was no noticeable difference between those who had received the placebo or the anabolic substance at the same time.

Discussion. On the whole, in the study under consideration, the androgenic steroid tried out on its own did not lead to any appreciable improvement in performance or in work capacity. From this it may be concluded that under the conditions of the experiment, the hormonal anabolic substance did not increase the strength of the athletes tested, so that its use by athletes is in no way justified.

... The conclusions of Fowler, Gardner and Egstrom differ from those of Johnson and O'Shea.

The latter, at the end of their study, came to the conclusion in fact that anabolic steroids can accelerate the acquisition of a certain muscular force and at the same

101

time allow the athlete to train to the maximum, or almost, of his possibilities with the greatest intensity desirable....

Conclusions to be drawn

From these different, often discordant studies, a number of conclusions may be drawn.

The anabolic steroid seems to possess a certain myotrophic power helping to increase strength, provided that certain vital factors are respected, i.e.:

1 a sufficient supply of calories,
2 an extra supply of proteins,
3 the absolute necessity of accompanying treatment with intense physical effort.

On the other hand, it would seem that the effectiveness of a hormonal anabolic substance is definitely more marked on an organism suffering from a nitrogen caloric deficiency, and we wish to stress this point for we consider it of the utmost importance. Hettinger has already put forward the hypothesis of a relationship between the action of a steroid and the low urinary elimination of 17 keto-steroids. Arcioni, as a result of Kerenski's work, thinks that these products have their maximum effect when the athlete's organism is in a state of deficiency; one has only to remember the spectacular effects of these steroids in cases of cachexia — in advanced cancers for example.

But in the healthy subject, the need being less or nil, the effect will be little or nil, unless as a result of a series of imbalances of the type:

Intensive training — resulting slight loss of weight, slight deficiency of the organism — taking of hormonal anabolic substance (+ proteins).

The athlete happens to create 'artificially' the same needs as a subject showing loss of weight caused by some disorder, in this way achieving the 'stimulation of an anabolic phase by a catabolic phase' as Vorobiev defined it earlier on. This is only an hypothesis, which might account for the small effect of a product like Dianabol — which is normally very powerful — when it is used alone, without any accompanying exercise. For this reason it is completely illogical for certain sportsmen to consume tremendous quantities of pills or to receive repeated injections of anabolic substances, since beyond a certain level (which some try to push further back than others by more intense training) the capacity for 'building' muscles will be exceeded and the illusory excess of weight obtained will in fact be nothing more than the consequence of sodium-hydro retention due to a secondary effect of the product.

It would seem therefore that the limits of the effectiveness of an anabolic steroid lie not so much in the dose which is administered, but in that they are rather bound up with the training targets, or limits, a sportsman may successfully set himself, and we know that these limits are pushed further back every day.

Finally, practically no author has stressed the dangers inherent in the use of such substances. One may moreover be sceptical concerning the expression 'studies carried out under medical supervision' .... Similarly, it would be disastrous for certain medical teams to sanction the use of hormonal anabolic substances by athletes under the pretext that they are issued in normal doses and under their responsibility.

What kind of check will there be in a few years time when one risks diagnosing the rupture of a tendon or worse a tumour of the prostate? None of the experiments carried out on androgenic steroids mention any examination of the prostate (questioning, rectal feeling, measurement of phosphatases) ... and yet this is a matter of vital importance....

Non-hormonal anabolic substances

The oral forms of non-hormonal anabolic substances have been known for several years now. Recently, injectable forms of this type have been made available to doctors.

Their advantage in therapy consists in the absence of toxicity and contraindications. It is very useful, for example, to be able to administer anabolic substances to babies without any fear of more or less serious side-effects. Harmful androgenic effects, in particular the stopping of growth or the production of tumours on the prostate, need never be feared.

... On the healthy individual, a study has been made in sports circles by Chailley-Bert and coll. The experiment was carried out on fifty-four students at the IREPS in Paris. A proper diet was worked out and given to each subject as well as a sufficient supply of proteins. Dibencozide was used in doses of 3 capsules per day for about four weeks, and clinical examinations of the subjects were carried out at rest and after each exercise. Laboratory tests were made, in particular measurements of the urea in the blood and the urine, of the glycemia and total lipids. The haematocrit, the blood count, the prothrombin and haemoglobin content were all recorded. These tests showed that tolerance of the product is good and that the product has an overall invigorating effect with improvement of physical fitness. Sleep is not affected; a better adaptation to effort with good recovery is also noted. The average gain in weight is about 2 lb and the appetite is increased. With regard to the pulse-rate, there would seem to be a slight acceleration of the pulse at rest but a drop in pulse-rate during effort, with an increase in the differential A.T. after treatment.

In Chaïlley-Bert's opinion, a dose of 3 capsules a day (9 mg) seems particularly favourable, and the trophic effect of the Dibencozide on the muscles is good.

The risks

Apart from the troubles referred to in the previous chapter, the athlete who uses — and frequently misuses — anabolic substances is liable to terrible after-effects. In particular, there is the danger of accidents to tendons, from the simple prolonged and recurrent tendinitis (especially in the knees) to complete ruptures of the tendons (brachial biceps and triceps, quadriceps, and sural triceps to mention but the main muscles involved).

This type of accident can be explained as follows: under the effect of the anabolic substance, the muscle hypertrophies. Consequently the tendinous 'attachments' do not develop. In any violent muscular contraction, this attachment is submitted to a stronger traction than normal. Very roughly speaking, the bigger the muscle, the greater the risk of rupture during a short, intense effort.

In addition, we have seen that the 'strong-man' type of athlete undergoes intensive training for his muscles, the joints — in particular those of the lower limbs — being placed under tremendous strain, during the series of squats (movement of alternate flexion and stretching of the legs with heavily loaded weightlifting bar on the shoulders). Many cases of evolutive coxarthrosis and gonarthrosis have been noted in this corpulent type of athlete carrying out these repeated exercises.

... To close, let us also point out that a male athlete using anabolic substances always runs the major risk of causing a prostatic tumour due partly to the dose and partly to individual susceptibility. This last factor is impossible to predict and so-called 'medical' supervision is unable as yet to detect it....

Sportsmen and anabolic substances

The motivations

For what reasons does a sportsman take anabolic substances? For greater convenience we shall consider the case of shotputters, discus, hammer and javelin throwers, weightlifters and body-builders, who are among the main consumers of these substances.

We know that in normal doses and used wisely these products can have a by no means negligible myotrophic effect on a healthy individual, with a consequent increase in stength. Whether he gets his supplies from the chemists or whether he goes to a doctor, the athlete concerned knows practically nothing of the product chosen except that at the end of his treatment (and he is often totally ignorant of the actual details of use), his performances should be considerably improved.

Certain champions think that anabolic substances are the equivalent of a highly perfected dietetic product capable of making up for the lack of a food properly adapted to the considerable efforts involved in highly concentrated muscular training (Castang ENSEP, Paris). Others like Drufin have followed several courses of treatment because all the other shotputters did the same (during a period of training in the USA a few years ago). Another shotputter, Beer, has said that:

'Nowadays all the really big shotputters take anabolic substances. The alternatives are as follows: either one takes them and one is competitive, or one doesn't and one ceases to be in the running.... No one is going to say "I have given up taking anabolic substances, I hope the others will follow my example". Everyone wants to be absolutely sure that he is competing on equal terms with everyone else.'

The course of treatment

The effect of an anabolic substance on an individual is not immediate. Unlike doping substances like amphetamines, their short-term action is not spectacular and a certain time of latency is needed before the effect becomes evident in a gain in weight.

... The taking of anabolic substances 48 hours before a competition, even in very high doses, is completely ineffective, and many ill-informed sportsmen have committed this error in the past. In such cases, if good performances have nevertheless been made, they are to be attributed entirely to the profound psychological effect created by the absorption of these substances. In actual fact, in most cases, the instructions laid down for a standard course of treatment are not respected, 'everyone wishing to go one better than the next...'.

And then we come to the inevitable abuse or misuse, first of all as regards the dose recommended and second as regards the length of treatment. Willy Holland, trainer of the British weightlifting team has categorically stated: 'I have heard it' said that certain competitors administered intravenously thirty times the dose recommended in hospitals for cases of rickets!' Assertions of this kind are alarming and need confirming.

The shotputter Beer mentions a course of treatment lasting thirteen days, at the end of which his weight had risen from 110 to 114 kg. In the same period of time, his weightlifting performances had all improved and he beat his own personal record. To quote his own words, he experienced an 'extraordinary need for action and he felt a tremendous appetite'. Harold Connolly, Olympic hammer champion in 1956, also followed a course of treatment with 20 mg of Dianabol per day for three months. His weight rose from 104 to 114 kg. He too improved his personal records.

For our part, we know certain athletes who swallow as many as ten Dianabol pills a day, a fortnight before the competitions. The unfortunate part of all this is that, far from causing any alarm, this practice tends to arouse an astonished, even admiring amusement on the part of certain strong men, as if it were a feat in itself in the same way as the achievement of a performance of real value.

... We would like to add a few words on the financial side of the practice, showing just how expensive the constitution of a veritable panoply of medical and dietetic products can be — in fact far too heavy a burden for a modest budget to bear.... Obviously the bill very seldom has to be footed by the athlete himself.... Taken as a whole, vitamins, dietetic products and anabolic substances, not to mention the tremendous quantities of meat consumed, add up to some $100 to $200 a month for those who use them.

The same is approximately true of a course of treatment with non-hormonal anabolic substances. The only difference being perhaps that the treatment needs to be a little longer than with steroids in order to produce the same results.

... We have made out a table showing the improvement (in per cent) of the world records in a number of men's events. We have divided our statistics into three sections, each corresponding to eleven years of competition:

1 1936–1947
2 1948–1959
3 1960–1971.

It was at the beginning of the last period that American supremacy in putting the shot and other throwing events became unparalleled. Three 'ceilings' were topped: the 20 m mark in the shot, the 60 m for the discuss, and the 70 m for the hammer. It was about this same time too that anabolic substances began to be used in Russian sports circles.

In Table 7.2, we see that the progress in the throwing events is far more marked than that in jumping and running (see also graph, Fig. 7.3). We have considered only three types of throwing event and three types of jumping for the figures for our graph, voluntarily excluding the javelin and pole-vaulting where the evolution of the equipment falsifies the calculations. We have not made any precise evaluation but the result is even more striking when one considers no longer the evolution of the

Table 7.2 Percentage of improvement in certain athletic events by series of eleven years men's world records)

	1936–1947* (in %)	1948–1959 (in %)	1960–1971 (in %)
Shot	1·5	8·3	11·2
Discus	4	7·6	12·4
Javelin	1·8	8·5**	7·2**
Hammer	0	14	10·1
High jump	0·9	2·3	5·8
Long jump	0	0	8·6****
Triple jump	0	4·1	4
Pole-vault	4·9	0·2	12 ***
110 m hurdles	0	3·7	1·5
400 m hurdles	0	2·6	2
200 m	0	1·5	1
400 m	0·7	1·5	3·2
800 m	2·9	0·8	1·2
1500 m	2·1	3·2	1
5000 m	2·3	2·9	2·3

* Results partly distorted by the 1939–1945 war.
** Modern javelins are not as good than those used in 1959 (Head 'gliding' javelins) hence only a slight improvement.
*** The advent of the fibreglass pole has radically changed performances and their significance. Comparisons are no longer valid in this speciality.
**** It should be pointed out that without the phenomenal leap of 8·90 m by Beamon at the Mexico Olympics in 1968, the world record would still be about 8·85 m, which would give an improvement of 2·6% for this event.

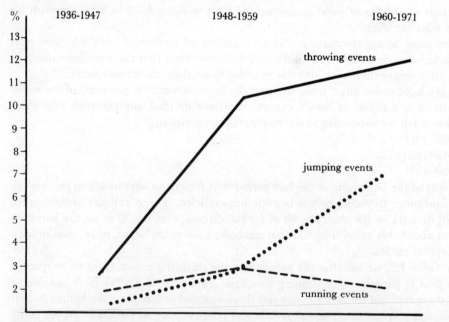

Fig. 7.3 Percentage of improvement in the three main types of athletic event (men's world records)

records alone but that of the twenty best world performances for each period. Today, the levelling out of international values at the top after the clear domination of the Americans during the 60s ... can be accounted for by many factors (training methods, preparation, etc....). The use of anabolic substances is no longer the monopoly of the USA.

In the field of weightlifting, heavy-weight category, in the three Olympic lifts we note an improvement in the world record of about ten per cent for the period 1951–1961, while for the period 1961–1971, this improvement is nearer twenty per cent. (It should also be pointed out that without the 'Anderson phenomenon' the increase obtained in the first period would be only five per cent.)

In terms of the period considered see Figure 7.3.

The problems raised by the use of anabolic substances

These problems are many and complicated.

Position of the medical profession. From the medical point of view, doctors are almost unanimous in their condemnation of the use of hormonal anabolic substances....

Positions of trainers and athletes. In countries where the use of anabolic substances is current, a line of conduct is adopted and the athlete has but two possibilities. Either he consumes this type of product, or as two young hopefuls of German sport did recently (Blaesius and Sasse), they cut themselves off from the race for records and give up competitive sport, because they refuse to use any form of doping to help them achieve rapid progress.

... As for the athletes, they are aware that, used wisely, anabolic substances can help them improve their performances but that the risk they are running is by no means negligible and many hesitate to take the step. However, all — and this is only logical — want to possess the same advantages as their foreign rivals.

Positions of sports authorities. After a certain hesitation regarding the line of conduct to be adopted, the heads of the world federations have reacted in their turn against the use of these products. In 1966, the British Amateur Athletics Association condemned the use of hormonal steroids, followed in 1967 by the International Olympic Committee, to which 123 countries belong. (This organisation considers that, except for medical reasons, such a practice consitutes doping according to the Olympic definition of the word.)...

Position of the specialised press. The part played by journalists in the fight against doping or against any other form of illicit and dangerous aid to athletic progress is of the greatest importance. Condemned in the United States and in the countries of the East, the use of anabolic substances in sport is also severely condemned by journalists in Western Europe and by those of France in particular....

Control and regulations

At the present moment it is impossible to carry out an effective check on an athlete suspected of using anabolic substances. What are the difficulties?

Unlike the antidoping checks, where any trace of amphetamine is rapidly detected in the urine, for the product had been taken recently in order to be effective, tests for anabolic substances are futile, since a course of treatment may be completed and stopped several weeks before the actual competitions, i.e. before the tests are carried out, without the effectiveness of the product being diminished in any way; the myotrophic effect still continuing (long-term effect). In the urine or blood tests, the steroid has already been eliminated and even if a few traces remain, it is quite impossible to try to detect them.

... With regard to regulations, countries like the United States and Germany have just officially placed anabolic substances in the category of doping substances, which now represents an added difficulty for anyone trying to obtain them.

In France the problem remains unsolved. There is obviously something very wrong in a situation where it is possible to obtain a hormonal product with a powerful anabolic effect as easily as a tube of aspirin, without medical prescription. As far as we are concerned, we hope that the whole of the medical profession will become aware of the situation and try to do something about it.

... On the international level, it would seem that appeals to reason as well as the words of warning uttered by sports and medical bodies have not yet succeeded in obtaining any results, so all efforts will have to be concentrated on rigorous methods of detection, and checks will have to be made afterwards as a deterrent rather than before as a preventive measure. One can only hope that new techniques will make it possible to detect and measure tiny traces of hormones or substances modified for some considerable time by the introduction of steroids into the organism.

We see no other solution and we think that nothing will be settled until then.

References

[1]Quoted by Dumas, P. (1968), *Vie Medicale* June, special no. devoted to sport. France.
[2]*Sport et Vie*. (1956). July, no. 2. France.
[3]'For or Against Anabolic Substances?' (1971). *Athletica*, March, no. 3. Italy.
[4]Garnier and Delamare. *Dictionary of Medical Terms*. France.

The use of anabolic steroid hormones in sport

New Zealand Federation of Sports Medicine

This paper was first published by the New Zealand Federation of Sports Medicine in 1975.

A serious increase in the number and severity of injuries, if the use of anabolic steroid hormones is not banned in sport, is forecast in a statement from the President and Executive of the New Zealand Federation of Sports Medicine, in conjunction with an Auckland Hospital Board endocrinologist.

In recent years many athletes in international competition in field events, weight lifting and rowing have been using synthetic anabolic hormones over periods of several months and years to boost muscular development with a view to improving their performances.

These drugs are derivatives of the male sex hormone, testosterone, and the effects of this natural hormone are seen most dramatically in the young boy undergoing puberty. His voice deepens, male hair develops in the pubic, armpit and facial regions, the genitalia enlarge and the growing ends of the long bones seal off. These are the masculinising effects of testosterone. In addition there are the body-building or anabolic effects, which comprise an increase in muscle bulk and the strengthening of the bones.

Pharmaceutical chemists have developed the anabolic steroid hormones from testosterone with the aim of retaining the body-building effects for use in patients with chronic diseases while reducing the undesirable masculinising effects. Unfortunately the undesirable sexual effects have not been completely abolished. Doctors are unwilling to prescribe anabolic steroids to children, because of the danger of stunting growth, and to women, because of the permanency of the voice change and facial hair.

In our present knowledge, there seems little short-term risk for a male athlete taking anabolic steroids. The known complications are a mild jaundice and infertility, although virility is maintained. These side effects usually disappear when the drug is stopped.

As a group of doctors looking at the problem from a medical point of view, we are very uneasy about the long-term use of synthetic anabolic steroids in young adults for four reasons:

1 Our knowledge of the long-term complications of these drugs is limited. While the risk of using anabolic steroids over a short-term period in a sick patient is acceptable, we are seriously concerned at the undefined risks of unsupervised administration over periods of two to ten years to healthy youngsters showing promise in the field of sport.

2 The second reason relates to the impression gained by some doctors attending sportsmen who have taken anabolic steroids, that large and powerful muscles have developed without compensatory increase in the strength of the tendons. These tendons seem to be more vulnerable to strain and rupture.

3 Unless anabolic steroids are now firmly barred from sport, it seems likely that their use will spread widely into the body contact sports with a serious increase in the frequency and severity of injuries because of the enormous size of the participants.

4 A final cause for anxiety is the health of these 'supermen' after their retirement. Are they more prone to diseases which will compromise their health and longevity in the second half of their lives? Some evidence is beginning to come forward to suggest that this is so.

Unlike other drugs sometimes taken by athletes on the day of, or during, the event, and readily detectable, there is no proven method of detecting these hormones, especially weeks and months after their administration. It has been stated that a group of workers in London are examining the urine of a number of athletes who attended the Commonwealth Games in Edinburgh, with the aim of evaluating a method for detecting anabolic steroids. Should this method prove reliable, it could be used for unannounced urine checks on athletes during their training programme as well as prior to national and international meetings. One suggestion for the pharmaceutical industry is to incorporate into the tablet or injection an easily detectable marking substance which would be retained without harm in the body for several months.

One can easily imagine the difficult situation which could arise if the Olympic Committee does not take more positive steps to ban anabolic steroids. The countries in which the use of the hormones is encouraged, and where they are freely available for purchase, are going to have a great advantage in certain athletic events over the countries such as New Zealand where the use of artificial drugs is generally unacceptable from the medical and ethical points of view, and where their availability is limited to supply by a doctor's prescription.

In conclusion, we are uneasy about the unknown, long-term complications of the use of synthetic anabolic steroids from the medical point of view. From the ethical standpoint, we condemn their use, along with other doping substances. By a strong ban and vigorous detection drives, the international and national sporting bodies have a vital role to play in safeguarding the health of individual athletes and in upholding the noble ideal of sport.

Anabolic steroids: doctors denounce them, but athletes aren't listening

N. Wade

The following article by Nicholas Wade was first published in *Science* (June 1972), Volume 176, pp. 1399–1403. Copyright 1972 by the American Association for the Advancement of Science.

The scene is the auditorium of the Masonic Temple in Detroit, filled to near capacity with a turbulent audience. A brisk succession of scantily-clad young men step up on to the spotlighted podium and exhibit, to music, their physical endowment. In a minute's worth of briefly held poses, each displays to best advantage his outsized arm and chest muscles, Herculean thighs, and a back that resembles a tangle of knotted ropes. The victor of this unusual modelling show will be Mr America 1972. He can cherish the ambition of becoming Mr Universe, an example to the world of how the human frame can be improved upon by only exercise and temperate living. Except that in recent years several Mr America's have carried off the proud title not by their own unaided efforts, but with the help of anabolic steroids, powerful drugs that are synthetic derivatives of the male sex hormone.

Anabolic steroids feature heavily in a drug sub-culture that includes body-builders, professional footballers, and strength athletes, such as weightlifters, shot-putters, and hammer and discus throwers. Among U.S. Olympic competitors, particularly the weightlifters, consumption of anabolic steroids is probably reaching a peak this month — in a few weeks, athletes will have to lay off the drug in order to be sure of flushing all traces out of their system before the Olympic games in August. U.S. athletes will have no monopoly on steroids. Rumour has it that the drugs are widely used by South American, Russian and European athletes. According to one member of the committee responsible for selecting the U.S. weightlifting team, victory in the Olympics has become a question of which country has the best doctors and chemists.

Just what anabolic steroids do to the human frame is a question that receives different answers from athletes, from the sports and medical establishments, and from the scientific literature. The few scientific studies that have been done are a mixed bag, some suggesting that steroids do no good for athletes, others that they are effective. The athletes who take them believe that anabolic steroids help to increase weight and muscular strength. They do so despite the warnings of sports officials and senior sports doctors, who insist that steroids do not increase muscle but do have a variety of unpleasant side effects. The American Medical Association 'categorically condemns' the use of steroids by athletes. 'Use of steroids is a complete waste of time and money,' says Allan Ryan, team physician at the University of Wisconsin and a past president of the American College of Sports Medicine. Daniel Hanley, official doctor to the U.S. Olympic team, believes flatly that steroids have 'zero effect' on muscle strength. Hanley is also a member of the International Olympics Committee medical commission, which, in a recent booklet entitled *Doping*, warned: 'Anabolic steroids can severely harm the health, causing liver and bone damage, disturbances in the metabolic and sexual functions, and, among women, virilisation and menstrual upset.'

For a drug that, according to informed medical opinion, is both ineffective and hazardous, anabolic steroids are rather widely used. Any amateur athlete caught taking a non-therapeutic drug is liable to disqualification, so most estimates of usage depend largely on anecdote and training room gossip. Between 10 and 25 per cent of weightlifters use steroids, according to Russell Wright, president of the medical committee of the International Federation of Weightlifting. But Donald Cooper, medical committee chairman of the National Collegiate Athletic Association (N.C.A.A.), says that 80 to 90 per cent of all weightlifters in the world are taking steroids. The weight of opinion seems to favour the higher estimate. Pat O'Shea, an exercise physiologist and member of the U.S. Olympic Weightlifting Committee, told *Science*: 'If we were informed we could not select an athlete taking steroids, we simply wouldn't have a team.'

Reliance on anabolic steroids appears to be equally widespread among bodybuilders. John Grimek, a former Mr America and now editor of *Muscular Development*, estimates that a preponderance — 'between 99 and 101 per cent' — of the entrants in the Mr America contest held in Detroit last month were taking or had experimented with steroids. (Grimek himself believes the drugs are hazardous and offer little, if any, benefit to the physique.)

Professional footballers (about 75 per cent, according to one estimate) are another group who use steroids to build up or retain body weight. Use of the drug is not confined to professionals; in Alabama, even high school coaches are rumored to advise young men to put on some weight with Dianabol in order to be considered for the football team.

Many of these users take steroids in large, sometimes massive, doses. In supervised trials, the usual dose is less than 10 milligrams per day for a 6-week course. But private users are tempted to keep on raising the dose. Some athletes are reported to take five, ten, or twenty times the recommended amount. The most popular brand of anabolic steroid is Ciba's Dianabol, followed by Winthrop's Winstrol and Searle's Anavar. South American athletes are said to prefer stanozolol. The approved use of all these drugs is confined to treatment of debilitated patients and specific diseases such as pituitary dwarfism. The ready availability of the drugs to athletes appears to be largely though not entirely on a black market and under-the-counter basis.

Anabolic steroids have a murky history of use, which may, in part, account for the scanty interest shown in them to date by medical researchers. The first use of male steroids to improve performance is said to have been in the Second World War, when German troops took them before battle to enhance aggressiveness. After the war, steroids were given to the survivors of German concentration camps to rebuild body weight. The first use in athletics seems to have been by the Russians in 1954. John D. Ziegler, a Maryland physician who was U.S. team physician to the weightlifting championships in Vienna that year, told *Science* that Soviet weightlifters were receiving doses of testosterone, a male sex hormone. The Russians were also using it on some of their women athletes, Ziegler said.

Besides its growth-promoting effect, testosterone induces male sexual development such as deepening of the voice and hirsuteness, which might account for the manifestation of such traits in Soviet women athletes during the 1950s. Present-day anabolic steroids stem from the discovery that testosterone can be chemically modified to diminish its sexual function, while preserving its growth-promoting, or anabolic, effects. Ziegler was probably the first in the United States to test the new anabolic steroids on athletes. 'I thought they were great at first,' Ziegler told *Science*: 'I had some weightlifters who said the Dianabol helped them a lot. But then I gave them placebos and they said it helped them the same amount.' Ziegler acknowledges the remarkable effect of Dianabol on debilitated patients, but believes that with normal people its influence is mostly psychological. He gave up experimentation with athletes when he learned that some who had taken twenty times the recommended dose had developed a liver condition. 'I lost interest in fooling with IQs of that calibre. Now it's about as widespread among these idiots as marijuana,' Ziegler says. Ziegler's experiments were conducted in 1959; since then anabolic steroids have grown increasingly popular. By 1965, the drug was widely used among body-builders and weightlifters, and it now seems to have become almost universal.

Universality has not brought enlightenment as to the drug's effects, at least on the normal physiology. There seems little doubt that for debilitated patients the anabolic steroids afford notable gains in both weight and strength. But, like vitamins, they are not necessarily helpful in excess. What metamorphosis can the man in the street expect from anabolic steroids — will they turn him into a Hercules, as the athletes believe, or will they damage his libido and make him sing soprano, as the sports medicine publications insinuate? That the most basic facts about the drug are still in dispute is due to a combination of circumstances, of which athletes are the chief victims. The manufacturers of anabolic steroids are presumably not unaware of the drugs' market among athletes, but, because this use is not approved by the Food and Drug Administration (F.D.A.) pharmaceutical companies neither promote anabolic steroids among athletes nor assume any responsibility for how the drugs are taken. A spokesman for Ciba, makers of Dianabol, said the company has never conducted any studies into the effect of the drug on athletes. The package insert for Dianabol warns specifically: 'Anabolic steroids do not enhance athletic ability.' An F.D.A. official told *Science* that the warning was required because the manufacturers had failed to provide evidence that anabolic steroids are effective for athletes. Thus the 'do not enhance' in the package warning means only 'have not been proved to enhance.'

Medical researchers have shown little interest in the messy task of sorting out the psychological effects of anabolic steroids on athletes from the physiological effects. As for sports organisations such as the N.C.A.A. and the Amateur Athletic Union (A.A.U.), the use of any drug is contrary to their ethos, and official attitudes range from reluctance to discuss the issue to an outright denial that the drugs are efficacious.

Such controlled studies as there are, most of them conducted by team physicians or physical educators, do little to resolve the salient issues of steroid efficacy. A recent double-blind study by S.W. Casner, former team physician at the University of Texas, indicated that an anabolic steroid caused subjects to put on weight but that the weight gain, Casner and his colleagues inferred, was in the form of retained water, not extra muscle[1] (the steroid used was stanozolol).

The most extensive series of experiments with anabolic steroids has been conducted by O'Shea and his colleagues at Oregon State University. In a 1969 study with Dianabol, O'Shea found that treated subjects gained significantly in weight and strength over matched controls.[2] (Crucial to O'Shea's treatment is that the athletes are fed a high protein diet and are made to train intensively during the anabolic treatment.) The design of this study has been criticized because athletes knew whether or not they were receiving steroids. O'Shea has now repeated the study according to a double-blind design with essentially the same results.[3] After a 4-week course of 10 mg of Dianabol per day, treated subjects increased their body weight by 5 per cent (untreated controls gained less than 1 per cent). The weight gain was presumably in the form of muscle, since the subjects, who were trained weightlifters, increased their weightlifting ability by an average of 18 per cent. It seems not unreasonable to infer, O'Shea concludes, 'that a nutritional and physiological basis exists for the use of anabolic steroid agents for the purpose of improving physical performance.'

With the moderate doses he used in these studies. O'Shea has observed no sexual effects, and the subjects reported no reduction in sexual appetite. (Paradoxically, administration of male sex hormone tends to reduce sexual drive by activating a hormonal counter-response.) The only side effect that turned up in O'Shea's studies is muscle cramps, which can be overcome by magnesium tablets. The long-term effect of moderate doses, if any, is unknown.

Excessive doses of anabolic steroids are likely to result in the liver and bone damage described in the Olympic Committee's anti-doping booklet. Other unpleasant effects include shrinkage of the testicles and swelling of the prostate gland. These symptoms seem partly or wholly reversible. Those who believe steroids help an athlete put on muscle say that about a third of the extra muscle is lost when steroid treatment is stopped. One effect that is not reversible is in young boys; the drugs cause premature ossification of the long bones and may, in certain cases, stunt growth. O'Shea believes anabolic steroids, should not be taken under the age of 22, and in any case only after careful medical evaluation. But he dismisses as 'scare tactics' the warnings put out by the medical committee of the N.C.A.A.

In O'Shea's hands, anabolic steroids are both effective (at least with weightlifters) and free of side effects (apart from muscle cramps), while in the studies cited by official sports doctors the drugs are inefficacious.

O'Shea's studies clearly need to be repeated by others before the efficacy of anabolic steroids can be proved or disproved. It would probably require a clear disproof, or discovery of a particularly damaging side effect, to shake athletes from their attachment to steroids. Even if the drugs gave only a fractional boost to performance, this might make the difference between winning an event or breaking a record. The steroids are also said to induce a feeling of well-being, which alone would guarantee a measure of popularity.

Opinions on the efficacy of anabolic steroids tend to run parallel with respective positions on ethics. Official athletic organisations such as the Olympics Committee, the N.C.A.A. and A.A.U., all of which exist to serve the ideal of the amateur in sports, state flatly that the use of any drug for a non-therapeutic purpose is unethical. In weightlifting and body-building, which have always been more players' sports than gentlemen's, the athletes see a distinction between steroids, which may be taken weeks before an event, and drugs such as amphetamines, which affect performance more instantaneously. Steroids, they say, are fair play.

The ethics issue is likely to remain an academic point until a practical test is developed to ascertain whether an athlete has been taking steroids. Steroids, in any case, are part of a larger phenomenon, which some describe as faddism, others as a special drug culture, among athletes. Bill Bates, former head trainer of the New England Patriots, dismisses steroids as 'just another example of faddism among athletes, like ice massage, isokinetics, brewer's yeast or vitamins.' But Bill St John, a Mr America finalist of Glassboro, N.J., says of steroids and other drugs used by athletes: 'It's crazy the way some of these guys abuse these medicines — it's like a real drug culture we live in.' Athletics has certainly not remained entirely free of the drug culture in society at large. Last fall, for example, a spot check of the Delaware State University football team revealed that about a fifth of the players had been taking drugs, including LSD, amphetamines, barbiturates, and heroin. Among professional footballers, the use of amphetamines is rife — the drugs are sometimes put out in the training room, according to Bates — and there are rumours that cocaine is taken too. Amphetamines have also been popular among weightlifters, at least until the National Championships in Columbus, Ohio, last year. Holders of the top six places had to be disqualified after the event, when analysis of urine samples revealed that all had taken Dexedrine. A drug problem of a different nature, affecting professional footballers, is the use of pain killers such as novocaine to enable a player to continue playing even when injured. Vince Lombardi, for example, took the line that no player was ever injured: 'A man would have to have a bone sticking out of his skin for Lombardi to let him off,' says one football trainer.

Though amphetamines and steroids are taken primarily in the belief that they will improve performance, both drugs impart a psychological kick and to this extent are no different from heroin, marijuana, and the drugs used by society at large. That athletes, the supposed exemplars of clean living and respect for their own physiology, should be so deep into drugs is presumably a consequence, at least in part, of the pressures to which they are subjected. In professional football, the advent of big gates and superstars has led some managers to use any means available to keep a player on the field. In athletics, the unceasing upward march of world records has compelled trainers to demand more and harder training schedules of their athletes. Swimmers may be required to swim 5000 yards a day, long- and middle-distance runners to run 150 miles a week. 'You can't ask this of these guys and expect them to submit to the average man's diet,' says O'Shea. 'At every meet you go to you see world records broken in one class or another. How far can you go before something gives way?' asks St John. If athletics is already approaching the limits of normal physiology, it is maybe inevitable that athletes will turn to artificial means to coax the last twitch of energy out of a fatigued muscle or to improve upon the masculinity of potential Mr Americas. But the gentlemen who set the rules seem happier denouncing steroids than trying to understand the trials and temptations that push today's athletes into drugs.

References

[1]Casner, S.W., Early, R.G. and Carlson, B.R. (1971). *J. Sports Med. Phys. Fitness*, 11, p. 98.
[2]Johnson, L.C. and O'Shea, J.P. (1969). *Science*, 164, p. 57.
[3]O'Shea, J.P. (1971). *Nutr. Rep. Int.*, 4, p. 363.

International Olympic Committee's testing list

The following is an up-to-date testing list of drugs considered by the International Olympic Committee to be dope. Any drug or drug preparation which is used with the intention of modifying advantageously the performance of a competitor may be considered as a 'doping substance'. Particular attention is drawn to the dangers of taking the following:

Psychomotor stimulant drugs
e.g.

Amphetamine	Methylphenidate
Benzphetamine	Norpseudoephedrine
Chlorphentermine	Pemoline
Cocaine	Phendimetrazine
Diethylpropion	Phenmetrazine
Dimethylamphetamine	Phentermine
Ethylamphetamine	Pipradrol
Fencamfamin	Prolintane
Meclofenoxate	and related compounds
Methylamphetamine	

Sympathomimetic amines
e.g.

Chlorprenaline	Isoprenaline
Ephedrine	Methylephedrine
Etafedrine	Methoxyphenamine
Isoetharine	and related compounds

Miscellaneous central nervous system stimulants

e.g.

Amiphenazole
Benigride
Doxapram
Ethamivan
Leptazol

Nikethamide
Picrotoxin
Strychnine
and related compounds

Narcotic analgesics

e.g.

Anileridine
Codeine
Dextromoramide
Dihydrocodeine
Dipipanone
Ethylmorphine
Heroin
Hydrocodone
Hydromorphone
Levorphanol
Morphine

Methadone
Oxycodone
Oxymorphone
Pentazocine
Pethidine
Phenzzocine
Piminodine
Thebacon
Trimeperidine
and related compounds

Anabolic steriods

e.g.

Methandienone
Nandrolone Decanoate
Nandrolone Phenylpropionate

Oxymetholone
Stanozolol
and related compounds

Beta-blockers

e.g.

Acebutalol
Metoprolol
Oxprenolol
Pindolol

Propranalol
Sotalol
and related compounds

Let us look at just a few of these drugs and some of their side-effects, under their respective headings.

Amphetamine.

Unwanted (immediate) side-effects:

1 Cardio-vascular reactions
2 Delirium
3 Convulsions
4 Coma
5 Cyanosis
6 Respiratory failure
7 Depression

Caffeine.

Unwanted side-effects:

1 Nausea
2 Vomiting
3 Insomnia
4 Restlessness
5 Excitement
6 Headache
7 Sensory disturbance
8 Tachycardia (increased heart-beats)
9 Possible increased urine output

Dexamphetamine.

Unwanted side-effects:

The unwanted effects of this drug are similar to those of amphetamine except that dexamphetamine has a relatively weaker peripheral action and therefore exhibits an apparently greater stimulating and toxic effect on the central nervous system.

Ephedrine.

Unwanted side-effects:

Some people can exhibit mild symptoms of overdose, even after taking a normal dose. Some of the effects in overdose (immediate):

1 Vertigo
2 Headache
3 Vomiting
4 Sweating
5 Palpitation
6 Irregular heart-beats
7 Anorexia
8 Restlessness
9 Insomnia

Central nervous system stimulants. Athletes have been known to take this form of medication, hoping that it will enhance their performances. As with other stimulants, these medications can be detected in urine specimens. As most large sports meetings now advise athletes that random tests will be performed following events, many athletes have been deterred from using central nervous system stimulants, although some may require them for medical reasons.

(The following sections do not appear on the I.O.C. drug list but they play an important part in the athlete's all-important build-up, in theory physiologically, definitely psychologically.)

Diuretics. Athletes usually take diuretics in conjunction with other drugs. For example, if an athlete discovers his body weight to be in excess of his desired weight on the eve of an event he will take a diuretic to assist urine output, thereby quickly removing body fluid. Increased urine output by means of a diuretic is a usual sign of an athlete's having taken anabolic steroids. Weightlifters have been known to lose a considerable number of grams within 12 hours prior to their weigh-in. What these athletes do not realise, however, is that this increase of urine output depletes the body and cells of electrolytes. It is not uncommon for an athlete to thereby experience severe cramps, resulting in a poor performance due to lack of strength during the event.

117

Vitamins. There are many different vitamins in the A to K group, and all are essential for a balanced diet. The most common vitamins administered to athletes are the vitamin B-complex and vitamin B_{12}.

Vitamins are organic compounds required by humans usually in small quantities. The term 'vitamin' was first used by Casimir Funk in 1912 to describe various food properties, and as most vitamins are amines, or related to them, the word has come into common usage.

Vitamins can be divided into two groups as follows:

1 Fat-soluble: Vitamins A, D, E, K:

2 Water-soluble: thiamine (B_1), riboflavin (B_2), niacin-nicotinic acid, pyridoxine (B_6), pantothenic acid (the important co-enzyme A, present in all cells, presumably cannot be made by man, and intake is therefore essential), biotin (widely distributed in food and made by gastrointestinal bacteria), inasitol (occurs in many foods, in cereals it is a component of phytic acid which renders food calcium less absorbable), para-amino benzoic acid (forms part of the less essential vitamin, folic acid), and cyancobalamin. All these water-soluble vitams form the B-complex.

Usually, only vitamin B-complex and vitamin B_{12} are taken by athletes participating in cycling and track and field events. Athletes, following injections of these substances, claim that they perform better because of an increased haemoglobin content in their blood.

Vitamin B_{12}. The chemical nature of this vitamin was evaluated by two teams working in co-operation under Dorothy Hodgkin at Oxford University and under Sir Alexander Todd at Cambridge.

In nature, B_{12} occurs usually in combination with protein. It is present in the body in several forms. With regard to its physiological action, it probably affects every cell in the body, but its deficiency is felt most severely in tissue where cells are normally dividing rapidly, for example, in the blood-forming tissues of the bone marrow, and in the gastrointestinal tract.

The nervous system is also affected. Biochemical lesion results in an arrest in the development of new red corpuscles and sometimes causes degeneration of nerve fibres in the spinal cord and peripheral nerves. Quite clearly, vitamin B_{12} participates in some essential enzyme system or systems, as the amount needed to restore to health a patient dying of Addisonian anaemia is amazingly small.

Cecil and Loeb state that :'When therapeutic diets are incomplete and need supplementation, the amount should be in small, simple multiples of the recommended allowances. Large amounts of vitamin A and D must be avoided. It is probable that vitamin B_{12} is not needed in amounts beyond that supplied by normal food intake, and that it is of therapeutic value only in the treatment of pernicious anaemia, when it must be given parenterally.'[1]

References

[1]Cecil, R.L. and Loeb, R.F. (1963). *A Textbook of Medicine*, 11th edition. Philadelphia: W.B. Saunders and Co., pp. 1211–1213.

Doping in sport

Dr A.P. Millar

This article was first published in 1970 in the *Australian Journal of Sports Medicine*.

Athletes have been engaged in a battle for superiority over their fellows from time immemorial, for rewards that varied from a life-time honour to financial security. They have striven to do the impossible knowing that results that bear that title today will not wear it tomorrow. One has only to review the records of recent achievements in the mile race to realise that the 4-minute time which was such a barrier for so many people until broken by Bannister does not even rate a mention when broken nowadays and indeed, it is pointless in many countries to compete unless one could smash this barrier at will.

This competition has brought notable developments in training methods so that now interval and circuit training are everyday words. There has been more emphasis placed on selection of athletes for events that suit their structure and on education of all personnel involved in competitions. This has raised the overall standards and has tended to bring many competitors to the same levels so that each is looking for any small advantage over the other. In a technological society such as ours, it is only to be expected that competitors and trainers will study fringe subjects such as pharmacology to find that added principle that leads to supremacy.

The use of drugs is not new. 5000 years ago the Chinese used Ma Huang to stimulate their performance. It was not until 1924 that ephedrine, the active principle of Ma Huang, was isolated and studied. The Romans fed their horses hydromel, a mixture of water and honey, to improve their stamina, and problem of fatigue in strenuous exercise was tackled by the Indians of Central America with a chew of coca, with gratifying results.

The use of drugs has become a relatively widespread although abnormal custom in the athletic field, and the problem of the use of drugs or doping in athletics is a matter which has caused consternation in both amateur and professional fields. For the purposes of this paper doping has been defined as:

(a) the use of any chemical compound which may alter a competitor's performance provided that:

1 the compound is not a normal metabolite

2 the compound is a normal metabolite but is given in excess or by an abnormal route;

(b) the use of any abnormal mechanism the object of which is to alter a competitor's performance, excluding at all times measures necessary to maintain health, taken under medical direction.

This presentation will approach doping from the point of view of those factors paramount in athletic performance. The most important of these are the psychological factors involving motivation and fatigue, and this is the area where the greatest danger lies. The selection of athletes for specific events has lead to doping to enhance body build artifically. The production of energy depends upon the substrates available and the mechanism for energy release. The actual movement itself is dependent upon strength, speed of action and co-ordination or skill.

The choice of drug has been based on its published actions as determined by animal and laboratory tests and its use in the ill population. As a result of this, the effects in athletes, who differ physically and emotionally from the population at large, are not always readily predictable and side effects are often correspondingly exaggerated.

The greatest problem has been the inability to match a qualitative effect to a quantitative dose — usually the athlete is given a dose generally in use, rather than titrating the dose to the athlete, so that the choice of drug has been based on its effect in non-athletes and results have not always been as desired, particularly with central stimulants which produce excessive excitement in some performers.

The dominant psychological factors needed for performance at high levels, and which can be influenced by doping, are motivation, a certain emotional tension to render the athlete keyed up and ready to go, and an ability to overcome fatigue. These factors have all been attacked by drugs with varying success. When emotional tension is too great the tendency to use tranquillisers or sedatives arises. No balanced studies are available on these drugs except for comparisons between barbiturates and placebos. These have shown, at the doses used, that performance overall has deteriorated when using the active material. It would appear that emotional tension is best managed by correct conditioning.

For athletes in whom this tension is lacking there is generally a lack of motivation, for it appears that without a heightening of emotional tone, peak performance is impossible. For that reason, amphetamines have been widely used and many competitors report an increased tuochiness after using the drug in varying doses and say they develop a feeling of increased drive and invincibility although this latter has not always been borne out in results.

Cocaine is a central stimulant which improves the readiness of performers. Here the balance with other effects is such that cocaine is a difficult compound to titrate to a patient. It is known to cause restlessness and excitement and affects the heat-regulating mechanism and is followed by a deterioration in performance — factors which on their own would point out the inadvisability of even a single dose before competition. It appears in some to lessen fatigue in its early effects.

Caffeine increases coronary blood flow but its use in sport can be attributed to its mild central stimulant action and it also interferes at times with heat regulation. Alcohol has been known to reduce inhibitions in some people and it may in theory be useful for that purpose, but its other effects when taken before competition readily militate against its use.

Fatigue relief or alternately an increased tolerance to fatigue, is a desire of all athletes and the stimulants aforementioned are helpful here. Controlled trials are available for the amphetamines but results are conflicting. Doses and time of administration have varied to a degree that makes comparisons difficult. Smith and Beecher in their experiment showed improved performance, more marked in throwers (3·4 per cent) and less noticeable in runners and swimmers. However, Golding and Barnard with large doses, using a treadmill, and making performers run to exhaustion, found no benefit — but their subjects were not trained at this pastime. This variation can be seen in other studies.

Probably the most surprising and uniform result of studies is the relative absence of side effects with the doses used. Use of amphetamines in the reported doses in my experience has been almost universally associated with side effects but perhaps athletes expected to be over-stimulated and ignored the significance. There is no doubt that until something better appears, the amphetamines will continue to be used.

The lack of motivation and readiness, and even fatigue, can be altered by hypnotic suggestion in suitable subjects, and hypnosis is a form of doping. Its use is limited by its very nature and needs, and documented material is extremely difficult to find.

Physical size and body proportions. It is obvious that shape and size play an important part in selection for specific sports and specific positions in team sports. The differences in physique in sprinters, throwers and marathon exponents is evident on brief reflection. To increase muscle bulk the anabolic steroids have been used in many centres. Reports have been very variable and in all successful instances it has been impossible to credit the drugs with results achieved as so many other variables have been involved.

The provision of substrates for metabolism is paramount in exercise. Drugs such as ronicol and priscol that increase peripheral blood flow do so at the expense of flow in vital centres and are physiologically unsound, and death has been reported with their use. The type of food has not been a consistent factor in improving performance whether by increasing or decreasing specific fractions. The use of diets leaving an alkaline residue has been claimed to be helpful in combating acidosis. Vitamins have been administered in all conceivable doses and combinations, but opinions, and not proven facts, hold sway. Alcohol as a substrate has no benefit over normal foods.

The mechanism of energy release at the cellular level depends upon the Krebs cycle, and increasing the intake of aspartates has not been found to improve performance. Creatine and ATP, which are important sources of energy, have been administered without benefit. In Sweden, ultra-violet light has been used to improve energy availability but it is again difficult to assess.

The strength of movements is generally unaffected by drugs as it involves the resultant force of a number of factors, and the most definite increment has been gained by training. However, bulk of muscle is a factor and if this can be increased by anabolic steroids, they must improve strength. Smith and Beecher's experiments suggest that an increase in strength occurs with amphetamine as throwers showed the greatest improvement. This is a quite unexpected result which warrants further study.

Speed of action is dependent on reflexes and synapses in the central nervous system and the conduction of impulses across neuro-muscular junctions. This is an extremely rapid process now and drugs affecting it such as acityl choline, prostignune and others have too many side effects to be useful.

Co-ordination can only be learnt by practice and adequate supervision.

The future of drugs in athletics will depend on finding new preparations which relieve fatigue and allow a feeling of well-being without side effects. This field is being actively cultivated. Compounds which act peripherally by improving the metabolic pathways are possibilities for the future which may allow a greater tolerance to fatigue.

However one views the problem of doping in sport, the practice is to be deprecated, as having once used drugs without any conscious deleterious effect, the temptation will always be present to repeat the dose when problems burdens the ex-athlete later in life, and this will lead to disaster.

Comments on artificial aids in sport

Dr T. Anderson

The late Dr T. Anderson was selected by the New Zealand Olympic and Commonwealth Games Association as Medical Officer to the New Zealand team at Munich in 1972. He died in 1978.

When it comes to the administration of drugs to athletes, I must admit to being amongst the guilty ones. In the early 1950s, whilst coaching a senior rugby team in Christchurch, I used local anaesthetic injections for certain injuries in order to keep key players in action. Later these were used on the Canterbury team which held the Ranfurly Shield in the mid-1950s, and on two players in the 1956 Springbok team. No harmful results occurred although I am sure that these injections must be used with care and discretion.

Prior to the Olympic Games in Mexico in 1968 I looked after the health and fitness of the New Zealand oarsmen during their training period at Kerr's Reach, and, being aware of the problems of altitude in Mexico City, I gave all of them supplies of ferrous gluconate tablets in the hope that these would provide them with iron reserves to help the build-up of haemoglobin. I also gave them vitamin B-complex as I have long felt that with the hard and exhausting training schedules which they undergo, they may need more of these vitamins than the average person. In addition, I have always advocated a high protein diet for these athletes.

In 1968, they stood up to their vigorous schedule very well, and I have repeated the procedure with each rowing team subsequently training in Christchurch. I can see no harm in the administration of these and other vitamins, although I must admit that any benefit gained could be psychological.

Other athletes in Munich asked me to give them injections of vitamin B_{12} and other vitamins, and this I did without demur. To have refused, and there was no reason to refuse, would undoubtedly have upset them as they were fully convinced of the efficacy of these substances.

Anabolic steroids are another kettle of fish. They can, it seems, have unwanted side effects.

From my own observations in Munich I found that the incidence of muscle and tendon injury was much higher in athletes taking these drugs, and in addition, response to treatment of their injuries was much delayed.

Undoubtedly these substances do build bulky muscles, but I am convinced that they are less efficient muscles in events which require endurance and speed.

8 Management of head and spinal injuries

The prevention and first aid of head and spinal injuries

Dr G. Martin

Graham Martin FRCS, MRCR, FRACS, is Consultant Neurosurgeon at Wellington Hospital, and is both a Fellow of the Royal College of Surgeons and a Member of the Royal College of Physicians. He has written this paper specially for this book, and describes here one of the most important areas of sports injury management. These injuries are mostly associated with running contact sports, mainly those involving scrummaging.

It is hoped this paper will be a source of instruction to those without medical training, and a source of reference to those who are trained. Some aspects of the management and prevention of head and spinal injuries are important for coaches and medical personnel in most branches of sport; in boxing they are essential.

Head injuries

Pathology
Pathology is the study of changes wrought upon the body by disease or injury, and is the theoretical basis for the prevention and treatment of injuries.

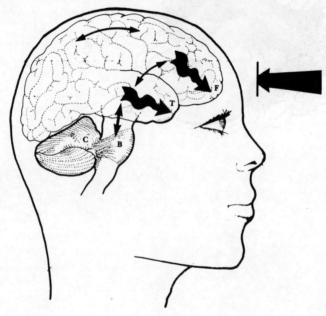

Fig. 8.1

The brain floats within the skull, supported by a thin film of fluid around it, called the cerebrospinal fluid (usually abbreviated to C.S.F.). This fluid cushions the brain from shocks, but also permits a certain amount of movement within the skull.

When a violent blow strikes the head (Fig. 8.1), the brain is free to move a little in the directions shown. This stretches the brain stem (B) and may bruise the temporal lobes (T) and frontal lobes (F). If the blow is hard enough the damage can be fatal; usually it is not, but there is an interruption to consciousness and memory, known as concussion.

In the brain stem (B) there is a structure, called the reticular formation, which maintains alertness and consciousness. The reticular formation is a network of many millions of nerve cells which are disconnected by the stretch, resulting in loss of consciousness. Their disconnection may be for ten seconds, ten weeks or permanently, depending on the severity of the blow.

The temporal lobes (T) are where memories are recorded and indexed. These may be bruised by a blow, causing the brain to be unable to lay down new memories for a period, and causing recent memories to fade, without actual loss of consciousness.

The frontal lobes (F) are where foresight, planning, caution, good manners and emotional control are situated. Injuries to these lobes may impair these social graces.

Also, there is the cerebellum (C), a co-ordinating centre for movement, containing the fine control that makes movement skilled and accurate.

When the head is injured by a severe blow the damage to the brain may be divided into two phases.

1 The first phase is that of the moment of impact, the damage being the physical destruction or injury of some nerve cells and sometimes the tearing of blood vessels.

2 The second phase is that of the complications occurring after the impact. If we cannot prevent the impact the only treatable things are these complications occurring after the impact.

The first treatable complication is obstruction of the unconscious person's airway preventing breathing, depriving the already injured brain of oxygen, thus injuring it still further. This is by far the commonest complication of head injury and should be preventable.

The second complication is swelling of the brain after it has been injured; this does not begin till the second day or later and is outside the scope of this chapter.

The third complication is rare but dramatic. A blood vessel, torn by the original impact, continues to bleed, instead of sealing itself off as they usually do. This produces an increasing clot within the closed box of the skull, which compresses the brain, thus further injuring it. Finally the pressure in the skull rises so high that it stops the blood flow to the brain, which then dies. Obviously the treatment of this situation is to drain the clot and stop the bleeding.

Thus it can be seen that there are treatments for the complications of head injury, but it needs a trained person to recognise them and act appropriately.

It may seem surprising to the non-medical reader that the subject of fractures of the skull has been left to last. This is because many fractures are not very significant in themselves — it is the injury to the underlying brain which is significant and there may be quite gross injury to the brain without a fracture, or conversely quite severe fracture without much brain injury. Moreover, only a few fractures require any special treatment.

The two types of fractures requiring special treatment are depressed and compound fractures. Depressed fractures are those where the fragments of the skull have been driven inwards on to the brain, and it may require an operation to lift them out again. Compound fractures are those where the skin is lacerated over the fracture; apart from putting a dressing on the laceration these are problems for a doctor.

Finally a rare sporting injury which may mimic a head injury is carotid thrombosis following blows on the neck. One of the two main vessels to the brain is disrupted, thus depriving half the brain of its blood supply and so mimicking a head injury.

Clinical features of sporting head-injuries

There are three main types of sporting head-injuries:
1 Minor concussion.
2 Repeated concussion.
3 Complicated head injuries, including fractures.

1 *Minor concussion*. These are common in body contact sports. After a blow on the head the player loses consciousness for a brief period. After the return of consciousness there may be a brief phase of confusion and failure to remember events for that time. Questioning the player later may show that memories of events have been lost for periods before and after the blow, often even during a time that the person was clearly conscious and rational.

Usually the period for which consciousness is lost is roughly related to the time for which memories are not laid down. It is only roughly related because the inability to lay down memories is due to bruising of the temporal lobe, and the loss of consciousness is due to stretching of the brain stem. Naturally, these two usually go together, but not all blows injure both equally. It seems that the temporal lobe converts short-term memories to long-term memories and this failure of conversion of short- to long-term memory may sometimes be observed after a concussion. The player may recall immediately the events leading up to the blow, only to lose the memories without trace an hour or so later.

Sometimes concussion impairs memory formation without any loss of consciousness; during the game the player may seem to be playing normally but later may have no memory of the game.

2 *Repeated concussion*. The evidence suggests that each concussion inflicts some permanent damage on the brain and subsequently the brain is more susceptible to injury. The importance of this in boxing is obvious, but it is also important for those playing team sports where head injury is likely — players who have suffered concussion in the last few weeks may suffer a second concussion more readily from lighter blows than would normally cause it. If they have suffered more than two concussions they may have to give up the sport for that season. There is good evidence that concussion is cumulative. There are demonstrable changes and loss of nerve cells in the brain after even minor head injury. This has been shown by post-mortems on people who have died of an unrelated disorder shortly after having had a minor head injury.[1] Also, it has been shown that concussion slows the speed of mental performance and that people having their second bout of concussion, even years later, are slowed down more than those having their first concussion.[2]

126

Lastly there is the evidence of the punch drunk syndrome, which is the rare end result of many bouts of concussion.

3 *Complicated head injuries.* From the point of view of a coach at the playing field, any person who is not clearly recovering consciousness within five minutes has a potentially complicated head injury.

Fractures by themselves do not present much difficulty unless there are associated complications when one can clearly see that something out of the ordinary has happened, e.g. paralysis of part of the body, clear fluid (the cerebrospinal fluid) running out of the nose or ears, or a laceration over the fracture. Otherwise it is not possible to diagnose the fracture anyway at the ground, and the only significant thing is the patient's conscious state.

The most important complications of head injury are those that are treatable if recognised promptly; as explained above, these are obstruction of the airway and bleeding within the skull compressing the brain.

Obstruction of the airway can be recognised and prevented. The signs of airway obstruction are more easily demonstrated than described, but an attempt will be made to do so. Obviously at a late stage the patient goes blue, but obstruction should be recognised before it reaches that stage.

The chest can be seen to heave and struggle against obstruction, and respiration may appear deceptively deep and fast. Even a little air may get in and out of the mouth past the obstruction so that feeling the breath at the mouth is not a reliable method of diagnosing obstruction. What is reliable is the see-saw pattern of chest and abdominal movements.

When a normal breath is taken in the diaphragm goes down and pushes the abdomen out and the chest wall expands to take the air in. Both chest and abdomen move out together. In obstructed respiration the diaphragm descends, pushing the abdomen out, but the chest cannot inflate as the airway is obstructed. Hence the careful observer may see greater respiratory effort, but it is ineffective, because the chest wall is sucked in while the diaphragm descends. This gives a sort of see-saw movement, abdomen moving out as the chest wall is drawn in, which is characteristic of obstructed respiration, instead of the normal simultaneous outward movement of chest and abdomen together.

The other detectable complication is intracranial bleeding. The earliest sign is a deterioration of consciousness. If the patient was originally conscious he becomes drowsy and progressively loses consciousness; or if unconscious from the time of the blow, the unconscious state progressively deepens, and the patient becomes less and less responsive to painful stimuli.

It is this deterioration in consciousness that is the earliest and best sign of intracranial bleeding and the patient should be sent directly to hospital as soon as it is recognised. Later signs are that first one pupil, then the other, stops reacting to light; and later, one after the other, they both dilate. These are late signs indicating that the situation is very urgent and should have been recognised earlier as being serious by the deterioration of consciousness before the pupils stopped reacting.

Two other alleged signs of intracranial compression are known to many people, namely a slow pulse and a rising blood pressure. While they do occur, they are not reliable enough to base decisions on. A slow pulse is only an indication to watch the patient carefully and many factors other than the head injury may affect the blood pressure. These two signs are best forgotten.

What to do about head injuries when they happen

Minor concussion . If the player has lost consciousness he should not play again that afternoon. Though he may seem all right and conscious, it is not uncommon to find later that there is no memory of events from the time when he was apparently conscious.

It is not necessary to send to hospital, for observation, patients who are well after a brief loss of consciousness (nor do they need X-raying if they do present at hospital).

If there are symptoms, such as headache, vomiting, confusion or double vision, the player should be observed at hospital. If there are no symptoms he can be observed by family or friends. He should not be left alone for the next six hours, nor allowed to go home by himself. The author has seen two disasters from intracranial bleeding where the injured person was (a) sent home by himself, and (b) left at the ski hut by herself.

If there is a period of memory loss he should not play again for four weeks. If there is a second concussion that season he should not play again for six weeks.

These may seem to be drastic restrictions. However they can be justified on two grounds. The first is that the player is more liable to suffer recurrent concussion from a less severe blow. Secondly, the psychological tests mentioned above show that the speed of decision making is slowed after minor concussion for twenty to thirty days. This period is longer, up to fifty days, if there is a second concussion.

Though the player may seem all right, it is not worth putting at risk his ability to make decisions rapidly. It is better to continue training, without the risk of further concussion, and resume play when the ability to make rapid decisions is unimpaired — not an unimportant ability for players.

Most minor concussions are not followed by any symptoms, but a minority are followed by several weeks of headache, dizziness, slow thinking, difficulty in concentrating and a sensitivity to bright lights and loud noises. Further playing should not be permitted while these symptoms last, though training may be continued.

It should be recognised that ignoring these rules, though gallant, may be unwise, as the player may be doing less than his best for longer. When many players are students, dependent on the peak of their intellectual performance, there is an additional reason for not risking impairment of their speed of thought.

Unconscious head injuries. As long as someone is unconscious, it is very important to see that their airway is clear. Obstructed respiration with its typical see-saw movement of the chest and abdomen has been described above, but it should be prevented while the patient is unconscious by routinely rolling them over on their side and letting the head and face hang half turned towards the ground, so that any fluid in their mouth automatically drains if they vomit, and so that the tongue automatically falls forward and does not obstruct the airway.

This procedure should be automatic when someone is seen to be unconscious.

Lacerations of the scalp. Suturing these is something for a trained person, but first aiders can put a firm pad and bandage on them to diminish the blood loss. This dressing is quite appropriate even for severe head injuries (e.g. a hit on the head by a shotput).

At hospital it is not necessary to X-ray otherwise uncomplicated lacerations if the wound is carefully inspected in a good light and clean conditions. A depressed fracture will not be missed and a linear fracture will not need any treatment other than closing the wound.

Deteriorating head injuries. Head injuries that are not steadily improving after the impact **must** be sent to hospital.

Penetrating head injuries. Some sports, such as spear fishing, even darts, occasionally inflict penetrating wounds of the skull. Obviously any such wound of the head, such as a dart or spear gun wound must go to hospital. Unless clearly impractical (e.g. javelin) it is best to leave the missile in the wound till arrival at the hospital, as sometimes on withdrawing these missiles there is a torrential haemorrhage requiring transfusion.

Severe head injuries. These, such as may be produced by falls in climbing, or occasional football injuries, are identified by the depth of unconsciousness. A painful stimulus produces little or no response in the way of movements of the limbs.

The only thing that can be done as first aid is to keep the airway clear and prevent further damage from lack of oxygen, and to put a dressing on any lacerations, then transport the patient rapidly to hospital.

Once again, airway obstruction should be prevented by transporting them on their side, with the face half turned to the ground, so that mouth and nose drain by gravity and the tongue falls forward, not obstructing the airway.

Epilepsy

Since one in 200 of the population has epilepsy, coaches will sometimes have to deal with epileptic fits, especially since fits tend to be precipitated by those two factors often associated with sporting events — fatigue and hangovers.

There is no reason why epileptics should not play sport. Very few epileptics have their fits precipitated by trauma and, in fact, are least likely to take a fit while they are concentrating. There is a tendency for severe fatigue to precipitate fits but this is more likely after, rather than during, a game. The decision not to play sport on medical grounds for epileptics is one that can be left to the patient and his doctor.

A fit is a very dramatic event, guaranteed to distract all but the most devoted spectators, and most of the team as well. The person having the fit cries out, loses consciousness, falls to the ground, goes stiff and blue, then shakes all over, may wet himself or vomit, then relaxes and gradually begins to come around.

There is an old myth that something should be put between the epileptic's teeth to prevent him biting his tongue. While it is true that he may bite his tongue, tongues heal well and are never bitten right off; and it is too late to do anything once he has started to fit, for the teeth are tightly clenched and you are more likely to break teeth (which don't heal) prising his mouth open than prevent damage to his tongue (which will heal), and, anyway, it is already bitten by the time you get there.

There is some value in opening the mouth and turning him on his side, with his face half turned to the ground, during the stage of relaxation (but unconsciousness) which follows the convulsion. Vomiting sometimes occurs at this stage and there is a real possibility of the inhalation of vomitus if he is left lying on his back.

Someone who takes frequent fits may present real practical problems to a sporting group but there is no reason why most groups should not be able to cope with someone taking an occasional fit. Some sports are obviously unsuitable, such as rock climbing or gliding, but other sports such as football are very suitable for the epileptic.

Boxing

From the point of view of sporting head-injuries, boxing is in a class by itself as it is the only sport where the object is to inflict a concussion. Indeed, the rules which prevent hitting below the belt provide better protection for the testicles than the brain.

What has been said above about concussion applies especially to boxing, namely that the effects of concussion appear to be cumulative and that the reaction time is slowed by concussion.

There is well known and dramatic syndrome, the 'punch drunk' state, which is known to affect boxers who have had a long fighting career. It is estimated by some to affect between fifteen and twenty per cent of those who have fought more than 100 bouts.[3] However, the author's experience is that it seems to be rare in New Zealand and the small numbers of cases collected by others in centres of large population suggest that at least it is not common.

The pathology of this syndrome is characteristic: there is widespread wasting of the brain, with scarring of the cortex (the outer surface) on the under surface of the frontal lobes and medial (inner) parts of the temporal lobes, both areas which are particularly liable to injury by blows on the head. The corpus callosum is thinned; this being the great tract of fibres joining and co-ordinating the two halves of the brain, which is subject to damage as it is flung against the falx, the midline fibrous partition in the skull. The cerebellum may lose up to two-thirds of its Purkinje cells, the main functional cells in this region.

There is a curious and characteristic separation of the two halves of the brain — normally between the two frontal lobes there is a single tissue layer, the septum pellucidum. In the punch drunk it is always separated into two sheets, with a space between them called the cavum septum pellucidum, a very rare thing to find in normal brains.

The symptoms to be seen are what one might expect from the damage to frontal lobes, temporal lobes and cerebellum. There is deterioration of intellect, memory and personality. The patient is forgetful, apathetic, irritable and sometimes confused, and personal care and habits deteriorate. The loss of cells in the cerebellum produces slurred speech, unsteady gait and a tremor in movements. The symptoms may begin some years after boxing has stopped and may progress for several years.

This probably occurs in mild forms, possibly in other sports also, but the frequency of the mild form is quite unknown.

There are occasional deaths in boxing, as there are in most sports. Most of these are due to bleeding on to the surface of the brain, producing a rapidly increasing clot and resultant death from cerebral compression. A minority of deaths are not associated with clots but occur after a very severe hammering and seem to be due to widespread obstruction of small blood vessels, blocking the blood supply to many small but widespread areas of the brain.[4]

Prevention of boxing injuries

The weight of gloves varies, the heavier the glove the less severe the blow to the head. 8 oz gloves are prescribed for amateur fights and heavyweight professionals (6 oz for lightweight professionals) but 16 oz or even 12 oz gloves inflict less impact and run less risk of injuring the head. In amateur boxing the use of a head guard is becoming increasingly frequent.

The work of Gronwall and Wrightson, mentioned above, suggests that it takes about six weeks to be certain that recovery has occurred from concussion, and bouts should not be more frequent than this, though training can continue.

Rounds should be stopped, and generally are, when it is clear that one of the contestants is becoming groggy and cannot win.

After a knock-out the boxer should be able to leave the ring unaided; if he is not able to, or not clearly improving from minute to minute, then he should be observed in hospital.

Medical examination of boxers. It is hoped that coaches will excuse the necessarily medical terms used in this section.

International rules require the medical examination of boxers before being certified as fit to fight. On the whole it is unlikely that the trainer would put up for a bout anyone who is not in the best of condition but it does sometimes happen.

The signs which may indicate damage are nystagmus, intention tremor, inability to do the finger/nose test accurately with the eyes closed, inability to walk a straight line heel to toe with the eyes closed, difficulty in balancing on the toes of one foot with the eyes closed, and dysdiadochokinesis. Increased or diminished jerks, or up-going plantars may be found.

The routine for examination should be as follows. The boxer is questioned about headaches, his memory and hearing, any dizziness or sensitivity to bright lights and loud noises, about past concussion and periods of loss of memory. He is then examined for nystagmus and slurred speech, and given the following tests with his eyes shut (after first being given a chance to practise them with open eyes): the finger-nose test, and balancing on the toes of each foot with the other off the ground and walking a straight line heel to toe.

An electro-encephalogram has been repeatedly shown to be of less value than clinical examination and has little discrimination in deciding whether or not a boxer is fit.[5]

Ophthalmic injuries. Though a glove cannot enter the orbit a thumb can (this is of course a foul) and almost every conceivable traumatic injury to the orbit and its contents has been recorded.

Other sports. Head injuries may occur in most sports as accidents; most commonly in football in its various forms. In soccer heading the ball does not seem to produce injury when headed by trained players, but has sometimes when done inexpertly.

Spinal injuries

The main problems with spinal injuries on the sporting field are their recognition and first aid. There is little that can be done to prevent them, though in some sports there are certain practices, recognised as dangerous, such as collapsing a scrum, which risk producing spinal injury.

From a first aid point of view, spinal injuries divide into major injuries (those with paralysis, from cord compression, or the risk of paralysis) and minor back injuries. The management of minor back injuries is described elsewhere in this book.

Major spinal injuries with actual or potential paralysis

Vertebrae may be fractured or dislocated anywhere in the spine, depending on the sport, e.g. parachute jumping for lumbar vertebrae, football for fractures in the neck.

Most fractures or dislocations are **not** associated with damage to the spinal cord; a few are. Damage or potential damage to the spinal cord may be recognised by inability to move a limb, or numbness or tingling in a limb or limbs. Thus, if the injured person can stand and walk away they should be allowed to do so, being carefully helped to their feet, providing they do not get worse in so doing, and helped off the field. If they get too much pain then they should be carried away on a stretcher, on to which they are rolled carefully, and not carried off by four hefty players each taking a corner.

The most important thing after injuring the spine, with or without damage to the spinal cord, is not to force movement of the painful part, and to keep the spine in the neutral position. Restricting movement avoids the risk of displacing a fracture and damaging the spinal cord.

This need not be taken to elaborate lengths — some people seem to have been taught that even the slightest movement of a spinal fracture may lead to instant paralysis and even death. In fact, providing the patient is conscious this is very unlikely, any movement of a fracture or dislocation is intensely painful and a displacement of the fracture or dislocation sufficient to damage the cord is not likely to be permitted without great protest.

All that is needed is that the injured person is moved with reasonable gentleness and care. He should not be heaved around. It is unlikely that the force used in moving the patient carefully will be anything like as great as the forces producing the fracture. If these forces did not displace the fracture far enough to damage the cord at the moment the fracture occurred, then careful movement with a conscious and protesting patient is very unlikely to displace the fracture. Naturally greater care must be taken if the patient is unconscious, or if there is already damage to the spinal cord.

References

[1]Strich, S.J. (1970). 'Lesions in the Cerebral Hemispheres After Blunt Head Injury.' *Journal of Clinical Pathology*, vol. 23, suppl. 4, pp. 166–71.
Oppenheimer, D., (1968). 'Microscopic Lesions in the Brain Following Head Injury.' *Journal of Neurology, Neurosurgery and Psychiatry*, vol. 31, pp. 299–307.
[2]Gronwall, D. and Wrightson, P. (1975). 'Cumulative Effect of Concussion.' *The Lancet*, 2, pp. 995–97.
[3]Jedlinski, J., Gatarski, J. and Szymusik, I. (1971). 'Encephalopathia Pugilistica,' (*punch drunkenness*) *Acta Medica Polonica*, 12, pp. 433–451.
Robert, A.H. (1969). *Brain Damage in Boxers*. Pitman Medical Scientific Publishing Co.

4Unterharnscheidt, F.E. *Handbook of Clinical Neurology*, ed. Vinken and Bruyn, vol. 23, pp. 523–93.

5Johnson, J. (1969). 'The EEG in the Traumatic Encephalopathy of Boxers.' *Psychiatric Clinics*, 2, pp. 204–211.

Other reading

Corsellis, J.A., Bruton, C.J. and Freeman Browne, D. (1973). 'The Aftermath of Boxing.' *Psychological Medicine*, 3, pp. 270–303.

'The Punch Drunk Syndrome.' (1973). Editorial, *British Medical Journal*, Nov. 24., p. 439.

Critchley, M.C. (1957). 'Medical Aspects of Boxing, Particularly from a Neurological Standpoint.' *British Medical Journal*, vol. 1, pp. 357–62.

Mawdsley, C. and Ferguson, F.R. (1963). 'Neurological Disturbances in Boxers.' *The Lancet*, vol. 2, pp. 795–801.

9 Oh, my aching back

The sportsman and his back

M. Hood

Malcolm Hood, physiotherapist, of Pukekohe, is a Member both of the New Zealand Manipulative Therapist Association and of the Chartered Society of Physiotherapists. He has written this paper specially for this book.

The spinal column

For a very long time the spinal column has been regarded as thirty-two vertebrae, most of them moveable, with a gelatinous disc between most joints. Problems arising from the joints have been attributed to torn muscles, torn ligaments, or a 'slipped disc'. For society in general, and the sportsman in particular, this concept of the pathology cannot continue and still allow the high levels of performance expected of the athlete in today's competitions to be maintained. Poor results in the treatment of back pain will occur unless the cause is specifically isolated. Isolate the cause, cure the condition. A bad diagnosis and a bad result is almost always the end result.

The above-mentioned conditions may create a painful back in many cases, but by far the most common sources of pain are the small joints on either side of the bodies of the vertebrae. Between each two vertebrae that move, in the spine, two small joints are found as well as the main flattened area of the vertebrae; these are termed 'facet joints'. They may move too much (hypermobile) or too little (hypomobile); both situations may cause pain.

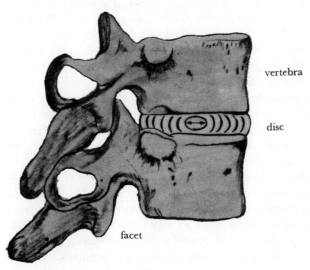

vertebra

disc

facet

Fig. 9.1

135

As there are usually twenty-three vertebrae which move and have facet joints; this means a total of sixty-nine little joints which must be considered when spinal pain occurs in the sportsman. However, added to these are the joints in the rib area, which join the ribs to the thirteen thoracic vertebrae and also, lower down, the five fused joints of the sacrum join the 'dangling monkey's tail' of the four fused joints of the coccyx. One also must not forget the super-strong sacro-illiac joints (which take about 8 tons to separate), these can cause pain, especially in females after child-birth. Then there is the symphysis pubis to the front — a rare but acutely painful place to receive an injury.

In all, ninety-nine moving joints must be regarded when treating the spine, and for this considerable post-graduate training and expertise in diagnosis is required for effective treatment. It will be appreciated why so many players have spinal prob-lems.

Incidence of backache

Studies of the general public have shown that about eighty per cent of the popula-tion will suffer, or are suffering, from backache sufficient to cause them to seek treatment.

However, in the most common forms of backpain, which are less severe and are non-permanent, there is little doubt that sport will induce a healthier outlook than non-competition. Only mental illness and 'rheumatism' cause more absenteeism than spinal problems. It can be regarded as almost normal to suffer a painful back.

World Health figures, on the other hand, show that, apart from fractures, spinal pain is almost non-existant in the so-called primitive societies — the societies which are reliant on physical activity involving full-range joint movements.

Cause

Why should humans suffer backache, when living an easier life, now than in preced-ing years? The sportsman's spine, like any other person's spine, was made to move; it tilts, it rotates, it glides and shears, it works in several directions. When all the joints are moving, it is able to move 110^0 forwards and 140^0 backwards. In those who are extra-mobile, which many sports people are, the added range may be noted (e.g. Olga Korbut, the Russian athlete). The problem occurs when the athlete has not recently moved the joints required in his particular sport during training, espe-cially immediately prior to a competition.

All joints, including the ninety-nine of the spinal column, are covered with cartil-age. This cartilage is similar to silver or brass. It requires gentle rubbing to main-tain the shine. As the athlete ages so the shine on the joint surfaces wears naturally, and with this the small canals bringing nutrients to the joint space themselves, fill in with minute calcium deposits and 'block' this process. This action is more notice-able at the outside edges of the joints, where movement is less likely to occur, and this enables small stalagmites and stalagtites to form. This is termed osteoarthritis, although usually there is little or no inflammatory reaction occuring.

After a time a sudden force, such as may occur on the sports field, may push the joint through this dull area, and as well as the joint surface reacting to this unpleas-ant situation, the small ligaments and muscles, that in turn have shortened about the area, set up a painful reaction. The cartilage, surprisingly, has no pain fibres and acts merely as a shock absorber to the joint.

By compressing the two joint surfaces together daily, the ageing process is minimised as polishing is maintained and the transfer to the joint of good nutriments, and the removal of bad waste products, is maintained. The associated soft tissues have little chance to permanently shorten.

Atmospheric pressure changes preceeding rain may lower this action, and this is probably one of the reasons aching joints are more noticeable before rain.

Sportsmen in sedentary jobs do **not** get the spinal joints to pass through full ranges unless specifically intended and so unless action is taken to do this their incidence of spinal trouble may result.

At the same time as the cartilages of the joints are ageing, so the over-rated disc is wearing out too. This is particularly so at the two lowest lumbar joints where most of the bending forward occurs (L4 — L5, L5 — S1).

Fig. 9.2

The disc

Discs are found between most of the joints in the spine where the main vertebral bodies are found. The main exceptions are in the very top joints of the neck, and in the lowest part of the spine about the pelvis. The lowest disc immediately above the fused sacrum area is the point where the main part of the body hinges, and because of leverage, amounting to ¾ ton in simple toes-touching, tremendous pressure occurs in this lowest bag of jelly, the disc. This action on the disc can be demons-

137

trated by having a bag of jelly between two pieces of wood and applying pressures. (Fig. 9.3)

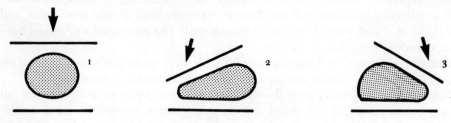

Fig. 9.3

The discs are shock absorbers of the body, analogous to hydro-elastic suspension in cars. As the body becomes older the ligaments holding the jelly in place wear, and with certain bending-forward pressures the bag may divide and the jelly push backwards on to the nerves in close proximity to the spinal cord. The further it pushes backwards, the further down the leg the pain passes. In the severest of sporting injuries the spinal cord may snap and paralysis may occur.

In any injury occuring in the sporting situation, it is vital to establish that the sportsman has normal sensation in the legs. Back pain is usually indicative of a lesser injury. If loss of sensation occurs in the legs in injured players, don't move them. Check with ambulance officers first.

Generally the younger sportsman need not worry too much about disc pain as it takes until about the age of forty to wear this region of the spine sufficiently to cause many problems. However, be cautious of any pain arising in the legs when associated with back pain. This is **nerve root pain.**

Prevention

Preventing pain before it occurs is obviously far more important than treating the afflicted sportsperson.

As eighty per cent of people will get back pain in their lives we can see a considerable number of people are not looking after themselves as well as they should. Exercises for preventing back pain concern mobility and strength.

Mobility

The small spinal joints on the sides of the vertebral bodies must be polished to maintain their integrity. The following exercises are polishing exercises and should be done on a daily basis taking only 1 to 2 minutes for each.

These exercises are certainly important at training sessions with the team, preferably done in the first quarter of an hour of training, before the body is expected to undergo the more stressful aspects of training.

1 *Neck mobility*. Neck circling works only the lower part of the neck joints and barely brings the top six vertebrae into play. There is nothing wrong with the exercise, but a better one is: with the hands behind the neck and the elbows raised, to push the fingers down the spine to below the shoulder blades. This stretches the strong neck and shoulder flexors to the front of the chest wall, and by reducing the tension here

allows the neck to move much more freely when rotated, side bent and rocked backwards and forwards later.

If one arm does not travel backwards as far as the other, this is an indication as to which side the rotations of the neck should be concentrated.

Fig. 9.4

Fig. 9.5

2 *Thoracic mobility.* The joints which attach to the ribs will be included as this exercise is performed.

Hook a stick in the elbow joints behind your back. Side rocking, turning and bending backwards can be included. The advantage of this method of exercise over others is that by raising or lowering the stick along the backbone, the level of joint movement can be selected.

3 *The lumbar spine.* The lumbar spine, or lowest part of the back with important movement, is best worked by a 'hula' action in both directions. As well as moving all the little joints, it has an important action on the disc, as well as moving the whole of the lumbar-sacral pelvis area. Again this exercise can have the level of the area of the back to be worked specified by hand placement.

Fig. 9.6

4 *Total mobility.* Hanging relaxed from an overhead bar elongates the whole spine, and certainly makes training bars worthwhile. Immediately before a game, in the pre-game warm-up situation, full overhead stretching is most useful, as most joints of the spine work; as well as the stretching having a considerable effect on heart/lung efficiency.

Strength

The back is very dependent on strength for performance in the sporting situation.

Strangely, a sportsperson is more likely to injure the back in tying bootlaces after the game than from poor action in the competitive situation. This is because the small joints previously mentioned are left unsupported by the muscles once the player relaxes after the game, then jam as the muscles take up the slack to move from the changing room.

If the muscles which support the spine are strong in the first place, then they are less likable to fatigue, and the case can be made that they will in turn assist the mechanics of the spine far better.

The spine is rather like a flagpole being held upright by guy-ropes. The guy-ropes are the muscles of the stomach, the back and the sides. Loosen a guy-rope and added stress occurs at the base of the flagpole, the lumbar spine in this case, and troubles are likely.

New Zealand athletes are generally remiss in this respect. The easy living style; over-eating and drinking, and sedentary occupations all add to slack abdominal muscles. The strain placed on the lower portions of the back is vastly increased and not well-accepted, and injury problems occur more easily.

While toes-touching has been recommended for muscle strength in the past, it is now advised against. It does nothing of value to strengthen the spine and may add to players' woes in the field of backache because of the tonnage stress placed on the unsupported back.

Strength exercises.

1 For abdominals, lie on the back with the knees bent slightly. Raise the head and shoulders off the ground, with the arms extended to the knees, and with the small of the back still on the ground hold the position. This should be held for 7 seconds at least, and repeated about twenty times per workout.

By hitting the stomach reasonably hard with the fist, any give will indicate muscle flab (fat) which should be eliminated by this exercise.

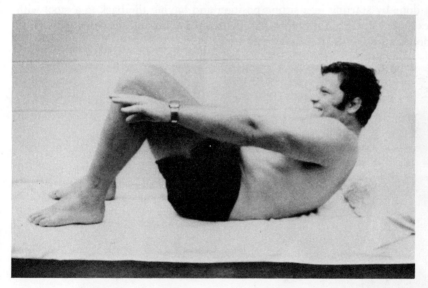

Fig. 9.7

A variation is to do the exercise with both arms one side. This builds the side flexors of the spine.

2 The back muscles themselves are fairly strong, having to hold a man upright during the day against a pressure of 32 lb per square inch. For added strength, back arches performed slowly until tired can assist (and after all the sportsperson is trying to build strength above the average).

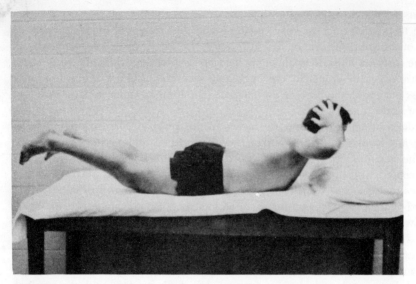

Fig. 9.8

3 The strong latisimus dorsi muscles and trapezieus muscles, which aid considerably in the working of the neck and thoracic spine, can be built up in strength by 'backward press-ups'.

This is done by starting in a sitting position and having the back to a stool with the legs extended straight out in front. Straighten the arms and raise the body. Hold the position for 7 seconds. Repeat twenty times.

Fig. 9.9

This exercise, done immediately before competition a few times, will stretch much of the structure around the shoulder, thus reinforcing the value of stretch activity.

Pushing/pulling/body placement

In rucking, scrummaging, rowing, tugs-of-war, and weightlifting, important body placement and angulation will not only aid in injury reduction but will enable a far greater improvement in performance.

Joints have a position of weakness and a position of strength. The elbow, for example, works best at a 90^0 angle, termed the 'carrying angle'. On either side of right angles the joint strength diminishes with the same load. The back is similar.

If the back can be maintained at about 45^0 with the hip, no matter the activity, then greater leverage can be made on the back with little side effect. In a rugby scrum for instance, the coach may require the forward pack to position very closely to the ground, which is fine; however, when the pushing strain is placed on the footballer, the push should be at 45^0 for maximum performance.

Weightlifters when lifting push the abdominal muscles firmly against the wide belt worn. This action is not merely to tighten the muscles to the front, but also to 'lock' the small muscles of the spine. This action allows much greater force to apply to the spine before collapse occurs. All sportsmen involved in explosive action should apply this technique of spinal support, and in fact use it in everyday activities if lifting. Few spinal problems in lifting would occur if this method of tension were employed by all.

Over a period, with correct training, and breathing with the spinal and abdominal muscles taut, breathes can be held for considerable times. The endeavour is worthwhile for increased performance alone.

Treatment of spinal problems

Treatment is varied for the spine. This is typified by the extremes of statements made by 'authorities', such as: 'All disease comes from spinal malalignments', to: 'All backs are psychological in nature'. Any practitioner with these comments to make is probably in need of academic revision.

The spine is delicate and complex. No one cause can be attributed to poor spinal hygiene, so it is important to the sportsman, especially at top levels, to ensure that any treatment taken is from the person best qualified to treat the particular condition.

If the facet joints on the sides of the spine are hypomobile (jamming), they can be freed quite easily by manipulation, which should be followed up by a specialised home programme of treatment aimed at maintaining normal mobility. Jamming is the commonest cause of back pain, thus the fact that many have been able to establish some type of reputation with little or unorthodox treatment.

The problem with manipulation is that only the affected joint should be manipulated. If the pain is in the lowest lumbar and first sacral region of the spine on one side, a common problem, then only the affected joint should be manipulated. If another joint is manipulated as well, the tissue may unduly stretch and the normal support will lead to trouble by making that joint unstable (hypermobile).

A hypermobile joint requires some form of support, such as, in extreme cases, a plaster jacket for up to six weeks, a corset, adhesive strapping or such like. Hypermobile joints are not easily righted and, left to develop, may even neccesitate surgery to fix the damaged bones.

Manipulation is graded 0–5 in intensity, 5 being very strong. Most manipulations if applied correctly will be about grade 2.

When the disc is involved, which is thankfully not too frequently, a longer period of treatment is usually required. Here, rotation manipulations are of little use and may be detrimental to the overall rehabilitation of the patient. The disc, being jelly-like, needs slow pressures, such as traction, applied to affect it.

Sometimes surgery is necessary, and this is similar to lancing a boil to let the pressure out, except that, being in the spinal cord region, it is not as easy and only a surgeon can do it, and also, infection is not apparent.

In other pathologies, such as tumours, paralysis or fractures, very special care is required and so will not be discussed in detail here. However, always be most careful of TABLETS:

1 T temperature changes or fever
2 A after a heavy blow or fall
3 B bladder, loss of control
4 L loss of sensation and feeling in arms or legs
5 E extensive or continuing pain in the back especially 4 inches above the small of
     the back or 2 inches below the hump in the neck
6 T teenage pain which comes on and off
7 S sickness and nausea

X-rays may be required in the worst conditions although they seldom show the cause of pain.

Training when injured

When injured, the sportsman **must** train harder than ever. The fit sportsman has little need to train, the injured must. Two weeks without training require ten weeks' training to regain peak fitness.

In most cases of the usual types of back pain seen, some form of training can still occur, indeed must. Swimming is an ideal form of training with an injured back. The postural muscles usually supporting the spine rest in the water, and with this, associated muscle spasm reduces, enabling painful joints to move for greater ranges, in turn easing the pain.

Most of the mobility and strength exercises described can be employed with only benefit arising.

The heart and lungs must be made to work hard, so, if possible, gentle jogging should occur fairly soon after injury, particularly if the back problem is one of loss of joint movement, the usual case.

Bed rest should only be employed in **extreme** cases of damage. It is surprising that some countries ever obtain great heights in sport with the conservative approach to back pain exhibited in their standard text books. But advice is essential before running.

If running causes pain, stop, especially if pain was present prior to activity. If the pain is noted very early in the season at the start of the training programme, lean forward to run. This common problem is caused by the lower part of the back taking some of the shock of the leg to road action on a part which has not yet been conditioned to it. The pain should reduce within ten days by forward running and if it doesn't, follow-up assessment is advised.

Heat in the forms of hot packs, microwave and infra red can be used immediately. Very seldom is soft tissue damage seen, so ice is soon dispensed with, although it can be used as first aid and will not harm the patient.

Massage has been over-rated in the past as a form of treatment, but despite being over-rated it still has an important part to play in reducing muscle spasm associated with joint damage. The massage should be deep and to the point of pain. The massage obtained in certain commercial situations is of little value physiologically.

The liniments applied can be worthwhile, particularly the hot forms. They have the effect of increasing the blood flow to the area and act as a counter-irritant. The counter-irritant effect is to give a superficial pain to replace the deep pain, although care in hot bathing after application must be taken.

In the on-field situation, the utmost care must be taken in any player having pain, paralysis, or partial loss of feeling after a direct blow is sustained. **Do not** move the athlete without medical advice if this is the case as further irreparable damage can result.

With a winded player, bear fracturing in mind and do not force the legs to the chest. Let the injured person bend his own legs, but assist in gentle head support and get the player breathing outwards to get the diagphragm working again.

Sportsmen in the seated sports such as motor racing, or those travelling distances by car, should have some form of support in the hollow of the back to help maintain a good sitting posture. Car seating is very poor with two exceptions: the Triumph Stag and the Alfa Romeo 2000 G.T.V. If you don't own one of those two cars, obtain a small pillow or folded towel and place in the small of the back to hold body shape.

Travelling exercises.

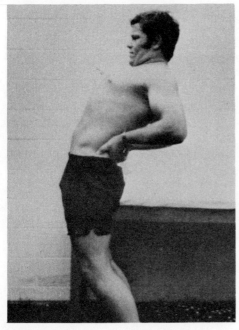

Fig. 9.10

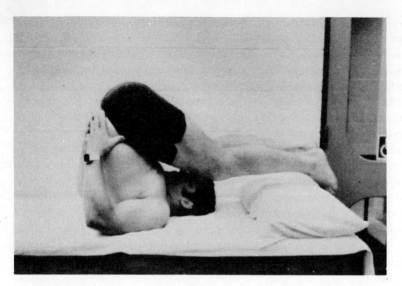

Fig. 9.11

When travelling distances by bus or car to distant sporting fixtures, alter the driving posture; this helps if you wish to arrive in some form of readiness competition wise. At stops, extend the back over the bonnet of the vehicle if possible, or failing that, over the hands supporting the small of the back. This takes the spine to one extreme, while lying flat on the back and rolling the feet over the head will take it to the other flexion extreme and increase the blood flow to the region. This will reduce muscle spasm from prolonged inactivity and psychologically assist in breaking the routine of travel.

10 Oh, my aching feet

Avoiding injuries of the feet

E. McKeown

Mrs Ellen McKeown is a Member of the New Zealand Society of Chiropodists Inc., and a part-time tutor at the New Zealand School of Chiropody, Central Institute of Technology, Lower Hutt. She has had wide experience in dealing with foot injuries incurred by sportsmen, and has written this paper specially for this book.

Professional sportsmen have become sensitive to changes in their physical well-being because modern training methods focus on a high standard of health and fitness. This concept is promoted by a team of trainers, doctors and para-medics who form a protective shield against injury. Amateur sportsmen, also striving for a competitive standard, are often handicapped by unrecognised disorders; their training sessions are usually sandwiched between occupational work-loads and family responsibilities, and preventive medicine is rarely available. In both categories, injury to the feet is quite common and in many cases need not occur.

Injury may be pertinent to a specific sport or may be due to lack of knowledge about stress factors relating to the human foot. Injuries may arise from unsuspected anatomical defects or may be related to footwear. And further, such injury may be progressive from childhood trauma to adult life, remaining unchecked and unidentified.

Avoidance of foot injury means that the sportsman must be aware of his own feet. This basic fact is ignored while following a particular fashion of sports shoe, ignored in the pressure of competition and ignored by the individual because he is reluctant to admit anything is wrong until pain stimulates his awareness and incapacity accentuates his loss of function.

In applying the principles of preventive medicine in this context, the sportsman may wish to consult the para-medic who is particularly concerned with feet. Consultation with a chiropodist/podiatrist should be included in every training schedule so that feet may be examined for anatomical defects, muscular imbalance and the effects of postural strain. The professional sportsman cannot afford to miss regular appointments with this specialist who will correct malfunction, consider the type of sports shoe suitable for a particular foot and give advice on how to combat stress and trauma.

The amateur sportsman frequently seeks assistance when his occupation and sport combine to increase the work-load on his feet. Consider the geologist who is also a harrier; the policewoman who is a netball player or the butcher who is a short distance runner. In each case, the occupation requires heavy footwear and in each case the workload is increased by the sporting activity. Deep-seated haematoma, bursitis, blisters and callouses, or just painful, burning feet are often the result of this overloading. It is important therefore, not only that the correct type of shoe is chosen for the occupation but also that sufficient cushioning is provided in the work shoe or boot to eliminate stress, and that the lacing, fit and composition of the sports shoe is adequate to combat compression and shearing stresses.

Treatment for traumatic conditions resulting from overloading may be palliative and curative. A modern therapeutic approach to specific problems lies in the use of polyethylene and silicone substances, which, as replaceable appliances, or as insoles combined with other materials, can be used to cushion the foot, to act as shock absorbers, or to redistribute the stresses.

Many athletic activities are repetitive — the jarring of the heel in joggers, the pivoting movement of the skater and the pounding of the forefoot in the runner. Ground surfaces vary, from the grass of the cricket and football fields to the bitumen of the tennis and netball courts, and to the synthetic composition of some athletic tracks. Surfaces are uneven in such sports as cross-country running, skiing and mountaineering, causing inevitable strain on seldom used muscles. All these may lead to conditions like heel spurs, stress fractures of the metatarsals, sesamoiditis and plantar fasciitis, as well as sprains and strains. In each case the importance of correct footwear, which will cushion and stabilise the foot, is clear.

It is of little use to pound the city streets in worn-out running shoes and save the new pair for the cross-country trial. It is of little value to wear low slung football boots in the interest of speed if, as sometimes happens, they are left behind on the field or result in ankle injury. And it is of little consolation to the woman golfer who changes from her high-heeled city shoes to lace-up brogues to find that she cannot complete the course because of pain in her calf muscles.

Golf is a sport which may cause harm to the younger foot. Pivoting while the epiphyses are developing may cause trauma to the great toe. Short football or cricket boots, handed down by a team-mate, may cause similar damage, while shrunken socks and stretch hose may weaken the lesser toes causing them to claw and retract. The young athlete, and those who are responsible for his training, must also be aware that overloading and the competitive urge can cause irreparable damage. Often knee and calf pains in the young person are symptomatic of conditions in the feet. Shoes must be correctly fitted and adequate room left for the growing foot.

Another condition frequently incapacitating the young sportsman is an inflamed toe with an ingrowing nail. Among the causes of this condition are inadequate trimming of the nails leaving a spicule, trauma from short or narrow shoes and an involuted nail. Once the inflammation is resolved, a nail-brace may be applied to straighten the curvature of the nail or if the condition is recurring, radical removal of the involuted portion of the nail and phenolisation of the matrix may be carried out under local analgesia by a chiropodist/podiatrist trained in this technique.

A commonsense approach to the care of the feet would eliminate many minor injuries. It is perhaps unnecessary to suggest the importance of personal hygiene, of frequent changes in socks, of letting shoes dry out completely after wear and of discarding worn insoles: yet ignoring these basic things often leads to fungus, tinea, and other infective organisms invading the skin and causing problems.

The skin of the foot may need extra care, especially between the toes or around the heels. Pre-training treatment with surgical spirit for moist areas or a prescribed powder for excessive perspiration, the use of silicone-based creams for excessive dryness around the heels, and the use of witch hazel, icepacks, or elevating of the limbs for burning and tiredness in the feet are some of the simple methods which any sportsman may adopt for foot care.

The use of hot and cold alternate foot-baths at five minute intervals will tone up the skin and make it less susceptible to soft-tissue injury. The use of strapping or bandaging for weakened structures and the importance of rest for sprains, strains and conditions like bursitis and tenosynovitis are essential for the return to good foot health. Finally, it is important to realise that there is a degree of imbalance when compensatory muscles are brought into action after injury and it is necessary to seek treatment for regaining strength and muscle tone.

Perhaps one of the worst features of injury is the fact that in some sports it is accepted as part of the game. This is negative thinking, for if modern research has resulted in the development of a style of footwear which fulfils a basic need for lightness and speed at the price of stability, and if synthetic, non-absorbent and heat-producing materials are used in its manufacture, then the player should not be content.

Avoidance of injury to the feet means therefore, that the sportsman should seek advice about foot problems, he should personally care about his feet and he should be selective in choosing the type of footwear which is suitable for his own needs and for his particular sport.

The shoe problem

R.C. Sutton

Mr Robert Sutton is a retailer of athletic footwear in Wellington and has written this paper specially for this book.

Before proceeding with this article, I feel I should qualify my being here — my qualification to write is purely and simply one of experience. From the hundred metres to the marathon, over a period of more than twenty years, with many hundreds of miles under my feet, I have experienced the inside story of feet and of shoes. Over the last few years this knowledge has broadened through coaching and retailing, where I have witnessed first hand the shoe problem as it affects the New Zealand athlete.

When we talk of shoes, we're really talking about feet — how to make those feet go and how to keep them from getting hurt. Shoes are nothing more than a go-between; a medium between the foot and the ground. Surveys have shown that two in every three runners have suffered a serious injury related to running stress. Nearly all these problems can be related to the foot — that intricate masterpiece containing twenty-six bones and a multitude of ligaments and tendons that we all tend to take for granted. Since running starts with the feet, the feet have to be cared for. In the modern running environment bare feet won't do, and any old pair of sneakers won't do: runners need specialised footwear for their special work.

For my part, I wish to discuss shoes related to the serious runner, i.e. the long distance runner, the regular jogger, the sprinter, and the other specialist shoes areas such as high jump, shot and discus. All these in turn should bear some relation to most sportsmen or women, as running forms the basic background to, and fitness build-up for, most active sports, whether rugby, rowing, netball, volleyball, etc. As basic fitness build-ups increase with intensity for many of today's sports, an ironic twist occurs — the high injury rate caused to athletes in training by unsuitable surfaces and poor footwear.

At this point it is interesting to note the current round-the-world situation relative to sport and general physical fitness. In New Zealand we have introduced 'Come Alive'; however, in the athletic world we 'came alive' about fifteen years ago because of the Snell era, and the resulting general boom in athletics and fitness created by men such as Lydiard in New Zealand and Bowerman in the U.S.A. Overseas they call it the 'running revolution'. The running population took a sudden jump and road running grew into a mature sport for men and women.

Along with the running revolution came the shoe revolution. Within a few years the interplay of supply and demand changed, making running shoes from little more than a cottage industry into a big business. However, a leading U.S. authority at a recent trade fair said on the subject of running shoes: 'While the shoes are theoretically made for running many of them are worn by people who do everything *but run*'. Yes, a new fashion was created by the running and shoe revolution and it became fashionable to wear athletic-looking shoes, bright colours, stripes and stars. This was a world wide situation which New Zealand retailers of course were quick to catch on to. However, with reference to New Zealand manufacturers the reverse of the previous quote became obvious: 'While the shoes are theoretically called running shoes most are suitable for everything *except* running'.

With the New Zealand manufacturer jumping on the band wagon numerous brands appeared on the scene; however, precious few manufacturer, if any, had even talked with runners or specialists and, while the prices were lower than imports, mainly due to the high duty rate imposed, the shoes should not have been allowed on the market labelled as running shoes, as with the bargain price came the curse of the runner — resultant injuries such as blisters, feet, ankle and knee problems.

Why then the need for specialist shoes? *Encyclopaedia Britannica* states: 'All athletes require shoes that give traction, protection, and minimum weight. The quality of shoes has improved steadily, becoming at the same time lighter, more colourful, and more specialised in purpose. Both the spiked shoes worn by runners and jumpers and the flat-soled shoes of runners and throwers have contributed to record-breaking.'

Dr Harry Hlavac, chief podiatrist at the sports clinic in San Francisco says: 'Shoes are for protection, support, traction, cushioning from the ground, balance of foot deformities and the accomodation of foot injuries. A proper shoe should provide support and cupping of the heel, firm arch support, protection of the ball of the foot and flexibility of the front sole for easy push-off. Also the upper shouldn't tear up the feet, and the total weight of the shoe shouldn't be like that of a hiking boot'.

We see, then, that the answer to the question 'Why the need for specialist shoes?' involves two items:

1 Performance of the athlete.
2 Protection from injuries.

The main objective of the athlete is to perform at his or her very best level. Today, the scene is forever changing, with new methods, techniques, running surfaces, equipment and, of course, shoes. Shoes play a major role in the performance of the athlete whether in training or racing. 100 miles or more per week is common practice these days in training, and certainly seven days a week is a regular regimen. Most of this is done on hard all-weather surfaces, tracks, roads, etc. plus grass or sand where necessary. This continual training puts the stress on the body and assistance is required in the form of good shoes, e.g. high jumpers need heel spiked shoes to eliminate the slip factor in their fast run-ups for the Fosbury Flop, hurdlers need built-up heels for the heavy landing factor of the event and so the list goes on.

Regrettably, although satisfactorily for them, the athletes who could assist with this problem, the topliners, do not have such a problem as they are on the well-known free list from notable overseas companies. The next strata of athletes, the New Zealand champions fringing on the big time, and all those below striving to do their best, are just not able to buy the shoes that they require to assist them to improve their performances or to eliminate the injury risk factor. This does not mean that the shoes are not available at all; the big cities have their supplies but these are very limited and quickly snapped up by those eager to purchase a good shoe for running or those on the fashion scene as described earlier.

So it can be seen that the athlete needs a specialist shoe just as a golfer needs a putter or a wedge.

The New Zealand athlete is indeed at a competitive disadvantage in relation to the overseas athletes and has to persevere with overseas mail orders, the very limited retail stock, the high New Zealand cost or the sub-standard (in many cases) quality of New Zealand-made shoes.

11 Prevent injury by motivation and good coaching

The skill of coaching

A.P. Freeman

During a recent trip to the U.S., Peter Stokes saw that the American approach to coaching emphasised motivation. The contentions is that good coaching motivates the athlete throughout training, resulting in reduced injuries during the training session. A player motivated is 'switched on', thinking at all times throughout training, resulting in better adaptation to unusual and potentially injurious situations. Mr A.P. (Bill) Freeman, National Coach of the New Zealand Rugby Football Union has given permission for the following papers to be reproduced here.

The game of rugby is one of the few sports that incorporates almost every natural body movement: running, dodging, pushing, pulling, kicking, catching, and passing with body contact, and it caters for all shapes, sizes and ages. Not all will play it well, but at least they will be able to go through the motions.

A great many players participating today are playing only on natural ability and are not what we call 'highly skilled players'. Do not blame the player for this, as it is only with experience that he will improve his all-round playing skill if left to his own devices.

Playing experience, coupled with natural ability, will produce a capable player, depending mainly on the amount of natural ability the player has. The process may be accelerated by a skilful coach, a man who knows *what* to advise, and, more importantly, *how* to advise.

Until recently, the success of a coach depended solely on his personality, his ability to motivate, and a little psychology sprinkled with a certain amount of rugby knowledge. With these ingredients he will certainly have a measure of success. With the advent of the National Coaching Organisation, the coach may now widen the scope of his knowledge by capitalising on the knowledge of others (the resource personnel) and by using aids. Armed with this information, the coach becomes more competent; competence brings confidence; and this in turn brings favourable response from the players.

With emphasis being placed on skill, and skill being the dominating factor, the forward unit, with the individual learning and completely understanding his positional responsibilities in all facets of the game, will contribute knowledgeably.

With evasive running, canny use of the ball, deception, and moves giving the player on the outside an advantage, the back unit (in combination with the forward unit) will complete the fifteen-man attacking machine.

If a player practises without knowing the results of his actions, improvement in his performance is unlikely.

When a ball is kicked, the kicker immediately knows whether or not it is a good kick. A player attempting a side-step or swerve will soon know if he went about it

154

the correct way. It is important for a player to know:

1 if he has made a mistake.

2 precisely where the mistake was made.

This brings us back to the coach, for his knowledge of correct technique and faults that may develop enables his players to distinguish right from wrong.

In team games it is difficult to give adequate information to each and every individual. Thus, the player who goes on improving is often the one who can best assess the results of his own actions.

If a player passes the ball to a team-mate and the potential receiver does not accept it, the passer must decide whether it was his fault or that of the receiver. Consequently, it is an important part of a coach's job to assist a player to analyse the results of his actions.

If a beginner has good players, like the All Blacks, to compare himself with, then he may be able to improve through observation. Usually he requires the help of a coach who will praise him when his form shows improvement, psychologically stimulating him to feel he has achieved a skilled movement.

With major advances being made in coaching techniques and organisation, the constant improving and updating of existing material, and work being undertaken on new projects, we are assured that coaches and players will always have the benefit of the best of information and instruction available.

The definition of a rugby coach should be the person who is prepared to learn, study all facets of the game, understand the positional responsibilities of all his players, capitalise on audio visual aids and physical training aids, and to cap it all, use all available resource personnel.

Notes for coaches

A.P. Freeman

These notes were written in 1977 for the National Training School of the New Zealand Rugby Football Union.

The secret of a successful campaign is planning. You decide who you want to reach and what you want them to do. Then you decide on the best 'tools' for the job and use them in the most effective manner.

We will cover:

Organisation

Learning

Communication

Coaching

Motivation

Leadership.

Organisation

Planning.

what — who — when — where

Where. We learn best in a comfortable environment without too many distractions.
Salesman.
1 Do you know your subject?
2 Sell a quality article.

Principles of learning

involvement — intensity — distribution
'See and remember — listen and forget.'

Teaching methods.
1 Variety of methods (do not become predictable).
2 We learn best with practical application.
3 Use of aids.
4 Keep them interested (we learn best when interested).

Communication

Selling yourself and your material.
1 Because of the development of new attitudes and social mores, special stress will
have to be laid on the skills of dialogue between coach/trainer and personnel.
'Communication' involves a knowledge of human relations, and also the attitude of the
young person to the sport.
2 From this follows the need for the coach to learn how to instruct in technicalities
with knowledge and skill, and how to impart the knowledge in such a manner that it
will be understood and accepted.
3 Another very important aspect of communication is how to plan and run
imaginative and effective training sessions, special clinics, club planning for the season involvement, etc.

Principles of coaching

1 Observation and analysis.
2 Planning.
3 Organisation.
4 Understanding how technical and knowledge skills are acquired.
5 Understanding the motivation of a rugby player.

Criteria for a good coach. Generally speaking, a coach should not be judged solely on
his grasp of technicalities and knowledge of skills but on his ability to impart such
knowledge.

Therefore he must:

1 have enthusiasm and dedication
2 understand the technical aspects
3 understand the principles of coaching
4 accept that the sport is for the participants
5 acknowledge that he himself must be coached
6 be prepared to co-opt special advice and assistance in fairness to himself and the participants.

Results.
1 Learning skills and becoming efficient takes time.
2 Don't become a perfectionist.
3 Don't blame others for your failures.
Winning isn't everything, it is the only thing!

Motivation

Training can be very tedious if the coach does not institute a planned programme of individual and group motivation. Athletes will maintain their enthusiasm, and desire to keep up their regular training, if they have gauged results.

It is of importance that the athlete understands the reasons behind every method that is designed to improve his technique and skill. Furthermore it is advantageous for him to see for himself the results of the methods in others.

Competition between individuals and between groups can be arranged in a variety of ways and will greatly stimulate morale and enthusiasm.

Creativity. There is eloquence in action, no matter what words we speak.

Sometimes we create our own problems by stimulating the world around us without knowing what we're doing.

Streams of information pour into the brain through the eyes and ears.

If you watch a dramatic scene with total attention, you afterwards recall parts of the scene which you had not consciously taken in.

Players form their own opinions about their coaches and this influences how much advice they follow.

The success of the player often depends on the attitude of the coach.

The coach lacks time to simply listen.

Boredom may be created by coaches' giving lessons that are too complicated for the individual to understand.

You can never afford to stop learning.

If it is right, do it boldly; if it is wrong, leave it alone.

You make a great many mistakes and will probably make a good many more, but you will always learn something from them.

Leadership

Leadership is the ability to direct people, but more importantly to have those people so directed that they accept it.

The difference between the group and the leader is not so much lack of knowledge, but rather lack of will. Unless you maintain discipline, and unless you enforce it in an accepted manner, you are a potential failure at your job. The effect you have on everybody should be: 'I don't know how I will feel tomorrow but right now I could take on the world'.

A leader is pictured as an aggressive, intelligent human being who determines objectives, organises people and selects methods and instruments for implementation. He makes vital decisions and co-ordinates action.

The leader unifies his followers for co-operative action in order to achieve his objectives. He asserts himself and makes others aware of this confidence in himself; he feels he could do the job better than anyone else, knowing what he wants and how to do it.

The possession of an abundance of energy or enthusiasm is a definite asset for the person who sets his sights on the top.

The effective leader must actually experience the weight and loneliness of leadership; a decision without responsibility is easy to make.

Leaders create confidence, devotion and respect, and having produced such attitudes, foster continued enlargement of them, so that the power of leadership grows with the passing of time.

The qualities for successful leadership involve intellectual capacity, self-significance, vitality, training, experience, reputation and loyalty, plus respecting the dignity of others.

12 That first aid box

Suggested contents of a first aid box

P.G. Stokes

type	size	description	order no.	amount	uses
Plasters					
Elastoplast	1" X 1·6 yd	Stretch, brown	1004	2	Taping fingers, thumbs
Elastoplast bandage	4" X 3 yd	Elastic, adhesive	1003	2	Taping knees
	3" X 3 yd		1002	3	Taping ankles, knees, shoulders
	2" X 3 yd		10025	2	Taping small ankles, wrists
	2½" X 3 yd			1	Taping small ankles, wrists
Leukoplast	1" X 10 yd	Zinc oxide, non-stretch	1627	3	Taping split boots, artificial ligaments, keeping socks up, head bands (waterproof)
Elastoplast	Selective		4554	1	Blisters, painful skin areas, grass burns, etc.
Cooling agents for acute injuries					
Ice	Plenty	Best carried in a Thermos flask		1	Freezing acute muscle, joint, ligament injuries—provided skin is not broken
Ethyl chloride	100 ml	Spray liquid		1	Do not place ice and slicker pads directly on to skin—place in damp towel
Slicker pad	2" X 4"	Cold pack		1	
Liniments					
Radion 'B'	100 g	Cream tube		3	Pre-game massage cream — mild reaction on skin
Finalgon	50 g	Cream tube		1	Pre-game massage cream — strong reaction on skin *N.B. read instructions*
Finalgon	20 g	Ointment tube		1	Pre-game massage ointment, very strong reaction *N.B. read instructions*
Lin-menthol-sal and Eucalyptus	½ litre	Liquid		1	Pre-game massage liquid. Mild reaction but leaves oil layer over skin. Also helps clear nasal passages by odour given off. Easily obtained
Antiseptics/disinfectants					
Savlon solution	Small bottle	Liquid		1	For cleaning of grass burns, grazes, wounds, prior to dry dressing

Item	Size	Type	Qty	Usage
Acriflavine	Small bottle	Liquid	1	Application following cleaning of area with Savlon and when not requiring further treatment or a dry dressing
Neosporin	7·5 g	Antibiotic powder	1 / On prescription	This is a restricted drug and does necessitate a prescription from club's doctor. Apply to grazed area
Dry dressings				
Telfa	2" X 3"	Sterile, pad-type	1 box / 6017	Good following cleaning by Savlon of grass burns, especially under clothes.
	4" X 3"	Sterile, adhesive edges	7643	Discard and replace regularly
Bandages				
Crepe	3"	Elastic, non-adhesive	2	For pressurising joints, muscles following sprain, strain, kick and other injury
	4"		2	
	6"		2	
Extra				
Aspro or Disprin	1 pkt, small	Relief of pain	1	May help ease pain following an acute injury
Sling	Large	Triangular cloth	2	Will help immobilise/rest an acute shoulder or upper limb injury. Also handy in case of clavicle fracture
Scissors	Medium		1	Cutting tapes before and after application. Many uses
Soap	Large	Lather	1	Prevents painful feet in boot on hard grounds and good for washing
Laces	Long	Rugby boot type	2	Good for boots and socks ties and saves sticking plaster
Vicks	Small jar	Jelly	1	Helps clear nasal passages prior to game
Vaseline	3 lb tin	Jelly	1	Place about exposed areas to help prevent grass burns, etc.
Cotton wool	4 oz	Small roll	1	To assist cleaning with Savlon solution of small grazes, grass burns, small wounds, etc.
Towel (clean)	12" X 18"	Small hand towel	1	Keep clean for the purpose of cleaning, in case ice pack required — do not use with liniment N.B. Do not use during the game for cleaning faces, etc.
Towel	12" X 24"	Large	1	Team to clean hands on, prior to taking the field
Emergency gear				
Johnsons' 'Resusitube Airway' (special instructions required)				For emergency only. If player is unconscious and airway appears restricted N.B. read instructions
Teeth divider	For epileptic fit			To keep the teeth separated to prevent epileptic from biting tongue

Liniments in sport

P.G. Stokes

The effects of counter-irritants (liniments) are extremely problematic in relation to sport and sportsmen.

Liniments on the market today vary considerably in the way in which they achieve results. One question that does arise is: 'Is it the liniment or is it the massage when applying the liniment, that is of value?'

Liniments contain large amounts of oil of camphor, turpentine, oil of pine, menthol-salicylate and capsium, plus many additives. They may be presented in liquid, cream, ointment or powder form. Some of the newer ointments contain newly-developed drugs which penetrate the skin into the deeper tissues. Again, it is debatable as to how far penetration of these applications goes, and what the exact subsequent effects are.

As stated by B. Savage, M.Sc., M.C.S.P. (*Practical Electrotherapy for Physiotherapists*, Faber and Faber, London, 1960): 'The mechanism by which counter-irritation is produced is uncertain. It was once assumed that a superficial vasodilation produced a deep depletion, but the work of Harris has shown this to be unfounded. Further, the phenomenon was described as due to an "axon reflex" producing a vasodilation as a result of sensory skin stimulation, but this again has been practically disproved. Nevertheless as a practical phenomenon it remains that a superficial dilation does help in combating pain due to deep congestion. This may be produced by various means.'

One definite effect of liniments in cream or liquid form, containing a thick oily base, is that treated skin which is exposed to considerable air movement (or in other words is uncovered whilst athletes are actually participating in their sport) will prevent loss of body (surface) heat. This means that the oily layer offers insulation, thereby reducing heat transfer loss.

This method of maintaining body heat (or preventing the loss of body heat) is used by long-distance swimmers, and should be applied to more sporting activities especially rugby and cycling, and other sports where sportsmen participate in low temperatures and high velocity winds.

The psychological effects of liniments are important too. By tradition, athletes knew that their fathers used them prior to performing, and their fathers before them, and so on.

The ease of mind that comes from the application of liniments, and the associated smell when applied to the anatomy prior to activity, is all-important to the athlete. The same psychological effect is induced by massage immediately prior to an event or game.

Other reading

Rugby World magazine. Feb. 1977, pp. 42–43.
Williams. *Injuries in Rugby Football and Other Team Sports*. Dublin: Green and Co. (16 Clare St, Dublin 2.)

13 Massage techniques for the sportsman

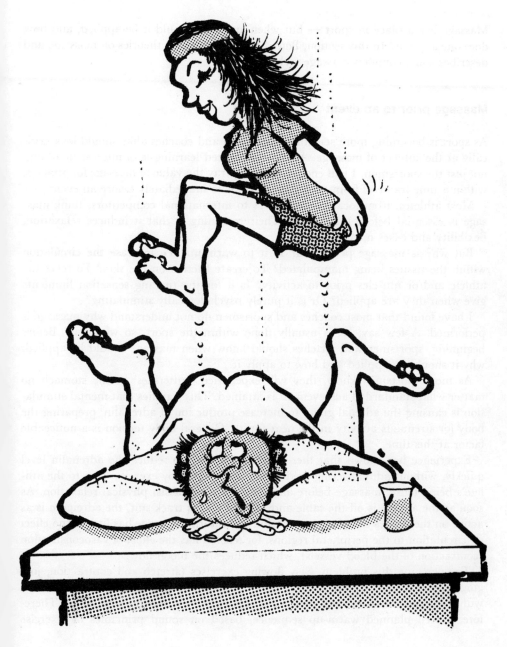

Massage techniques

P.G. Stokes

Massage has a place in sport — but when and why should it be applied, and how does one apply it? In this section, Peter Stokes outlines his theories on massage, and describes some common massage techniques.

Massage prior to an event

As sport is becoming more scientific, sportsmen and coaches alike should look critically at the subject of massage. As more advanced learning is of interest to all and not just the sportsman, I will endeavour to portray the value of massage for athletes, within a time frame of from twelve hours prior to immediately before an event.

Most athletes, from local grade players to international competitors, think massage is essential before their event. Their reasoning is that it induces relaxation, flexibility and eases mental tension.

But why is massage performed? Is it to warm-up? To increase the circulation within the tissues being manipulated? To create friction on the skin? To relax the athlete and/or muscles prior to activity? Is it for the tingling sensation liniments give when they are applied? Or is it purely psychologically stimulating?

I have found that most coaches and sportsmen do not understand why massage is performed. A few say: 'It is usually done within the sport, so we do it.' Before beginning, sportsmen and coaches should know when massage should be applied, why it should be applied and how to apply it.

As most sportsmen know, they will experience 'butterflies' in the stomach no matter what standard of achievement is attained. This signifies that mental stimulation is causing the adrenal gland to increase production of adrenalin, preparing the body for strenuous activity in the near future. General body tension is a noticeable factor at this time.

Experience has shown that there is only one way to reduce the adrenalin level quickly, without administering medication, and that is by exercise. Due to the athlete's being tense, massage before an event will never assist physical relaxation. As soon as the athlete is off the table and has put on his track suit, the adrenalin is as active on the tissues as before and tension will return. Massage has little or no effect on circulation to the peripheral regions, for tension has the effect of vasoconstriction (contraction of the blood vessels), which reduces the blood flow.

To overcome this problem, easy flowing exercises (stretch and contraction, jogging, isometric muscle contractions, etc.), designed to create a simple 'pump' action within the muscle tissue, will produce an increase in peripheral circulation. Therefore, a well planned warm-up sequence, based on sound principles of 'exercise physiology', is of more value immediately prior to an event. Certainly, massage, whether it be percussions or the long sweeping stokes of effleurage, does create friction and thereby generates heat, though this is lost very quickly.

An important effect of massage immediately prior to an event is its psychological benefit. The athlete on the table is thinking: 'It feels good — therefore it must be doing good.' The liniment is irritating and the smell associated with it stimulates his ego — somebody is going out of their way for him, assisting him, preparing him for a win.

For these reasons, immediate pre-event massage may have merit in top-level competition, for it is at this time that an athlete requires a little subconscious and conscious stimulus and assurance. By receiving massage at this time, the athlete is psychologically assisted to achieve his best. The adrenalin, still circulating in excess, is needed, and a better result will be attained provided the athlete is mentally prepared to his own requirements. His coach will know the best way to achieve this conscious and subconscious stimulation.

After the event

Massaging following the event is of more value therapeutically. When fatigue levels rise, resulting in increased lactic acid and carbon dioxide retention within the cells and tissue, massage by the coach is logical, provided there is *no acute injury*.[1]

Massage at this time, when all physical and mental tensions have gone, assists in the removal of waste products.

Effects of massage on an athlete at rest (*after the event or 48 hours before*)

Although various massage techniques produce slightly different effects, only the overall effects need be considered, as a massage would rarely, if ever, be confined to the use of one technique.

1 The sensory nerve-endings in the skin may be stimulated or sedated, the latter method assiting both local and general relaxation.

2 A local hyperaemic effect may be produced, either directly through the stimulation of sensory nerve-endings, or indirectly through slight cellular damage leading to the liberation of H-substance (H – hystermine).

Both of these effects result in arteriole dilation.

3 Venous and lymphatic return is given mechanical assistance by alternate pressure and relaxation.

4 The skin and subcutaneous tissue are moved. This has a stretching and softening effect, particularly on fibrous tissue.

The skin

The depth of the skin is no more than three-sixteenths of an inch (on the eyelids, less than two-thousandths of an inch). The skin contributes to body health and has its special functions:

1 It is almost waterproof and covers the body to prevent dehydration.

2 It has receptors — nerve-endings — which receive sensory stimuli from the environment. These receptors create nerve impulses which are transmitted to the brain. The impulses are set off by pressure, changes in temperature and tissue damage, and produce sensations of touch, warmth, cold and pain, as well as an awareness of comfort or discomfort.

3 It regulates body temperature.

4 It is a barrier against external injury and disease.

Within the skin and subcutaneous layers there are nerve-endings, small blood vessels, hair follicles and roots, sweat glands, sebaceous or oil-producing glands which give the skin its softness and pliancy, and fat globules.

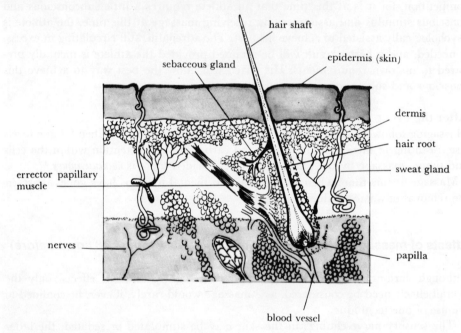

Fig. 13.1 Transverse section of the skin

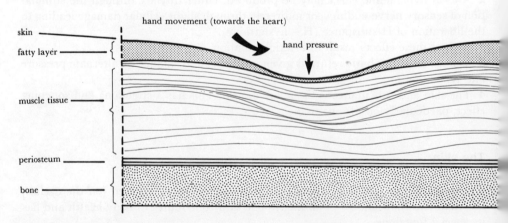

Fig. 13.2 Diagrammatic representation, showing a transverse section of tissue layers and how they are compressed by massage

Positioning of the athlete for massage

The athlete should be positioned for the convenience of the physiotherapist/masseur/coach, between hip and chest level. The physiotherapist need not bend excessively to perform efficiently the various techniques. Position comfortably the limb to be massaged, so that it is relaxed.

Prior to performing the technique chosen, check the skin for abrasions, for massage may be contra-indicated (see below). If any form of dermatitis or skin changes from previous massages are observed, discontinue.

If the operator is to use a counter-irritant (liniment), select one appropriate for the condition or occasion and apply it to the skin. Select your technique and (as many sportsmen say) carry on 'slapping' and 'tickling'.

Contra-indications to massage
Never use massage over:
 1 Sensitive skin.
 2 Dermatitis (inflammatory conditions of the skin).
 3 Open wounds or sores.
 4 Sunburn.
 5 Extremely hairy limbs or torso.
 6 Necrosed or damaged skin (blisters).
 7 Immediate acute haematomas.
 8 Immediate joint injuries (strains/sprains).
 9 Immediate muscle tears or strains.
10 Immediate acute ligamentus injuries.

Common massage techniques

Effleurage
1 *Single-handed.*

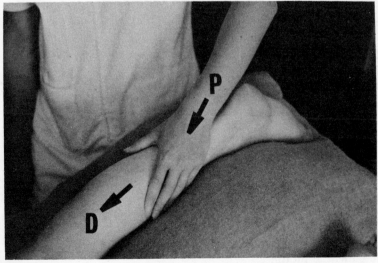

Fig. 13.3

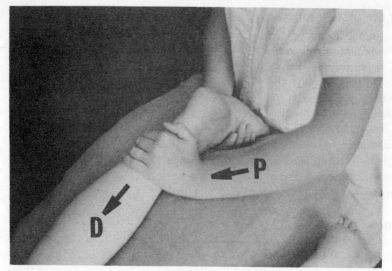

Fig. 13.4

P — Pressure application via the operator.
D — The direction of movement of the operator's hands.

Description. This technique uses a long flowing action commencing with the palm of the hand at the heel, flowing up the leg to behind the knee or, if required further, to the bottom. The amount of pressure applied by the operator should be sufficient for the action to remain comfortable to the patient at all times, and for the skin not to be pinched.

2 *Double-handed.*

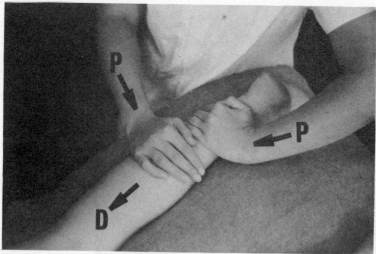

Fig. 13.5

Description. This double-handed method is an alternative to the single-handed methods. It also commences, this time using the palm of both hands, at the heel, and flows up to behind the knee or beyond, if required. The pressure should remain comfortable to the patient at all times.

168

Kneading

1 *Single-handed.*

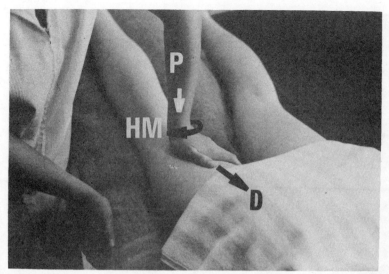

Fig. 13.6

P — Pressure application via the operator.
D — The direction of movement.
HM — Hand and arm movement of the operator.

Description. The pressure applied by the operator is at right angles to the tissue, with a steady applied action. The overall direction of the hand is from distal to proximal, yet local application and hand movement is in steady concentric circles with even pressure from the fingers and the heel of the hand.

2 *Double-handed.*

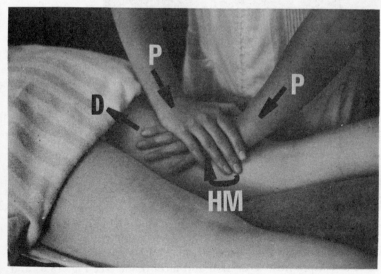

Fig. 13.7

Description. (See description of single-handed kneading.)

Skin rolling
(Fig. 13.8) Starting position of the hands and fingers.

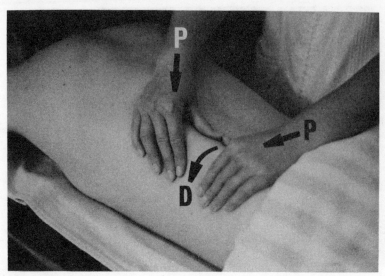

Fig. 13.8

P — Pressure of the hand, thumb and index finger during application by the operator.

D — The direction of movement of both hands.

(Fig. 13.9) The technique in action, down the side of the chest and trunk.

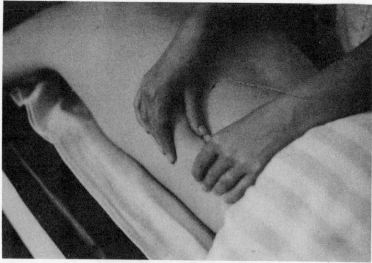

Fig. 13.9

Description. This technique is used on larger areas, such as the back, where the operator may be able to clasp a little loose skin and fatty tissue (see Fig. 13.8) and then by steady applied pressure via the fingers and thumbs, run off down the side to complete the movement.

Picking up

1 *Single-handed.*

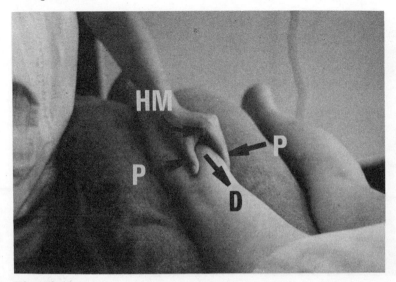

Fig. 13.10

2 *Double-handed.*

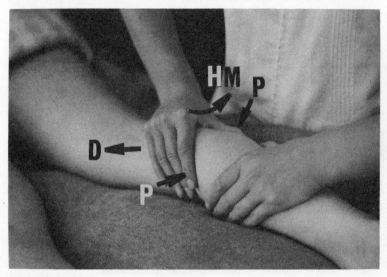

Fig. 13.11

P — Pressure applied to the tissues by the fingers and thumb (slight squeezing).

D — Direction of overall hand movement.

HM — Hand movement when steady pressure is applied via the fingers and thumb.

Description. The thumb and fingers gently squeeze the tissue at the same time as the hand is raised, lifting the bulky tissue beneath. This is repeated continually until the desired level is reached.

171

Percussion

1 *Hacking*.

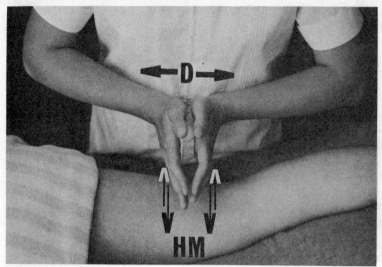

Fig. 13.12

D — Direction of the hands, moving backwards and forwards.

HM — The movement of the individual hands and fingers.

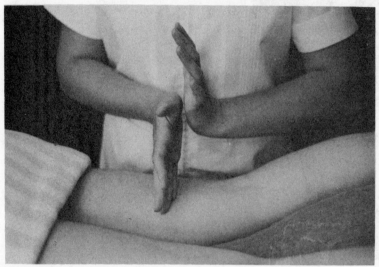

Fig. 13.13

Description. This technique is used to apply quick, steady pressure to the tissues on any part of the body. Fig. 13.12 shows the starting position, with wrists at right angles. Fig. 13.13 shows the alternate action of right and left hand and fingers.

172

2 *Clapping*.

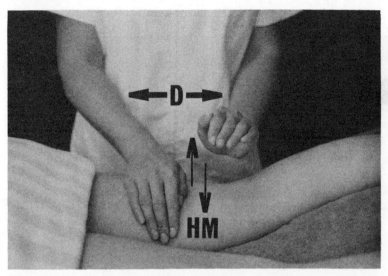

Fig. 13.14
D   — Direction of the hands, moving backwards and forwards.
HM — The movements of the individual hands and fingers.

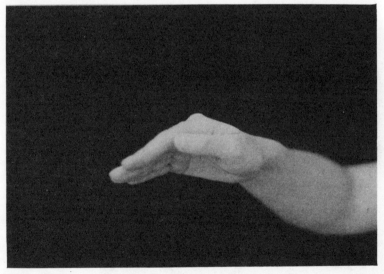

Fig. 13.15

Description. The hand is held in a cupped position (see Fig. 13.15). The hand movements are as for hacking: alternatively clapping the tissues. The hands are continually moving up and down the tissue being worked.

Frictions

1 *Single-handed*.

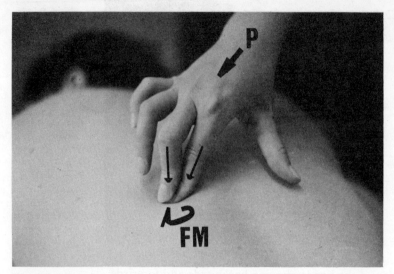

Fig. 13.16

2 *Double-handed*.

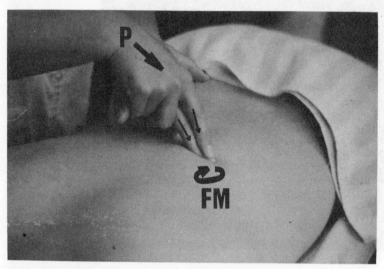

Fig. 13.17

P   — Pressure is applied locally via the tips of the fingers.

FM — Finger movements in concentric circles.

Description. The movement of the fingers is in concentric circles on a local area on the skin. These concentric movements (circles) are no larger than a ten cent piece.

174

References

[1]Stokes, P.G. (1973). *Rugby and Sports Medicine*. Wellington: Alistair Taylor Publishing Ltd.

Prevention rather than cure

K.S. Hay

K.S. Hay is an executive officer in the Safety Division of the Accident Compensation Commission. The Commission have kindly allowed the following paper to be included in this book.

The Battle of Waterloo may have been figuratively won on the playing fields of Eton, but for many New Zealanders the results of playing sport resemble a genuine and re-occurring battle casualty list. Sport may well produce a sound mind, but in an increasing number of cases it is definitely not resulting in sound bodies — a fact reflected in New Zealand's sports accident rate which is currently rising in excess of the country's population growth. From figures available, authorities are now predicting that an annual ratio of 135 New Zealanders out of every 100 000 will enter hospital for a variety of sports injuries. The impact of this figure on the community is only appreciated when compared to the fact that sixty New Zealanders out of every 100 000 will receive hospital treatment as a result of industrial accidents, a fact which can be cynically accepted as an indication that safe working practice is more readily acceptable to the working community than safety in sport.

It has become somewhat of a cliché to state that New Zealand is a nation of sportsmen and women, and sporting administrators. It is an historic and accepted fact that sport plays a major role in our community life. However, there have been changes. Attitudes towards physical fitness have become steadily more scientific and attitudes towards sport increasingly expert and professional at all levels. It can also be claimed with a strong degree of justification that many individual sportsmen and women display a decreasing and alarming lack of concern for their own safety and that of others on the field. High degrees of physical fitness have tended to produce a sense of euphoria towards safety and injury. A deeply instilled psychological approach towards sport has also had its effect on community attitudes towards the entire concept of sports injury and safety.

An Accident Compensation Commission survey indicated that during a single week in late winter 1976, 10·4 per cent of all accident patients treated by general practitioners were injured while playing some form of sport. The actual figure would have been probably higher as some of the accidents at home and school resulted from some form of sport.

Of those treated, 51 per cent were wage earners, 29·3 per cent school students and 9·4 per cent were housewives. The major causes were over-exertion and strenuous movement, falls and being struck by an object. The results were equally varied and included lacerations, sprains and back injuries.

Apart from the clinical aspects of sports injuries, the effects in terms of man-hours lost, economic loss, personal pain and discomfort, exact a continually high toll from the community. It is equally apparent that without a far-reaching and concerted attempt to examine the causes and formulate safeguards, these effects will quite simply became increasingly complicated and traumatic.

Sportsmen and women in other countries are faced with a similar dilemma. Many are covered by a variety of insurance and rehabilitation schemes, but no other society is covered as comprehensively as New Zealand. No other community possesses an accident compensation scheme which embraces not only the concept of adequate and prompt compensation for all cases of personal injury by accident but also the twin objectives of safety education and rehabilitation.

The Accident Compensation system has been in existence for four years. During that time, it has assisted in an innovative approach to safety and rehabilitation never before seen in New Zealand. The problem of personal injury through accident, described as 'one of the most disastrous incidents of social progress', will ultimately be overcome by a co-ordinated, cohesive approach. The Commission's role is largely educational and advisory, making any evaluation of success in the field extremely difficult. But a continuation of its programmes, either in isolation or in co-operation with sporting administrations and organisations, will undoubtedly result in the long term in changed attitudes and an increased awareness that safety requires motivation, application, constant example and increasing follow-through.

The implementation of this combined approach to dealing with sports injuries is however complicated by two factors. One, referred to during a symposium on sport and injury organised by the Irish Rugby Football Union in 1975, crystalises the predicament faced by all those directly concerned with the problem: 'No matter how stringent the rules or how strictly they are imposed, certain team games carry risks which cannot easily be circumnavigated. Nor is it desirable to avoid all risks and so emasculate the particular sport'....

The second factor is that each individual sport and recreation has an equally individual, often unique, hazard and safety requirement. The sole unifying factor is those injuries of a characteristic type and nature, frequency and severity which run like a thread throughout every type of sporting activity and recreation. In all cases, the opportunity for the 'non-safe' condition arises. Some injuries can even be described as virtually 'unpreventable', occurring even when the activity is being played in ideal conditions and under careful supervision.

Neither set of circumstances should prevent injury from remaining as the prime issue.

At the administrative level, rules should be framed in order to provide a controlled situation from which a proportion of risks have been excluded. Control at this level is indirect since it can only indicate what may, or may not, be done. It cannot physically prevent injury.

Direct control is provided by the umpire, the referee or the adjudicator, who can impose immediate sanctions as necessary. An effective deterrent can be provided by their presence and handling.

Finally, the most effective control of injury lies in the hands of the actual participant. The entire question of moulding and directly affecting the attitudes of all three groups remain with the instructor, the coach and team leader. These groups have the responsibility to promote fitness for the individual amongst players; to maintain high standards in equipment and clothing; to emphasise the strong need for first aid training for all involved in the sport and, above all, to press the continuing need for common sense and a practical attitude to the sport.

The Accident Compensation Act 1972 emphasises that the Commission must play a major co-ordinating role in 'all areas where accidents are likely to occur'.

Towards this end, the Commission is anxious to see the interdependence of all the agencies, organisations and groups involved. This attitude has grown during the past decade to the stage where sports medicine has assumed the role of a major clinical discipline within the concept of community health. The Commission's teams of trained safety advisors and specialists, at head office and throughout the various regions, continue to promote, inform and initiate. In addition, rehabilitation of the accident victim demands continued attention. Its importance is underlined by the fact that twelve months ago, eighteen A.C.C. liaison officers were assisting the rehabilitation of 1369 claimants. Currently, thirty-three officers are handling a caseload of 3000 cases. The figures reflect the extent of a complex situation, and indicate the effects of the Commission's responsibilities in this area.

The central policy of accident compensation also continues to develop. An umbrella of comprehensive, adequate and prompt compensation for every person in New Zealand regardless of how and when the accident occurred remains in its infancy. The schemes are in a continuing process of reassessment and re-examination especially those affecting sportsmen and women. For those involved in non-work accidents, costs involved in the immediate removal for treatment can be claimed, but there is no compensation for loss of earnings in the first week. If the incapacity lasts for more than one week, A.C.C. form C1 should be completed and sent to the nearest State Insurance Office together with a medical certificate.

The accident compensation scheme is justifiably regarded as one of the most advanced items of social legislation to be introduced in New Zealand. Its attitude to compensation treats the security and well-being of the individual as a matter of priority. The progress made on the associated questions of rehabilitation and safety in all areas of community life has been equally far-reaching. But this is not static policy. At its foundation lies a flexible approach towards the welfare of the indi-vidual, with its emphasis on prevention rather than cure, motivating rather than merely directing.

It might be appropriate to end these general remarks with a comment made by the Commission at the beginning of its operations:

'New Zealand's boldness in establishing so comprehensive a scheme, without the benefit of precendent elsewhere, must be matched by a willingness to keep the scheme under scrutiny so as to ensure that not only are the original objectives maintained, but also that we are prepared to examine and learn from our common example ... the willingness of the Commission to impart information should there-fore be reciprocated by the willingness of the public to offer its views.'

Four years later (1978), this philosphy continues. Its effects on the community are already being felt, but it is equally imperative that they should continue.

15 Champions of today and tomorrow

Eureka! That Gold

R. Gillespie

Ross Gillespie, MBE, who wrote the following paper specially for this book, played hockey for New Zealand from 1958–64, was the New Zealand National Representative Coach from 1971–76, and has been on the New Zealand Hockey Association's management committee since 1970.

The New Zealand Olympic hockey team at Montreal, 1976

Olympic record	1956	Melbourne	sixth
	1960	Rome	fifth
	1964	Tokyo	seventh
	1968	Mexico City	seventh
	1972	Munich	ninth
	1976	Montreal	first
World Cup record	1973	Amsterdam	seventh
	1974	Kuala Lumpur	seventh

(*left to right*)

Back row: **P. Ackerley, A. McIntyre, B. Maister, G. Dayman, J. Christensen, A. Ineson, E. Wilson**

Middle row: **N. McLeod, J. Archibald, R. Patel, T. Palmer** (*manager*)**, R. Gillespie** (*coach*)**, P. Stokes** (*physiotherapist*)

Front row: **S. Maister, A. Borren, W. Parkin, A. Chesney, M. Patel, T. Manning**

181

Words from the coach

'*Friday, 30 July 1976*: Hockey team has shock win in Final. New Zealand won the Hockey Gold Medal today in the upset win of the Montreal Olympics. The New Zealanders, who were not expected to make the semi-finals, scored a 1-0 win over Australia in today's final.'

These were typical of newspaper headlines throughout the country after that eventful day. Was it such a shock win?

Admittedly, when we left the country not many gave us a chance of making the semi-finals, but within the squad we had a wealth of experience, ability and determination to make this our Olympics.

Our success should serve as an inspiration, not only to future hockey teams, but to all New Zealand competitors, no matter what sport, that even in this age of semi-professionalism it is possible for a minor amateur code to overcome all the difficulties, lack of finance, poor facilities, limited public support and still come out on top.

New Zealand's introduction to international tournament.hockey was at the Melbourne Olympics, 1956. Up until this time our international experience had been games against Australia and India, a far cry from hard tournament hockey. In 1956 our team finished a very creditable sixth, but more importantly, the players returned home enthused with their foray into the Olympics, and this enthusiasm spread throughout the hockey community and established the mystical aura that only the Olympics can generate. Now young players had something to strive for.

Over the next twelve years New Zealand competed at Rome in 1960, Tokyo in 1964, Mexico in 1968; our best placing being a fifth at Rome. 'Always a hard team to beat,' 'played well but unlucky', 'good sports', 'lacked the necessary finish', 'a very popular side both on and off the field — but *No Gold*!' These were typical of comments on the New Zealand teams' performance in those years. However, the winds of change were blowing even if they were just a gentle breath at this stage.

In 1971, the N.Z.H.A. (New Zealand Hockey Association), through the generosity of the Rothmans Sports Foundation, appointed a full-time national coach, Ernie Barnes, an ex-New Zealand player and a sound coach with the personality to really get the message across on the teaching of basics. So for the first time coaching was standardised throughout the country and players became more aware of the necessity to spend session after session on mastering the basic skills. These players then filtered through the system: Hatch Cup, high school first elevens, Colts teams, provincial sides, national coaching schools and finally into national teams. Obviously this was supplemented to a great degree by the efforts of many enthusiastic provincial coaches at all levels. New Zealand now had players whose basic skills were up with the best in the world.

At the Mexico Olympics, 1968, New Zealand once again performed with distinction, but I think all were disappointed that we still were just not good enough to break into the top four.

We were most impressed with the performance of the rowers who had proved that, by adopting a more professional, planned and scientific approach, it was possible for dedicated weekend sportsmen to hit the big time. We had players with the skill, but compared to the European and Asian teams we were sadly lacking in two areas, namely international experience and physical conditioning. Unlike the rowers we were inclined to let our finances or lack of them dictate our four year build-up programme.

Consequently, prior to Munich the thing uppermost in administrators' minds was how to qualify for the games without too much expense to the average hockey player, for all were most conscious of our modest results to date at the Olympic level. Qualify we did, at an Asian tournament in Singapore, 1971, when we finished second to India, but this was not sufficient exposure at the international level, and we paid the penalty at Munich with another mediocre result.

Back home again, same noises, same excuses, but this time we were able to convince the administration that we did have the ability to do better, if more thought was put into the preparation of our team over the next four years. The N.Z.H.A., in conjunction with the coach, came up with a four year plan, in my opinion, the biggest breakthrough to date. Now we were serious about our intent, players knew what was required of them, associations and supporters knew of the financial commitment. So detailed planning for the next four years was set in motion.

We competed at the World Cup, Amsterdam, 1973; the International Tournament Christchurch, 1974; the World Cup Kuala Lumpur, 1975; the test series, Canada and India, 1975. At the same time we continued with our coaching schools on the domestic scene. Improvement was steady, if not spectacular; our players were now more confident in their ability and more familiar with the differing styles of play from the other countries.

Although we still adhered to our basic 5–3–2 formation, we were developing the individual flexibility within this pattern to enable us to exploit different styles of play, especially the European soccer-orientated approach. Our strength as always was a very solid orthodox assembled defence. Now, with the added confidence in individual ability plus the encouragement to channel natural flair in to our attacking play, we were a much more competitive team. In most games we were now creating more opportunities than our opponents whilst still retaining control of the game. All that was needed now was to a chance capitalise on these strengths.

This meant much more work, and emphasis on scoring goals both in field play and from corners. Our percentage of success in this department was still well below that of our European counterparts, but was improving with continued practice. At the completion of the test series against India, 1975, the team was playing some of the best hockey I have seen from a New Zealand side, and I was quietly confident that we had a good chance of making the semi-finals in Montreal.

My only reservation on this forecast was fitness. We had, in our travels, amassed a wealth of experience in terms of games played, but we had also noticed just how much more thoroughly other sides were prepared for these energy-sapping tournaments. All teams except New Zealand included in their squad a manager, coach, doctor or physiotherapist, depending on the numbers allowed at that tournament. Once again this demonstrated our casual Kiwi do-it-yourself approach in this important area. At most tournaments we were reduced to bludgeoning assistance from other teams or accepting the organisers' doctor or physio, which was far from satisfactory.

All hockey tournaments are an endurance contest, requiring players to be at peak fitness for ten days, often playing seven matches in that period. Our past performances had highlighted our lack of preparation. At most tournaments we started well, but faltered badly in the middle stages of the contest, due either to lack of training or the wrong type of training. Past New Zealand teams had used the expertise of qualified trainers, but only in a very limited manner and certainly in a way secondary to the actual hockey coaching. Prior to Munich, the selectors acquired the services of Sam Lewis of rowing fame. Sam set out training schedules for the players, at the same time keeping a check on individual progress through a series of specific tests. As well as the actual training programme, he was also able to bring home to the players on the few occasions we could get together that this type of training was essential at international level if we were to compete with any serious intent. Acceptance was slow by some, as for years their training had been either an individual commitment or through a coach not trained in physical conditioning. But at successive tournaments, especially Kuala Lumpur, 1975, the message got through to all players that we were being left behind by these other superbly fit and prepared sides. Obviously our physical preparation was suspect — not so much the programme, but the quality of effort by individuals in actually doing the work contained in that programme. Many of our players did not realise just how professional hockey is at this level, nor did they realise the personal sacrifice necessary to be a true international. Those were comments from my report at Kuala Lumpur, along with the recommendation that we appoint a suitably qualified trainer to be responsible for the fitness of the Olympic squad.

Brian Maunsell, ex-N.Z. hockey player, and Senior Lecturer in the department of physical education at Palmerston North Teachers College, accepted the appointment, and after discussions with myself on programmes and on my requirements launched himself with all his customary enthusiasm into this task. Players were each given a day-by-day schedule, and testing was done in groups on a regular basis, to check on individual progress and to maintain the momentum of the whole programme — peak fitness by July 1976 in Montreal. The success of the programme was evident in our performance at Montreal; we achieved all the plateaus in the programme whilst steadily improving, so that by the semi-finals we were, along with Australia, without a double the fittest sides in Montreal. We were forced into extra time in two vital games against Spain and Holland and on both occasions we won out on physical fitness.

I feel that in the past there has been a reluctance on the part of many coaches, not just in hockey, to avail themselves of the scientific knowledge on human performance that is now available. Hockey, with its success at Montreal, has proved beyond all doubt that such a marriage is possible, and to ignore this is to relegate one's sport to the also-rans. We have the individual ability, the scientific expertise and above all the enthusiastic amateur approach with which not too many countries are familiar any more.

I have endeavoured in this section to illustrate that success is not immediate. I was fortunate that the N.Z.H.A. perservered with my appointment as coach for that five year period 1971–1976, because the learning process never ceases, and the knowledge I gained in my playing career, plus my experiences whilst coaching, all contributed to my performance as a coach.

Coaching team sports is a difficult art, and in spite of all that has been written on the subject it still remains a very personal ability. The approach depends very largely on the coach's personality. I have found that flexibility, team consensus, commonsense, and above all sincerity, go a long way towards producing a successful team.

So haere ra (farewell) Montreal — haere mai (welcome) Moscow. The next challenge is there and preparations are in hand, with the certainty that standards will continue to improve and new records will be set. Can we stay with it?

In search of gold

B. Maunsell

The following conditioning programme has been specially written for this section by Brian Maunsell, head of the department of physical education at Palmerston North Teachers College. He was the trainer of the New Zealand Olympic hockey team for Montreal, 1976 (Gold Medal winners), and he has now succeeded Ross Gillespie as the New Zealand National Representative Coach.

The winning of the Gold Medal in the 1976 Olympic Hockey Final at Montreal was the climax of twenty years of international competition by New Zealand teams, and of thirty-two weeks of preparation by a group of extremely dedicated sportsmen.

The success of this team at Montreal is now history. Many factors combined to bring about this most exciting result. Previous New Zealand hockey teams have promised much in the international arena. Individual players had displayed skills that were the equal of most opponents they met but so often the Kiwis were left groping in the wake of greater speed and agility. At different times, the New Zealanders had successfully beaten every other international side including the regular leaders such as India, Pakistan, Germany, Holland and Australia. Never before had the team put it all together in any one tournament. The early matches had often been completed without defeat, though the teams would fade from recognition when sustained effort, was required to complete the qualifying rounds and then proceed to the play-offs for major placings.

During 1975, the New Zealand Hockey Association made a new appointment in the form of a trainer for the national team. In order to overcome the previous shortcomings there were many decisions to be made before the 1976 team stepped on to the 'Astroturf' of Montreal's Molson Stadium. Contact was made with experts in various fields of sports science both in New Zealand and other parts of the world.

Solutions were sought for many relevant concerns that had previously been observed:

1 What are the physical performance requirements for hockey?
2 How can running speed and agility be improved?
3 Are there any problems when playing hockey on 'Astroturf'?
4 What acclimatisation methods are appropriate when travelling from a mid-winter climate to compete in mid-summer?
5 Are there any appropriate testing methods for evaluating the physical fitness of hockey players?
6 Can carefully directed training assist in the prevention of musculoskeletal injuries sustained in hockey?

As a result of this research some ideas were developed regarding the responsibilities of a trainer and could be outlined as follows:

1 Preparation for optimum physical performance during an individual game and for a series of games during a tournament.

2 Prevention of injuries that can result from inadequate preparation and inability to cope with fatique.

3 Development of the ability to recover from temporary fatigue during a game and from game to game in a series, when the physical demands are high and the periods of lesser activity are minimal.

4 Consideration of the special environmental conditions so that individuals can adapt to, and cope with, the demands of increased temperature and humidity, faster playing surfaces, greater stress placed on weight-bearing joints brought about by increased traction when playing on artificial surfaces, etc.

5 Care and guidance of individuals sustaining an injury or illness that could impede preparation or participation.

6 Physical and psychological guidance to ensure sound attitudes to training and competition.

Preparation for competition in all sports has now reached the point where development of physical performance is a carefully monitored and directed campaign. Physical fitness, while important for every individual, is essential for the competitive sportsman. Physical fitness reduces the chance of injury and speeds up recovery following trauma. Physical fitness enhances skill performance. Physical fitness helps the player to cope with the psychological stresses of intense physical activity.

Modern field hockey requires the sort of training followed by many other athletes. During a game of hockey a player could be required to run, pass, stretch, tackle, turn, sprint, and dribble many times, with little opportunity for recovery and always without allowing the stress of fatigue to interfere with the skills of stick and ball manipulation.

Any conditioning schedule must be based upon physiological principles that will improve the response of the body systems involved during periods of intense activity. Physical training aims to condition the heart, lungs, joints, skeletal muscles, and nervous system to function at maximum efficiency while sustaining considerable stress and strain. The schedule for the Montreal Hockey Squad was carefully planned and scientifically based on such foundations.

The decision of the selection panel to choose a medium sized training squad, later to be reduced to the final travelling group, meant that the training programme would need to proceed in two phases:

Phase 1. Mid-December to the end of March when a 'mini-peak' of fitness would be reached to allow for sufficient performance during fitness testing and evaluation matches.

Phase 2. April to mid-July when the ultimate 'mark-peak' would be reached during the Olympic Tournament.

The programme was planned to achieve the following objectives:

1 To develop maximum individual cardiovascular endurance.

2 To develop muscular strength and muscular endurance necessary for the maintenance of skill performance during match play.

3 To increase flexibility in various body segments in an attempt to avoid musculo-skeletal injuries and also to reduce resistance to fast changes of body position.
4 To improve general speed and agility.
5 To develop 'speed-endurance' to the highest possible level.
6 To integrate fitness and skill training so that players could adapt to performing hockey skills during periods of semi-fatigue.

In the process of developing the training activities it was also necessary to consider the following scientific principles of physical exercise:
1 The principle of warm-up.
2 The principle of exercise tolerance.
3 The principle of progressive overload.
4 The principle of individual dosage.
5 The recording of training and performance achievements.
6 The principle of motivation.
7 The principle of warming-down and tapering off.

The decision to commence the training programme in mid-December was based on the need to allow sufficient time for a progressive development of all the necessary components of fitness. It was considered that any less time would have exposed the players to a level of stress that could produce physical strain and mental fatigue. The timing of the start of the schedule allowed thirty weeks of training until the opening ceremony in Montreal. At all times the squad members were encouraged to 'train don't strain' and accordingly used heart rate as a monitor to determine intensity and recovery period duration.

It was recognised that such a period of training would be a mammoth task and the squad members had to be highly motivated to start and continue when confronted with such a programme. In order to avoid exposing the group to the total programme and its concomitant psychological barrier, instalments of approximately six weeks duration were scheduled and evaluated with fitness tests before progressing to the next stage. The fact that the coach and trainer were able to visit groups of the squad regularly from mid-February to the time of departure in June provided very good incentives to the carrying out the training requirements. Physical performance tests were administered in order to evaluate individual progress and to provide objective evidence to the players that their workload was producing results. This latter consideration was very important from the point of view of motivation and incentive to continue with the training.

The performance tests were selected to simulate, as closely as possible, the conditions that could be experienced during a game of hockey, and at the same time to measure the various components of endurance, speed, and agility.

The total value of the training programme for the New Zealand Olympic Hockey Team in 1976 can never be accurately assessed. Obviously there are many variables that collectively produce a successful combination in hockey. However, this team achieved a greater result than any of its predecessors and was never found wanting in terms of physical performance. On two occasions matches went into extra time with the New Zealanders gaining a greater hold on the game the longer that play went on. Their opponents were literally 'run into the ground'.

The achievements of New Zealand rowing crews in recent years are well-known. The fact that the oarsmen have applied the principles and methods of modern sports science in their preparation has served to stimulate the action taken by the hockey players. Hopefully, other sports groups will adopt a similar approach in order that the performance of Kiwis in the international arena may produce more gold.

... Citius, Altius, Fortius.

Appendix

Training schedule

Weeks 1–8 (December–February).
1 Aerobic running four–five days per week.
2 General body flexibility exercises.
   Weeks 9–14 (February–March).
1 Aerobic running four days per week.
2 Interval running two days per week.
3 Flexibility exercises three days per week.
4 Circuit training three days per week.
5 Skill development.
N.B. The final evaluation and selection trials were held at the end of this period.
   Weeks 15–24 (April–May).
A period of fitness maintenance for most, and further build-up for those considered to be in need, as shown by the results of the fitness tests. Running, mainly aerobic in nature, with one session of interval training each week.

Increased emphasis placed on skill development and refinement. Some sessions devoted to performing skills under conditions of physical fatigue.
   Weeks 25–30 (June–July).
1 A period of final build-up.
2 Emphasis on interval training with distances varying from 50 m to 300 m.
3 Training schedules individualised to allow for differences in performance levels identified by tests conducted at the end of week 24. Some members were well advanced in their preparation and were given more sharpening work while a few continued with a heavy schedule in an attempt to produce a more desirable performance.
4 The team travelled to Toronto during week 27 and completed their final sharpening and match preparation under the direction of the team coach. During the seven days prior to the first match of the Olympic Tournament the training load was tapered off to allow the players to freshen up.

Training methods

1 *Aerobic running*. This was used as the foundation of all activities, and followed the principles of Cooper in progressing gradually to a level of desired cardiovascular endurance. The schedule required the players to progress from gaining 30 points per week in December to achieving 100 points per week by the end of March.

Heart rate was used to monitor the training load by periodically checking the pulse. The squad members were encouraged to work at a level that produced a heart response of 70 per cent of the difference between the resting heart rate and the individual maximum heart rate. The monitoring of heart rate also provided the players with further indication of their progress as training proceeded. This in itself was excellent feedback and motivation for continued efforts in their striving for increased performance.

2 *Flexibility exercises.* Introduced to increase the range of movement in various body segments and to reduce resistance to fast changes of body position.

3 *Circuit training.* Introduced to develop muscular strength and muscular endurance in the body segments considered important for hockey, and particularly to increase these qualities in the weight-bearing joints that would be likely to be exposed to increased stress when playing on an artificial surface such as 'Astroturf'.

4 *Interval training.* Introduced to develop the oxygen transport system of the body. Heart rate again used as a guide to work intensity and the duration of the recovery interval. As a general rule the heart rate was reduced to 130/min. before commencing the next repetition of running.

5 *Skill development.* Essential skills were developed and practised under conditions of fatigue or semi-fatigue in order to condition the players to operate in simulated match conditions.

6 *Fitness performance tests.* A battery of tests was selected to evaluate the progress of each squad member in order to prescribe training schedules that were suited to the needs of the individual. Testing was undertaken at the end of weeks 8, 14, 20, and 30 and provided a useful guide to the players, selectors, and trainer. The tests included:

1 A twelve minute run.
2 A five minute step test.
3 A progressive shuttle run with distances of 5, 10, 15, 20, and 25 metres. This was repeated six times with rest intervals of thirty seconds between each repetition.
4 Six sprints of 50 metres.
5 The 'Illinois Agility Run'.
6 Selected skinfold measures (supra-iliac, triceps, and sub-scapular).
7 Tests of body weight.

References

Astrand, P.O. and Rodahl, K. (1970). *A Textbook of Work Physiology.* New York: McGraw-Hill Book Company.

Cooper, K.H. (1970). *The New Aerobics.* New York: Bantam Books, Inc.

de Vries, H.A. (1975). *Physiology of Exercises*, 2nd edition. Dubuque: W.C. Brown Company.

Klafs, C.E. and Arnheim, D.D. (1973). *Modern Principles of Athletic Training*, 3rd edition.

Mathews, D.K. and Fox, E.L. (1976). *The Physiological Basis of Physical Education and Athletics*, 2nd edition. Philadelphia: W.B. Saunders Company.

Ryan, A.J. and Allman, F.L. (1974). *Sports Medicine.* New York: Academic Press.

On the brink of that world

J. Perrott

Jane Perrott is the sister of Rebecca Perrott, and herself represented Fiji in swimming at the Commonwealth Games in Christchurch.

Are Olympic and world record holders simply trained to reach high standards, or do they possess exceptional natural ability which is harnessed by a competent coach in such a way that all the necessary preparations are calculated with one specific peak in mind? In Peter Stokes' opinion, individuals can be genetically perfect for their sport, and, with careful guidance from a professional coach using training skills, motivation and technique, will achieve the necessary peak. Genetically perfect athletes are few and far between in New Zealand. When one such as Rebecca Perrott emerges, encouraged by her coach Tony Keenan and with the support of her family, prominence is inevitable. Settle back and view with interest; this is a world record combination.

Portrait of a champion

Photograph by courtesy of the Evening Post, *Wellington*

Rebecca has always enjoyed the water and first began competitive swimming at the age of eleven when the family was in Fiji. Her first major competition was the Commonwealth Games in Christchurch in 1974, where she represented Fiji. At twelve and a half, she had the distinction of being the youngest competitor at the Games, and although insignificant by international standards, her times of 4.54.43

mins. in the 400 metres freestyle and 10.14.67 mins. in the 800 metres freestyle were her personal bests by 13 and 24 seconds respectively. She also gained valuable experience in international competition which helped her considerably in later events.

Our whole family moved back to New Zealand later that year and Rebecca took up training in Wellington where our father had accepted a position at Victoria University. Under her coach, Tony Keenan, Rebecca's swimming improved steadily and she was asked to compete in the New Zealand Games in Christchurch in January 1975. She had not taken part in the trials but, at a 62·6 secs., she had swum the fastest 100 meter freestyle that season. In training at Christchurch she reduced this to 61·5 secs. and at the Games themselves she swam at 60·67 sec., tantalisingly close to breaking the minute. Later the same year she was chosen as a member of the New Zealand team to compete at the Second World Swimming Championships in Cali, Colombia. Here she broke the one minute barrier doing 59·5 secs. and became the first New Zealand woman to do so in a long course pool; this time placed her tenth overall. In the 400 metres freestyle she swam 4.28.05 mins. which placed her ninth, while in the 200 she qualified for the final with 2.06.51 mins. Which placed her seventh. In the final she swam 2.06.72 mins. for eighth place.

Rebecca's next big meet was the Montreal Olympics. The build-up for these began in March and her aim was to reach the final in each of her three events — the 100, 200 and 400 metres freestyle. Her coach felt that she had a sporting chance of a bronze medal in the 400. In fact she swam very close to the times predicted by her coach. In the 100 heats she recorded eighth fastest time with a 57·66 secs., but in the semi-finals she slipped slightly to 58·13 secs. and did not qualify for the final.

Her next event was the 400 where her coach had advised her to aim at a time of 4.16 mins. in order to be sure of qualifying. She won the first heat in 4.15.71 mins., six seconds faster than her previous best and a new Olympic record. As it turned out she was the fastest qualifier, but never before had she swam a personal best and then lowered that time again on the same day. Nevertheless in the final she took a further second off and missed a bronze medal by only 0·16 secs. She was swimming so strongly at the finish that it seems likely that had she had a little more experience she would have won a medal that day.

In the 200 she was ninth fastest, missing qualifying for the final by a mere 0·09 secs.

Immediately after the Olympics, Rebecca swam in the U.S. and Canadian National Championships and in each she won the 400 metre freestyle events. She also swam well in the other events, lowering the New Zealand record in the 200, 800, and 1500 metre freestyle events.

Perhaps the best indication of Rebecca's ability as a freestyler is the fact that in 1976 she was ranked in the top twenty in the world for the 200 and 800 metres and in the top ten for the 100, 400 and 1500 metres.

Before major events Rebecca spends as much as five hours a day in training, including dry-land work, and will swim up to twelve to fifteen kilometres a day. Obviously, her days have to be carefully planned to fit in such long hours of training, and it may be this high degree of organisation and necessary self-discipline which has helped Rebecca to keep abreast of her school work. It has to be fitted in wherever there are gaps in her programme and she knows that if she procrastinates she may not have another opportunity to do the assignment.

Due to the amount of time taken up by her swimming and the need for adequate sleep, Rebecca doesn't have much time left over for other activities. The more active ones are discouraged as she may injure herself at a crucial time in her training. So her main pastimes while not swimming are reading and watching television. None of us in the family have ever had our arms twisted to swim competitively or to undertake any other organised activity but we have been encouraged to follow our leanings and have been given the necessary support. Swimming, particularly, requires a great deal from parents, because so many swimmers are young and need assistance with transport to and from training sessions. As this can mean getting up at 5.30 a.m. or earlier, five days a week, and driving considerable distances to the pool, there are good reasons for not pressurising children to swim competitively!

Like the other members of the family, I have been interested in what motivates Rebecca, how she feels when she faces one of her important races and what her reactions were when, for example, she just missed an Olympic medal. Unfortunately, she is reticent about her feelings, but some things are fairly obvious. She really enjoys the water and during her lay-off periods at weekends she enjoys an opportunity to swim. She has been blessed (if that is the correct word) with abundant energy. Swimming provides a good outlet for this and her long training sessions are not the drudgery that they would be for others. Also, her coach ensures that there is variety and challenge in the programmes that he prepares. A lot of emphasis is placed on judgement of pace and this demands a high degree of concentration from the swimmer.

We know that Rebecca enjoys the travel around New Zealand, and, even more so, overseas, which is involved in competitive swimming. This and the prospect of challenging competition are the incentives that give purpose to her training. There is no doubt that she has a strong competitive instinct, combined with a temperament which copes with the pressures of top competition. These assist her when she mounts the starting block on a big occasion, preparing to put it all to the test in a race.

Tony Keenan   **Rebecca**   **Mr Perrott**

Photograph by courtesy of the Evening Post, *Wellington*

192

The high point of her career so far is clearly the 400 metre heat and final at Montreal. Both Rebecca and her coach were pleased with her two swims in this event. Tony Keenan regarded her first swim as a fine effort, and for her to have swum even faster later that same day was even more praiseworthy, bearing in mind her limited background of hard training and top level competition. Of course she was disappointed at missing a medal by such a small margin, but the knowledge that she has held an Olympic record, even briefly, gives her satisfaction. The fact that she maintained her condition for another month and won both the U.S. and Canadian 400 metre titles shows the determination and discipline that must be factors in her success.

It is hard for a sixteen-year old to say what she will be doing in two years' time but at this stage (1978) it looks as though Rebecca is keen to swim at the Moscow Olympics in 1980, and she has competed this year at the Commonwealth Games at Edmonton and at the Third World Swimming Championships at Berlin, having now taken a further six seconds off her 400 metre record.

Rebecca has always accepted our parents' view that school work is important too, and, having passed School Certificate in 1976, and gained University Entrance in 1977, she can now give more emphasis to swimming if necessary.

Rebecca has not yet chosen a career, nor have any decisions been made about where her swimming training should be carried out over the next three years. One thing that seems certain is that she, her parents and coach will discuss all the aspects very thoroughly before a decision is reached. To have any chance of success, the plan will need to have Rebecca's full approval.

Othopaedic snags in swimmers

The following article was first published in the magazine *Swimming Technique* (California) in 1976.

Miami Beach, Florida. The competitive swimmer subjects his body to repeated strains in unusual positions, and coaches, trainers, and physicians should be alert for early manifestations of orthopaedic difficulties, a Canadian specialist warned here.

In a survey that covered nearly 2500 members of prominent swimming clubs across Canada, the primary anatomic areas in ninety per cent of the competitors' complaints were the shoulder, knee, foot and calf. Dr John C. Kennedy, head of orthopaedic surgery at Victoria Hospital, London, Ont., told this to a postgraduate course on water-sports injuries sponsored by the American Academy of Orthopaedic Surgeons.

There were eighty-one specific shoulder complaints, he reported, with freestyle and butterfly stroke the common offenders and backstroke responsible for occasional pathology seventy specific knee complaints, with breaststroke the universal offender; and eighty-five foot and calf complaints divided among the four major strokes.

Most of the serious orthopaedic ailments were the result of one of two pathologic lesions: chronic irritation of the tendon or of the ligament due to repeated performance in an abnormal position.

The following is a summary of Dr Kennedy's comments on orthopedic problems in swimmers.

The shoulder

Studies suggest that the supraspinatus tendon is subjected to constant pressure from the head of the humerus, which 'tends to wring out its blood supply' when the arm is held in a resting position of adduction and neutral rotation.

'With maximum abduction, this area of avascularity in the supraspinatus tendon may impinge on the coracoacromial arch or, indeed, on the acromion itself.'

In the freestyle and butterfly strokes, the underwater pull of the arm in a repetitive fashion over months or even years of training invites early degenerative changes in a critical area of the supraspinatus tendon.

The intracapsular portion of the biceps tendon stretches in a similar manner over the head of the humerus and has an avascular zone passing from the supraglenoid origin over the prominence of the head of the humerus.

'Chronic irritation in this avascular area of either the biceps or supraspinatus leads to focal cell death; in turn, inflammatory response results, reflected in tendinitis of both supraspinatus and biceps tendon and eventually complicating subacromial bursitis, calcific tendinitis, and actual rotator cuff tear.'

Discomfort leads to pain

Usually, diagnosis is not difficult. Discomfort is first noticed only after swimming. This progresses to pain during and after training. Finally, performance of the stroke is difficult.

The treatment of a swimmer's shoulder 'is a most difficult problem'. It might be helpful to divide the shoulder problem into three phases: pain only after swimming activity; and disabling pain during training and after.

In phase one or two, swimmers should ice their shoulders after workouts and maintain range of motion of the shoulder (best done during the icing-procedure). They should change their training pattern by reducing yardage and training in another sport. Ultrasound and anti-flammatory drugs, such as phenylbutazone, should be used, particularly if a serious competition is scheduled for the near future.

In phase three, total rest may be necessary. This does not mean total cessation of training. The athlete may still do land exercise and pool workouts using the kick board and minimising arm activity.

One or two emergency injections of steroids, specifically centered on the trigger point of pain in the biceps or supraspinatus tendon, may be indicated.

The knee

The tibial collateral ligament is the main offender in the 'breaststroker's knee.' During the whip kick in the breaststroke, this ligament increases in tension as the knee moves from flexion to extension. Increased tension is aggravated by a valgus strain and, most important, by external rotation of the tibia, ankle, and foot.

With regard to diagnosis, point tenderness is usually located at the origin of the tibial collateral ligament from the adductor tubercule. Specific tests include pain on forced abduction and external rotation of the tibia with the knee in 20⁰ to 30⁰ of flexion.

Treatment calls for modifying the kick so that there is less external rotation of the tibia, and the training programme must be altered so that there is infrequent use of the whip kick. Here, too, icing is 'most important.' Ultrasound may help over a short period. Cortisone injections play only a minor role.

'Total rest may be necessary from time to time. Of all the competitive strokes, we feel that the breaststroke swimmer should have at least a total of two months' rest per year when the knee joints are not subjected to this very abnormal stress. Occasionally, this ailment has become so chronic that despite all forms of treatment the competitor must quit.

'This naturally applies to the mature swimmer and we would hope, with the adolescent age group competitor, that early diagnosis and intelligent management preclude this.'

Ankle and foot

During the backstroke and flutter kicks, the foot and ankle are forced down into extreme and abnormal plantar flexion stretching the extensor tendons in their narrow compartment. Chronic overuse in this peculiar position creates friction between the tendons and their surrounding sheaths, with resultant edema, inflammation, and adhesions. The diagnosis is quite obvious, and often crepitations are noted as the foot is passively brought from plantar flexion to dorsiflexion.

This disorder is not uncommon, and its chronicity is not worrisome. Should it arise, however, it may be necessary to change the style of leg kick. Local modalities are of great help, particularly icing after workouts and occasionally night wrapping of the foot at a 90⁰ angle.

An interesting case

A. Anderson

Adrian Anderson is a professional swimming coach in Hawera, and Barry Conway's case history was written specially for this book. It involves a new facet of thinking, now that retirement age is 60 years, as interest, recreation and maintenance of fitness, whether mental or physical, of superannuitants may be achieved in many fields, of which swimming is one.

Swimming, we hear, is a complete activity. It may be in the form of competitive sport, a recreation, or life-saving associated with boating safety. It may be used for medical reasons, such as for controlled breathing in asthma, or for rehabilitation, with many sporting injuries, from fractures to soft tissue problems of diverse origins. Swimming can assist, benefit and be enjoyed by all ages.

We have looked previously at swimming in a competitive atmosphere; now let's look at swimming as a recreation for the young and old.

Take the case of Barry from Hawera. Barry is sixty-three years of age, a returned serviceman, and a retired optician, spending all his spare time, till five years ago, on the mountain (Mt Egmont). He didn't like running, so he tried swimming one Christmas with his grandchildren. He enjoyed it very much but was able to swim only a length. The pool's professional coach taught him correct breathing, mastered by Barry in breaststroke, resulting in considerable progress. Barry became an everyday figure at the Hawera pool, commencing at 6.30 a.m. He swam for an hour each time and is now averaging 1500 metres per hour. In the warmer weather when the water temperature is up, he can achieve 1500 metres in fifty minutes. He enjoys company while swimming, not to talk to, but just to be in the water with him whether they be training squad kids or other superannuitants. He also likes his strokes to be checked by the pool coach from time to time, and he may be given some other point to concentrate on, to perfect.

One very important area of supervision, apart from motivation, is to see that he does not overdo the work-out, particularly in cold weather and/or cold water. (Older participants can be very determined.) Barry did once swim 1500 metres in 64°F, got very cold then went home to bed with an electric blanket. It took four days for him to feel comfortable and warm again. From this experience it was obvious and most important that when water temperatures were down, a limit was set for a specific number of lengths, so temperature and time spent in the water swimming are the governing factors, not distance travelled. Last season he swam 250 000 metres and only missed swimming on the very cold days. His wife says: 'He is hard to live with if he can't have that morning swim; also, he counts the days from the end of one season to the beginning of the next.' In the winter months Barry achieves ten kilometres each morning in running and walking. This keeps his cardio-vascular system in good shape and the intermittent walking relieves jarring, of the legs in general but specifically of the joints. Barry has a felling of well-being, of walking on a cloud and wants to share it with others.

What does Barry think?

'The stimulus of regular exercise interested me in a bid for more desirable management of asthma without using the ephedrine and adrenalin traditionally in use thirty to forty years ago. This new found preventative medicine involving a daily regime of walking/running achieved such an enhanced heart and lung stamina that the severe pulmonary disability of many years was overcome. Obviously, staying well proved to be far preferable to getting well after each debilitating attack of asthma. My blood pressure had been a little raised for some years but is considered to be stable now. No treatment was suggested until three years ago when suppression was accomplished with methyldoha.

'As the need to sustain cardio-vascular/pulmonary fitness was paramount, I looked to swimming as a supplementary discipline. I resolved to learn to swim correctly and was astonished to find that an environment of water provided a natural relaxant. Apart from attaining an incomparable aerobic capacity, a degree of animation never before experienced was to prove very good value emotionally.

'Success in this exercise regime has been made possible only by:

1 A very good medical practitioner who urged me into cardio-vascular/pulmonary exercise as a medicine.

2 A most professional swimming coach who has a personal interest ensuring that hydro-therapeutic medicine was taken.

3 Most importantly: a wife's constant admonition: "Stick at it!" '